behind the beautiful forevers

RANDOM HOUSE / NEW YORK

behind the beautiful forevers

katherine boo

Published in the United States by Random House,
an imprint of The Random House Publishing Group,
a division of Random House, Inc., New York.

RANDOM HOUSE and colophon are registered
trademarks of Random House, Inc.

LIBRARY OF CONGRESS CATALOGING-IN-
PUBLICATION DATA
Boo, Katherine.
Behind the beautiful forevers : life, death, and hope in
a Mumbai undercity / Katherine Boo.
p.   cm.
ISBN 978-1-4000-6755-8
eBook ISBN 978-0-679-64550-4
1. Urban poor—India—Mumbai.   I. Title.
HV4140.M86B66 2011
305.5'690954792—dc23   2011019555

Printed in the United States of America
on acid-free paper

www.atrandom.com

20 19 18 17 16 15

Book design by Barbara M. Bachman

For two Sunils
and what they've taught me about not giving up

contents

PROLOGUE   *between roses*   ix

PART ONE   *undercitizens*

    1. Annawadi   3

    2. Asha   17

    3. Sunil   31

    4. Manju   50

PART TWO   *the business of burning*

    5. Ghost House   71

    6. The Hole She Called a Window   84

    7. The Come-Apart   99

    8. The Master   117

PART THREE   *a little wildness*

9.   Marquee Effect   135
10. Parrots, Caught and Sold   152
11. Proper Sleep   166

PART FOUR   *up and out*

12. Nine Nights of Dance   177
13. Something Shining   190
14. The Trial   200
15. Ice   213
16. Black and White   221
17. A School, a Hospital,
     a Cricket Field   233

AUTHOR'S NOTE   247
ACKNOWLEDGMENTS   255

prologue: between roses

MIDNIGHT WAS CLOSING IN, the one-legged woman was grievously burned, and the Mumbai police were coming for Abdul and his father. In a slum hut by the international airport, Abdul's parents came to a decision with an uncharacteristic economy of words. The father, a sick man, would wait inside the trash-strewn, tin-roofed shack where the family of eleven resided. He'd go quietly when arrested. Abdul, the household earner, was the one who had to flee.

Abdul's opinion of this plan had not been solicited, typically. Already he was mule-brained with panic. He was sixteen years old, or maybe nineteen — his parents were hopeless with dates. Allah, in His impenetrable wisdom, had cut him small and jumpy. A coward: Abdul said it of himself. He knew nothing about eluding policemen. What he knew about, mainly, was trash. For nearly all the waking hours of nearly all the years he could remember, he'd been buying and selling to recyclers the things that richer people threw away.

Now Abdul grasped the need to disappear, but beyond that his imagination flagged. He took off running, then came back home. The only place he could think to hide was in his garbage.

He cracked the door of the family hut and looked out. His home sat midway down a row of hand-built, spatchcock dwellings; the lop-sided shed where he stowed his trash was just next door. To reach this shed unseen would deprive his neighbors of the pleasure of turning him in to the police.

He didn't like the moon, though: full and stupid bright, illuminat-ing a dusty open lot in front of his home. Across the lot were the shacks of two dozen other families, and Abdul feared he wasn't the only per-son peering out from behind the cover of a plywood door. Some peo-ple in this slum wished his family ill because of the old Hindu–Muslim resentments. Others resented his family for the modern reason, eco-nomic envy. Doing waste work that many Indians found contempt-ible, Abdul had lifted his large family above subsistence.

The open lot was quiet, at least—freakishly so. A kind of beach-front for a vast pool of sewage that marked the slum's eastern border, the place was bedlam most nights: people fighting, cooking, flirting, bathing, tending goats, playing cricket, waiting for water at a public tap, lining up outside a little brothel, or sleeping off the effects of the grave-digging liquor dispensed from a hut two doors down from Ab-dul's own. The pressures that built up in crowded huts on narrow slumlanes had only this place, the *maidan,* to escape. But after the fight, and the burning of the woman called the One Leg, people had retreated to their huts.

Now, among the feral pigs, water buffalo, and the usual belly-down splay of alcoholics, there seemed to be just one watchful presence: a small, unspookable boy from Nepal. He was sitting, arms around knees, in a spangly blue haze by the sewage lake—the reflected neon signage of a luxury hotel across the water. Abdul didn't mind if the Nepali boy saw him go into hiding. This kid, Adarsh, was no spy for the police. He just liked to stay out late, to avoid his mother and her nightly rages.

It was as safe a moment as Abdul was going to get. He bolted for the trash shed and closed the door behind him.

Inside was carbon-black, frantic with rats, and yet relieving. *His* storeroom — 120 square feet, piled high to a leaky roof with the things in this world Abdul knew how to handle. Empty water and whiskey bottles, mildewed newspapers, used tampon applicators, wadded aluminum foil, umbrellas stripped to the ribs by monsoons, broken shoelaces, yellowed Q-tips, snarled cassette tape, torn plastic casings that once held imitation Barbies. Somewhere in the darkness, there was a Berbee or Barblie itself, maimed in one of the experiments to which children who had many toys seemed to subject those toys no longer favored. Abdul had become expert, over the years, at minimizing distraction. He placed all such dolls in his trash pile tits-down.

Avoid trouble. This was the operating principle of Abdul Hakim Husain, an idea so fiercely held that it seemed imprinted on his physical form. He had deep-set eyes and sunken cheeks, a body work-hunched and wiry—the type that claimed less than its fair share of space when threading through people-choked slumlanes. Almost everything about him was recessed save the pop-out ears and the hair that curled upward, girlish, whenever he wiped his forehead of sweat.

A modest, missable presence was a useful thing in Annawadi, the sumpy plug of slum in which he lived. Here, in the thriving western suburbs of the Indian financial capital, three thousand people had packed into, or on top of, 335 huts. It was a continual coming-and-going of migrants from all over India—Hindus mainly, from all manner of castes and subcastes. His neighbors represented beliefs and cultures so various that Abdul, one of the slum's three dozen Muslims, could not begin to understand them. He simply recognized Annawadi as a place booby-trapped with contentions, new and ancient, over which he was determined not to trip. For Annawadi was also magnificently positioned for a trafficker in rich people's garbage.

ABDUL AND HIS NEIGHBORS were squatting on land that belonged to the Airports Authority of India. Only a coconut-tree-lined thoroughfare separated the slum from the entrance to the international terminal. Serving the airport clientele, and encircling Annawadi, were five extravagant hotels: four ornate, marbly megaliths and one sleek blue-glass Hyatt, from the top-floor windows of which Annawadi and several adjacent squatter settlements looked like villages that had been airdropped into gaps between elegant modernities.

"Everything around us is roses" is how Abdul's younger brother, Mirchi, put it. "And we're the shit in between."

In the new century, as India's economy grew faster than any other but China's, pink condominiums and glass office towers had shot up near the international airport. One corporate office was named, simply, "More." More cranes for making more buildings, the tallest of which interfered with the landing of more and more planes: It was a smogged-out, prosperity-driven obstacle course up there in the overcity, from which wads of possibility had tumbled down to the slums.

Every morning, thousands of waste-pickers fanned out across the airport area in search of vendible excess—a few pounds of the eight thousand tons of garbage that Mumbai was extruding daily. These scavengers darted after crumpled cigarette packs tossed from cars with tinted windows. They dredged sewers and raided dumpsters for empty bottles of water and beer. Each evening, they returned down the slum road with gunny sacks of garbage on their backs, like a procession of broken-toothed, profit-minded Santas.

Abdul would be waiting at his rusty scale. In the hierarchy of the undercity's waste business, the teenager was a notch above the scavengers: a trader who appraised and bought what they found. His profit came from selling the refuse in bulk to small recycling plants a few miles away.

Abdul's mother was the haggler in the family, raining vibrant abuse upon scavengers who asked too much for their trash. For Abdul, words came stiff and slow. Where he excelled was in the sorting—the crucial, exacting process of categorizing the purchased waste into one of sixty kinds of paper, plastic, metal, and the like, in order to sell it.

Of course he would be fast. He'd been sorting since he was about six years old, because tuberculosis and garbage work had wrecked his father's lungs. Abdul's motor skills had developed around his labor.

"You didn't have the mind for school, anyway," his father had recently observed. Abdul wasn't sure he'd had enough schooling to make a judgment either way. In the early years, he'd sat in a classroom where nothing much happened. Then there had been only work. Work that churned so much filth into the air it turned his snot black. Work more boring than dirty. Work he expected to be doing for the rest of his life. Most days, that prospect weighed on him like a sentence. Tonight, hiding from the police, it felt like a hope.

THE SMELL OF THE ONE LEG'S BURNING was fainter in the shed, given the competing stink of trash and the fear-sweat that befouled Abdul's clothing. He stripped, hiding his pants and shirt behind a brittle stack of newspapers near the door.

His best idea was to climb to the top of his eight-foot tangle of garbage, then burrow in against the back wall, as far as possible from the door. He was agile, and in daylight could scale this keenly balanced mound in fifteen seconds. But a misstep in the dark would cause a landslide of bottles and cans, which would broadcast his whereabouts widely, since the walls between huts were thin and shared.

To Abdul's right, disconcertingly, came quiet snores: a laconic cousin newly arrived from a rural village, who probably assumed that women burned in the city every day. Moving left, Abdul felt around the blackness for a mass of blue polyurethane bags. Dirt magnets, those bags. He hated sorting them. But he recalled tossing the bundled bags onto a pile of soggy cardboard—the stuff of a silent climb.

He found the bags and flattened boxes by the side wall, the one that divided his shed from his home. Hoisting himself up, he waited. The cardboard compressed, the rats made rearrangements, but nothing metal clattered to the floor. Now he could use the side wall for balance as he considered his next step.

Someone was shuffling on the other side of the wall. His father, most likely. He'd be out of his nightclothes now, wearing the polyester shirt that hung loose on his shoulders, probably studying a palmful of tobacco. The man had been playing with his tobacco all evening, fingering it into circles, triangles, circles again. It was what he did when he didn't know what he was doing.

A few more steps, some unhelpful clanking, and Abdul had gained the back wall. He lay down. Now he regretted not having his pants. Mosquitoes. The edges of torn clamshell packaging, slicing into the backs of his thighs.

The burn-smell lingering in the air was bitter, more kerosene and melted sandal than flesh. Had Abdul happened across it in one of the slumlanes, he wouldn't have doubled over. It was orange blossoms compared with the rotting hotel food dumped nightly at Annawadi, which sustained three hundred shit-caked pigs. The problem in his stomach came from knowing what, and who, the smell was.

Abdul had known the One Leg since the day, eight years back, that his family had arrived in Annawadi. He'd had no choice but to know her, since only a sheet had divided her shack from his own. Even then, her smell had troubled him. Despite her poverty, she perfumed herself somehow. Abdul's mother, who smelled of breast milk and fried onions, disapproved.

In the sheet days, as now, Abdul believed his mother, Zehrunisa, to be right about most things. She was tender and playful with her children, and her only great flaw, in the opinion of Abdul, her eldest son, was the language she used when haggling. Although profane bargaining was the norm in the waste business, he felt his mother acceded to that norm with too much relish.

"Stupid pimp with the brain of a lemon!" she'd say in mock outrage. "You think my babies will go hungry without your cans? I ought to take down your pants and slice off what little is inside!"

This, from a woman who'd been raised in some nowhere of a village to be burqa-clad, devout.

Abdul considered himself "old-fashioned, 90 percent," and censured his mother freely. "And what would your father say, to hear you cursing in the street?"

"He would say the worst," Zehrunisa replied one day, "but he was the one who sent me off to marry a sick man. Had I sat quietly in the house, the way my mother did, all these children would have starved."

Abdul didn't dare voice the great flaw of his father, Karam Husain: too sick to sort much garbage, not sick enough to stay off his wife. The Wahhabi sect in which he'd been raised opposed birth control, and of Zehrunisa's ten births, nine children had survived.

Zehrunisa consoled herself, each pregnancy, that she was producing a workforce for the future. Abdul was the workforce of the present, though, and new brothers and sisters increased his anxiety. He made errors, paid scavengers dearly for sacks of worthless things.

"Slow down," his father had told him gently. "Use your nose, mouth, and ears, not just your scales." Tap the metal scrap with a nail. Its ring will tell you what it's made of. Chew the plastic to identify its grade. If it's hard plastic, snap it in half and inhale. A fresh smell indicates good-quality polyurethane.

Abdul had learned. One year, there was enough to eat. Another year, there was more of a home to live in. The sheet was replaced by a divider made of scraps of aluminum and, later, a wall of reject bricks, which established his home as the sturdiest dwelling in the row. The feelings that washed over him when he considered the brick divider were several: pride; fear that the quality of the bricks was so poor the wall would crumble; sensory relief. There was now a three-inch barrier between him and the One Leg, who took lovers while her husband was sorting garbage elsewhere.

In recent months, Abdul had had occasion to register her only when she clinked past on her metal crutches, heading for the market or the public toilet. The One Leg's crutches seemed to be too short, because when she walked, her butt stuck out—did some switchy thing that made people laugh. The lipstick provided further hilarity. *She draws on that face just to squat at the shit-hole?* Some days the lips were orange, other days purple-red, as if she'd climbed the jamun-fruit tree by the Hotel Leela and mouthed it clean.

The One Leg's given name was Sita. She had fair skin, usually an asset, but the runt leg had smacked down her bride price. Her Hindu parents had taken the single offer they got: poor, unattractive, hard-working, Muslim, old—"half-dead, but who else wanted her," as her mother had once said with a frown. The unlikely husband renamed her Fatima, and from their mismating had come three scrawny girls. The sickliest daughter had drowned in a bucket, at home. Fatima did not seem to grieve, which got people talking. After a few days she re-emerged from her hut, still switchy-hipped and staring at men with her gold-flecked, unlowering eyes.

There was too much wanting at Annawadi lately, or so it seemed to Abdul. As India began to prosper, old ideas about accepting the life assigned by one's caste or one's divinities were yielding to a belief in earthly reinvention. Annawadians now spoke of better lives casually, as if fortune were a cousin arriving on Sunday, as if the future would look nothing like the past.

Abdul's brother Mirchi did not intend to sort garbage. He envisioned wearing a starched uniform and reporting to work at a luxury hotel. He'd heard of waiters who spent all day putting toothpicks into pieces of cheese, or aligning knives and forks on tables. He wanted a clean job like that. "Watch me!" he'd once snapped at their mother. "I'll have a bathroom as big as this hut!"

The dream of Raja Kamble, a sickly toilet-cleaner who lived on the lane behind Abdul's, was of medical rebirth. A new valve to fix his heart and he'd survive to finish raising his children. Fifteen-year-old Meena, whose hut was around the corner, craved a taste of the freedom and adventure she'd seen on TV serials, instead of an arranged marriage and domestic submission. Sunil, an undersized twelve-year-old scavenger, wanted to eat enough to start growing. Asha, a fighter-cock of a woman who lived by the public toilet, was differently ambitious. She longed to be Annawadi's first female slumlord, then ride the city's inexorable corruption into the middle class. Her teen-aged daughter, Manju, considered her own aim more noble: to become Annawadi's first female college graduate.

The most preposterous of these dreamers was the One Leg. Everyone thought so. Her abiding interest was in extramarital sex, though not for pocket change alone. That, her neighbors would have understood. But the One Leg also wanted to transcend the affliction by which others had named her. She wanted to be respected and reckoned attractive. Annawadians considered such desires inappropriate for a cripple.

What Abdul wanted was this: a wife, innocent of words like *pimp* and *sisterfucker*, who didn't much mind how he smelled; and eventually a home somewhere, anywhere, that was not Annawadi. Like most people in the slum, and in the world, for that matter, he believed his own dreams properly aligned to his capacities.

THE POLICE WERE in Annawadi, coming across the maidan toward his home. It had to be the police. No slumdweller spoke as confidently as this.

Abdul's family knew many of the officers at the local station, just enough to fear them all. When they learned that a family in the slum was making money, they visited every other day to extort some. The worst of the lot had been Constable Pawar, who had brutalized little Deepa, a homeless girl who sold flowers by the Hyatt. But most of them would gladly blow their noses in your last piece of bread.

Abdul had been bracing for this moment when the officers crossed his family's threshold—for the sounds of small children screaming, of steel vessels violently upended. But the two officers were perfectly calm, even friendly, as they relayed the salient facts. The One Leg had survived and had made an accusation from her hospital bed: that Abdul, his older sister, and their father had beaten her and set her on fire.

Later, Abdul would recall the officers' words penetrating the storeroom wall with a fever-dream slowness. So his sister Kehkashan was being accused, too. For this, he wished the One Leg dead. Then he wished he hadn't wished it. If the One Leg died, his family would be even more screwed.

To be poor in Annawadi, or in any Mumbai slum, was to be guilty of one thing or another. Abdul sometimes bought pieces of metal that scavengers had stolen. He ran a business, such as it was, without a license. Simply living in Annawadi was illegal, since the airport authority wanted squatters like himself off its land. But he and his family had not burned the One Leg. She had set herself on fire.

Abdul's father was professing the family's innocence in his breathy, weak-lunged voice as the officers led him out of the house. "So where is your son?" one of them demanded loudly as they stood outside the storeroom door. The officer's volume was not in this instance a show of power. He was trying to be heard over Abdul's mother, wailing.

Zehrunisa Husain was a tear-factory even on good days; it was one of her chief ways of starting conversations. But now her children's sobbing intensified her own. The little Husains' love for their father was simpler than Abdul's love for him, and they would remember the night the police came to take him away.

Time passed. Wails subsided. "He'll be back in half an hour," his mother was telling the children in a high-pitched singsong, one of her lying tones. Abdul took heart in the words *be back*. After arresting his father, the police had apparently left Annawadi.

Abdul couldn't rule out the possibility that the officers would return to search for him. But from what he knew of the energy levels of Mumbai policemen, it was more likely that they would call it a night. That gave him three or four more hours of darkness in which to plan an escape more sensible than a skulk to the hut next door.

He didn't feel *incapable* of daring. One of his private vanities was that all the garbage sorting had endowed his hands with killing strength—that he could chop a brick in half like Bruce Lee. "So let's get a brick," replied a girl with whom he had once, injudiciously, shared this conviction. Abdul had bumbled away. The brick belief was something he wanted to harbor, not to test.

His brother Mirchi, two years younger, was braver by a stretch, and wouldn't have hidden in the storeroom. Mirchi liked the Bollywood movies in which bare-chested outlaws jumped out of high windows and ran across the roofs of moving trains, while the policemen in pursuit fired and failed to hit their marks. Abdul took all dangers, in all films, overseriously. He was still living down the night he'd accompanied another boy to a shed a mile away, where pirated videos played. The movie had been about a mansion with a monster in its basement—an orange-furred creature that fed on human flesh. When it ended, he'd had to pay the proprietor twenty rupees to let him sleep on the floor, because his legs were too stiff with fear to walk home.

As ashamed as he felt when other boys witnessed his fearfulness, Abdul thought it irrational to be anything else. While sorting newspapers or cans, tasks that were a matter more of touch than of sight, he studied his neighbors instead. The habit killed time and gave him theories, one of which came to prevail over the others. It seemed to him that in Annawadi, fortunes derived not just from what people did, or how well they did it, but from the accidents and catastrophes they dodged. A decent life was the train that hadn't hit you, the slumlord you hadn't offended, the malaria you hadn't caught. And while he regretted not being smarter, he believed he had a quality nearly as valuable for the circumstances in which he lived. He was *chaukanna*, alert.

"My eyes can see in all directions" was another way he put it. He believed he could anticipate calamity while there was still time to get out of the way. The One Leg's burning was the first time he'd been blindsided.

WHAT TIME WAS IT? A neighbor named Cynthia was in the maidan, shouting, "Why haven't the police arrested the rest of this family?" Cynthia was close to Fatima the One Leg, and had despised Abdul's family ever since her own family garbage business failed. "Let's march on the police station, make the officers come and take them," she called out to the other residents. From inside Abdul's home came only silence.

After a while, mercifully, Cynthia shut up. There didn't seem to be a groundswell of public support for the protest march, just irritation at Cynthia for waking everyone up. Abdul felt the night's tension finally thinning, until steel pots began banging all around him. Startling up, he was confused.

Golden light was seeping through the cracks in a door. Not the door of his storeroom. A door it took a minute to place. Pants back on, he seemed to be on the floor of the hut of a young Muslim cook who lived across the maidan. It was morning. The clangor around him was Annawadians in adjacent huts, making breakfast.

When and why had he crossed the maidan to this hut? Panic had ripped a hole in his memory, and Abdul would never be certain of the final hours of this night. The only clear thing was that in the gravest situation of his life, a moment demanding courage and enterprise, he had stayed in Annawadi and fallen asleep.

At once, he knew his course of action: to find his mother. Having proved himself useless as a fugitive, he needed her to tell him what to do.

"Go fast," said Zehrunisa Husain, upon issuing her instructions. "Fast as you can!"

Abdul grabbed a fresh shirt and flew. Across the clearing, down a zigzag lane of huts, out onto a rubbled road. Garbage and water buffalo, slum-side. Glimmerglass Hyatt on the other. Fumbling with shirt buttons as he ran. After two hundred yards he gained the wide thoroughfare that led to the airport, which was bordered by blooming gardens, pretties of a city he barely knew.

Butterflies, even: He blew past them and hooked into the airport.

Arrivals down. Departures up. He went a third way, running beside a long stretch of blue-and-white aluminum fencing, behind which jackhammers blasted, excavating the foundations of a glamorous new terminal. Abdul had occasionally tried to monetize the terminal's security perimeter. Two aluminum panels, swiped and sold, and a garbage boy could rest for a year.

He kept moving, made a hard right at a field of black and yellow taxis gleaming in a violent morning sun. Another right, into a shady curve of driveway, a leafy bough hanging low across it. One more right and he was inside the Sahar Police Station.

Zehrunisa had read her son's face: This boy was too anxious to hide from the police. Her own fear, upon waking, was that the officers would beat her husband as punishment for Abdul's escape. It was the eldest son's duty to protect a sick father from that.

Abdul would do his duty, and almost, almost gladly. Hiding was what guilty people did; being innocent, he wanted the fact stamped on his forehead. So what else to do but submit himself to the stamping authorities—to the law, to justice, concepts in which his limited history had given him no cause to believe? He would try to believe in them now.

A police officer in epauletted khaki was splodged behind a gray metal desk. Seeing Abdul, he rose up, surprised. His lips, under his mustache, were fat and fishlike, and Abdul would remember them later—the way they parted a little before he smiled.

PART ONE

undercitizens

Everybody in Annawadi talks like this —

oh, I will make my child a doctor, a lawyer,

and he will make us rich. It's vanity, nothing more.

Your little boat goes west and you congratulate

yourself, "What a navigator I am!" And then the

wind blows you east.

—ABDUL'S FATHER, KARAM HUSAIN

1.

Annawadi

LET IT KEEP, the moment when Officer Fish Lips met Abdul in the police station. Rewind, see Abdul running backward, away from the station and the airport, toward home. See the flames engulfing a disabled woman in a pink-flowered tunic shrink to nothing but a matchbook on the floor. See Fatima minutes earlier, dancing on crutches to a raucous love song, her delicate features unscathed. Keep rewinding, back seven more months, and stop at an ordinary day in January 2008. It was about as hopeful a season as there had ever been in the years since a bitty slum popped up in the biggest city of a country that holds one-third of the planet's poor. A country dizzy now with development and circulating money.

Dawn came gusty, as it often did in January, the month of treed kites and head colds. Because his family lacked the floor space for all of its members to lie down, Abdul was asleep on the gritty maidan, which for years had passed as his bed. His mother stepped carefully over one of his younger brothers, and then another, bending low to

Abdul's ear. "Wake up, fool!" she said exuberantly. "You think your work is dreaming?"

Superstitious, Zehrunisa had noticed that some of the family's most profitable days occurred after she had showered abuses on her eldest son. January's income being pivotal to the Husains' latest plan of escape from Annawadi, she had decided to make the curses routine.

Abdul rose with minimal whining, since the only whining his mother tolerated was her own. Besides, this was the gentle-going hour in which he hated Annawadi least. The pale sun lent the sewage lake a sparkling silver cast, and the parrots nesting at the far side of the lake could still be heard over the jets. Outside his neighbors' huts, some held together by duct tape and rope, damp rags were discreetly freshening bodies. Children in school-uniform neckties were hauling pots of water from the public taps. A languid line extended from an orange concrete block of public toilets. Even goats' eyes were heavy with sleep. It was the moment of the intimate and the familial, before the great pursuit of the tiny market niche got under way.

One by one, construction workers departed for a crowded intersection where site supervisors chose day laborers. Young girls began threading marigolds into garlands, to be hawked in Airport Road traffic. Older women sewed patches onto pink-and-blue cotton quilts for a company that paid by the piece. In a small, sweltering plastic-molding factory, bare-chested men cranked gears that would turn colored beads into ornaments to be hung from rearview mirrors—smiling ducks and pink cats with jewels around their necks that they couldn't imagine anyone, anywhere, buying. And Abdul crouched on the maidan, beginning to sort two weeks' worth of purchased trash, a stained shirt hitching up his knobby spine.

His general approach toward his neighbors was this: "The better I know you, the more I will dislike you, and the more you will dislike me. So let us keep to ourselves." But deep in his own work, as he would be this morning, he could imagine his fellow Annawadians laboring companionably alongside him.

ANNAWADI SAT TWO hundred yards off the Sahar Airport Road, a stretch where new India and old India collided and made new India late. Chauffeurs in SUVs honked furiously at the bicycle delivery boys peeling off from a slum chicken shop, each carrying a rack of three hundred eggs. Annawadi itself was nothing special, in the context of the slums of Mumbai. Every house was off-kilter, so less off-kilter looked like straight. Sewage and sickness looked like life.

The slum had been settled in 1991 by a band of laborers trucked in from the southern Indian state of Tamil Nadu to repair a runway at the international airport. The work complete, they decided to stay near the airport and its tantalizing construction possibilities. In an area with little unclaimed space, a sodden, snake-filled bit of brushland across the street from the international terminal seemed the least-bad place to live.

Other poor people considered the spot too wet to be habitable, but the Tamils set to work, hacking down the brush that harbored the snakes, digging up dirt in drier places and packing it into the mud. After a month, their bamboo poles stopped flopping over when they were stuck in the ground. Draping empty cement sacks over the poles for cover, they had a settlement. Residents of neighboring slums provided its name: Annawadi—the land of *annas*, a respectful Tamil word for older brothers. Less respectful terms for Tamil migrants were in wider currency. But other poor citizens had seen the Tamils sweat to summon solid land from a bog, and that labor had earned a certain deference.

Seventeen years later, almost no one in this slum was considered poor by official Indian benchmarks. Rather, the Annawadians were among roughly one hundred million Indians freed from poverty since 1991, when, around the same moment as the small slum's founding, the central government embraced economic liberalization. The Annawadians were thus part of one of the most stirring success narratives in the modern history of global market capitalism, a narrative still unfolding.

True, only six of the slum's three thousand residents had permanent jobs. (The rest, like 85 percent of Indian workers, were part of the informal, unorganized economy.) True, a few residents trapped rats and frogs and fried them for dinner. A few ate the scrub grass at the sewage lake's edge. And these individuals, miserable souls, thereby made an inestimable contribution to their neighbors. They gave those slumdwellers who didn't fry rats and eat weeds, like Abdul, a felt sense of their upward mobility.

The airport and hotels spewed waste in the winter, the peak season for tourism, business travel, and society weddings, whose lack of restraint in 2008 reflected a stock market at an all-time high. Better still for Abdul, a frenzy of Chinese construction in advance of the summer's Beijing Olympics had inflated the price of scrap metal worldwide. It was a fine time to be a Mumbai garbage trader, not that that was the term passersby used for Abdul. Some called him garbage, and left it at that.

This morning, culling screws and hobnails from his pile, he tried to keep an eye on Annawadi's goats, who liked the smell of the dregs in his bottles and the taste of the paste beneath the labels. Abdul didn't ordinarily mind them nosing around, but these days they were fonts of liquid shit—a menace.

The goats belonged to a Muslim man who ran a brothel from his hut and considered his whores a pack of malingerers. In an attempt to diversify, he had been raising the animals to sell for sacrifice at Eid, the festival marking the end of Ramadan. The goats had proved as troublesome as the girls, though. Twelve of the herd of twenty-two had died, and the survivors were in intestinal distress. The brothel-keeper blamed black magic on the part of the Tamils who ran the local liquor still. Others suspected the goats' drinking source, the sewage lake.

Late at night, the contractors modernizing the airport dumped things in the lake. Annawadians also dumped things there: most recently, the decomposing carcasses of twelve goats. Whatever was in that soup, the pigs and dogs that slept in its shallows emerged with bellies stained blue. Some creatures survived the lake, though, and not only the malarial mosquitoes. As the morning went on, a fisher-man waded through the water, one hand pushing aside cigarette packs and blue plastic bags, the other dimpling the surface with a net. He would take his catch to the Marol market to be ground into fish oil, a health product for which demand had surged now that it was valued in the West.

Rising to shake out a cramp in his calf, Abdul was surprised to find the sky as brown as flywings, the sun signaling through the haze of pollution the arrival of afternoon. When sorting, he routinely lost track of the hour. His little sisters were playing with the One Leg's daughters on a makeshift wheelchair, a cracked plastic lawn chair flanked by rusted bicycle wheels. Mirchi, already home from ninth grade, was sprawled in the doorway of the family hut, an unread math book on his lap.

Mirchi was impatiently awaiting his best friend, Rahul, a Hindu boy who lived a few huts away, and who had become an Annawadi celebrity. This month, Rahul had done what Mirchi dreamed of: bro-ken the barrier between the slum world and the rich world.

Rahul's mother, Asha, a kindergarten teacher with mysterious

connections to local politicians and the police, had managed to secure him several nights of temp work at the Intercontinental hotel,
across the sewage lake. Rahul—a pie-faced, snaggle-toothed ninth
grader—had seen the overcity opulence firsthand.

And here he came, wearing an ensemble purchased from the
profits of this stroke of fortune: cargo shorts that rode low on his hips,
a shiny oval belt buckle of promising recyclable weight, a black knit
cap pulled down to his eyes. "Hip-hop style," Rahul termed it. The
previous day had been the sixtieth anniversary of the assassination of
Mahatma Gandhi, a national holiday on which elite Indians once
considered it poor taste to throw a lavish party. But Rahul had worked
a manic event at the Intercontinental, and knew Mirchi would ap-
preciate the details.

"Mirchi, I cannot lie to you," Rahul said, grinning. "On my side
of the hall there were five hundred women in only half-clothes—like
they forgot to put on the bottom half before they left the house!"

"Aaagh, where was I?" said Mirchi. "Tell me. Anyone famous?"

"Everyone famous! A Bollywood party. Some of the stars were in
the VIP area, behind a rope, but John Abraham came out to near
where I was. He had this thick black coat, and he was smoking cigarettes right in front of me. And Bipasha was supposedly there, but I
couldn't be sure it was really her or just some other item girl, because if the manager sees you looking at the guests, he'll fire you,
take your whole pay—they told us that twenty times before the party
started, like we were weak in the head. You have to focus on the tables and the rug. Then when you see a dirty plate or a napkin you
have to snatch it and take it to the trash bin in the back. Oh, that
room was looking nice. First we laid this thick white carpet—you
stepped on it and sank right down. Then they lit white candles and
made it dark like a disco, and on this one table the chef put two huge

dolphins made out of flavored ice. One dolphin had cherries for eyes—"

"Bastard, forget the fish, tell me about the girls," Mirchi protested. "They want you to look when they dress like that."

"Seriously, you can't look. Not even at the rich people's toilets. Security will chuck you out. The toilets for the workers were nice, though. You have a choice between Indian- or American-style." Rahul, who had a patriotic streak, had peed in the Indian one, an open drain in the floor.

Other boys joined Rahul outside the Husains' hut. Annawadians liked to talk about the hotels and the depraved things that likely went on inside. One drug-addled scavenger talked *to* the hotels: "I know you're trying to kill me, you sisterfucking Hyatt!" But Rahul's accounts had special value, since he didn't lie, or at least not more than one sentence out of twenty. This, along with a cheerful disposition, made him a boy whose privileges other boys did not resent.

Rahul gamely conceded he was a nothing compared with the Intercontinental's regular workers. Many of the waiters were college-educated, tall, and light-skinned, with cellphones so shiny their owners could fix their hair in the reflections. Some of the waiters had mocked Rahul's long, blue-painted thumbnail, which was high masculine style at Annawadi. When he cut the nail off, they'd teased him about how he talked. The Annawadians' deferential term for a rich man, *sa'ab*, was not the proper term in the city's moneyed quarters, he reported to his friends. "The waiters say it makes you sound D-class—like a thug, a *tapori*," he said. "The right word is *sir*."

"*Sirrrrrr*," someone said, rolling the r's, then everyone started saying it, laughing.

The boys stood close together, though there was plenty of space in the maidan. For people who slept in close quarters, his foot in my mouth, my foot in hers, the feel of skin against skin got to be a habit. Abdul stepped around them, upending an armful of torn paper luggage tags on the maidan and scrambling after the tags that blew away. The other boys paid him no notice. Abdul didn't talk much, and when he did, it was as if he'd spent weeks privately working over some little idea. He might have had a friend or two if he'd known how to tell a good story.

Once, working on this shortcoming, he'd floated a tale about having been inside the Intercontinental himself—how a Bollywood movie called *Welcome* had been filming there, and how he'd seen Katrina Kaif dressed all in white. It had been a feeble fiction. Rahul had seen through it immediately. But Rahul's latest report would allow Abdul's future lies to be better informed.

A Nepali boy asked Rahul about the women in the hotels. Through slats in the hotel fences, he had seen some of them smoking—"not one cigarette, but many"—while they waited for their drivers to pull up to the entrance. "Which village do they come from, these women?"

"Listen, idiot," Rahul said affectionately. "The white people come from all different countries. You're a real hick if you don't know this basic thing."

"Which countries? America?"

Rahul couldn't say. "But there are so many Indian guests in the hotels, too, I guarantee you." Indians who were "healthy-sized"—big and fat, as opposed to stunted, like the Nepali boy and many other children here.

Rahul's first job had been the Intercontinental's New Year's Eve party. The New Year's bashes at Mumbai's luxury hotels were renowned, and scavengers had often returned to Annawadi bearing discarded brochures. *Celebrate 2008 in high style at Le Royal Meridien*

Hotel! Take a stroll down the streets of Paris splurging with art, music & food. Get scintillated with live performances. Book your boarding passes and Bon Voyage! 12,000 rupees per couple, with champagne. The advertisements were printed on glossy paper, for which recyclers paid two rupees, or four U.S. cents, per kilo.

Rahul had been underwhelmed by the New Year's rituals of the rich. "Moronic," he had concluded. "Just people drinking and dancing and standing around acting stupid, like people here do every night."

"The hotel people get strange when they drink," he told his friends. "Last night at the end of the party, there was one hero— good-looking, stripes on his suit, expensive cloth. He was drunk, full tight, and he started stuffing bread into his pants pockets, jacket pockets. Then he put more rolls straight into his pants! Rolls fell on the floor and he was crawling under the table to get them. This one waiter was saying the guy must have been hungry, earlier—that whiskey brought back the memory. But when I get rich enough to be a guest at a big hotel, I'm not going to act like such a loser."

Mirchi laughed, and asked the question that many were asking of themselves in Mumbai in 2008: "And what are you going to do, *sirrrrrrrr*, so that you get served at such a hotel?"

But Rahul was shoving off, his attention diverted to a green plastic kite snagged high in a peepal tree at Annawadi's entrance. It appeared to be broken, but once the bones were pressed straight, he figured he could resell it for two rupees. He just needed to claim the kite before the idea occurred to some other money-minded boy.

Rahul had learned his serial entrepreneurship from his mother, Asha, a woman who scared Abdul's parents a little. She was a stalwart in a political party, Shiv Sena, which was dominated by Hindus born in Maharashtra, Mumbai's home state. As the population of Greater

Mumbai pressed toward twenty million, competition for jobs and housing was ferocious, and Shiv Sena blamed migrants from other states for taking opportunities that rightfully belonged to the natives. (The party's octogenarian founder, Bal Thackeray, retained a fondness for Hitler's program of ethnic cleansing.) Shiv Sena's current galvanizing cause was purging Mumbai of migrants from India's poor northern states. The party's animus toward the city's Muslim minority was of longer, more violent standing. That made Abdul's family, Muslims with roots in the northern state of Uttar Pradesh, twice suspect.

The friendship of Rahul and Mirchi transcended ethnic and religious politics, though. Mirchi sometimes raised his fist and yelled the Shiv Sena greeting, "Jai Maharashtra!" just to make Rahul laugh. The two ninth graders had even started to look alike, having decided to let their bangs grow into long floppy forelocks, which they brushed out of their eyes like the film hero Ajay Devgan.

Abdul envied their closeness. His only sort-of friend was a homeless fifteen-year-old boy named Kalu, who robbed recycling bins in airport compounds. But Kalu worked nights, when Abdul slept, and they didn't talk much anymore.

Abdul's deepest affection was for his two-year-old brother, Lallu, a fact that had begun to concern him. Listening to Bollywood love songs, he could only conclude that his own heart had been made too small. He'd never longed with extravagance for a girl, and while he felt certain he loved his mother, the feeling didn't come in any big gush. But he could get tearful just looking at Lallu, who was as fearless as Abdul was flinchy. All those swollen rat bites on his cheeks, on the back of his head.

What to do? When the storeroom grew too crowded, as it did in flush months like this one, garbage piled up in their hut, and rats came, too. But when Abdul left garbage outside, it got stolen by the scavengers, and he hated to buy the same garbage twice.

———

BY 3 P.M., ABDUL WAS FACING down the bottle caps, a major sorting nuisance. Some had plastic interior linings, which had to be stripped out before the caps could be assigned to the aluminum pile. Rich people's garbage was every year more complex, rife with hybrid materials, impurities, impostors. Planks that looked like wood were shot through with plastic. How was he to classify a loofah? The owners of the recycling plants demanded waste that was all one thing, pure.

His mother was squatting beside him, applying a stone to a heap of wet, dirty clothes. She glared at Mirchi, drowsing in the doorway. "What? School holiday?" she said.

Zehrunisa expected Mirchi to pass ninth grade at the third-rate Urdu-language private school for which they paid three hundred rupees a year. They'd had to pay, since spreading educational opportunity was not among the Indian government's strong suits. The free municipal school near the airport stopped at eighth grade, and its teachers often didn't show up.

"Either study or help your brother," Zehrunisa said to Mirchi. He glanced at Abdul's recyclables and opened his math book.

Recently, even looking at garbage made Mirchi depressed, a development that Abdul had willed himself not to resent. Instead he tried to share his parents' hope: that when his brother finished high school, his considerable wit and charm would trump the job-market liability of being a Muslim. Although Mumbai was said to be more cosmopolitan and meritocratic than any other Indian city, Muslims were still excluded from many good jobs, including some in the luxury hotels where Mirchi longed to work.

It made sense to Abdul that in a polyglot city, people would sort themselves as he sorted his garbage, like with like. There were too many people in Mumbai for everyone to have a job, so why wouldn't

Kunbi-caste Hindus from Maharashtra hire other Kunbis from Maharashtra, instead of hiring a Muslim of garbage-related provenance? But Mirchi said that everyone was mixing up nowadays, that old prejudices were losing strength, and that Abdul just couldn't see it, spending his days with his head in his trash pile.

Abdul was now working as fast as he could in order to finish by dusk, when strapping Hindu boys began playing cricket on the maidan, aiming their drives at his sorted piles, and sometimes his head. While the cricketers sorely tested Abdul's policy of non-confrontation, the only physical fight he'd ever had was with two ten-year-olds who had turf-stomped one of his little brothers. And these cricketers had just sent another Muslim kid to the hospital, after smashing his head in with their bats.

High above Abdul, Rahul was bobbling on another tree branch, trying to liberate a second resalable kite. The leaves of the tree were gray, like many things in Annawadi, on account of sand and gravel blowing in from a concrete plant nearby. You won't die to breathe it, old-timers assured red-eyed new arrivals who fretted about the spoon-it-up air. But people seemed to die of it all the time—untreated asthma, lung obstructions, tuberculosis. Abdul's father, hacking away in their hut, spoke of the truer consolation. The concrete plant and all the other construction brought more work to this airport boom-town. Bad lungs were a toll you paid to live near progress.

At 6 P.M., Abdul stood up, triumphant. He'd beaten the cricketers, and before him were fourteen lumpy sacks of sorted waste. As smoke clouds rose from the surrounding hotels—their evening fumigation against mosquitoes—Abdul and two of his little brothers hauled the sacks to the truckbed of a lime-green, three-wheeled jalopy. This small vehicle, one of the Husains' most important possessions, allowed Abdul to deliver the waste to the recyclers. And now out onto Airport Road and into the city's horn-honk opera.

Four-wheelers, bikes, buses, scooters, thousands of people on foot: It took Abdul more than an hour to go three miles, given calamitous traffic at an intersection by the gardens of the Hotel Leela, around the corner of which European sedans awaited servicing at a concern named "Spa de Car." A section of the city's first metro rail was being constructed here, to complement an elevated expressway slowly rising on Airport Road. Abdul feared running out of gas while in the gridlock, but in the last spidery light before nightfall, his wheezing vehicle gained a vast slum called Saki Naka.

Among Saki Naka's acres of sheds were metal-melting and plastic-shredding machines owned by men in starched kurtas—white kurtas, to announce the owners' distance from the filth of their trade. Some of the workers at the plants were black-faced from carbon dust and surely black-lunged from breathing iron shavings. A few weeks ago, Abdul had seen a boy's hand cut clean off when he was putting plastic into one of the shredders. The boy's eyes had filled with tears but he hadn't screamed. Instead he'd stood there with his blood-spurting stump, his ability to earn a living ended, and started apologizing to the owner of the plant. "Sa'ab, I'm sorry," he'd said to the man in white. "I won't cause you any problems by reporting this. You will have no trouble from me."

For all Mirchi's talk of progress, India still made a person know his place, and wishing things different struck Abdul as a childish pastime, like trying to write your name in a bowl of melted kulfi. He had been working as hard as he could in the stigmatized occupation he'd been born to, and it was no longer a profitless position. He intended to return home with both hands and a pocketful of money. His mental estimates of the weight of his goods had been roughly correct. Peak-season recyclables, linked to a flourishing global market, had bestowed on his family an income few residents of Annawadi had ever known. He had made a profit of five hundred rupees, or eleven dollars a day—enough to jump-start the plan that inspired his mother's morning curses, and that even the little Husains knew to keep close.

With this take, added to savings from the previous year, his parents would now make their first deposit on a twelve-hundred-square-foot plot of land in a quiet community in Vasai, just outside the city, where Muslim recyclers predominated. If life and global markets kept going their way, they would soon be landowners, not squatters, in a place where Abdul was pretty sure no one would call him garbage.

2.

Asha

RAHUL'S MOTHER, ASHA, took note in that winter of hope: The slumlord of Annawadi had gone batty and pious! Although Robert Pires beat his second wife, he let her live. He erected a Christian shrine outside his hut, then a second shrine, to a Hindu goddess. Before these altars every Saturday, he clasped his meaty hands in prayer and atoned for all past crimes by giving tea and bread to hungry children. Weekdays, the attractions of the underworld paling, he passed the hours in slack communion with nine horses he stabled in the slum, two of which he'd painted with stripes to look like zebras. Robert rented the fake zebras, along with a cart, to the birthday parties of middle-class children — a turn to honest work he thought the judging gods might factor in.

In this reformation, thirty-nine-year-old Asha Waghekar perceived an opportunity. Robert had lost his taste for power just as she was discovering her own. Let others thread the marigolds. Let others sort the trash. For the overcity people who wished to exploit Annawadi, and the undercity people who wished to survive it, she wanted to be the woman-to-see.

Slumlord was an unofficial position, but residents knew who held it—the person chosen by local politicians and police officers to run the settlement according to the authorities' interests. Even in a rapidly modernizing India, female slumlords were relative rarities, and those women who managed to secure such power typically had inherited land claims or were stand-ins for powerful husbands.

Asha had no claims. Her husband was an alcoholic, an itinerant construction worker, a man thoroughgoing only in his lack of ambition. As she'd raised their three children, who were now teenagers, few neighbors thought of her as anyone's wife. She was simply Asha, a woman on her own. Had the situation been otherwise, she might not have come to know her own brain.

Robert's chief contribution to Annawadi history had been to bring Asha and other Maharashtrians to the slum, as part of a Shiv Sena effort to expand its voting bloc at the airport. A public water connection was secured as an enticement, and by 2002, the Maharashtrians had disempowered the Tamil laborers who had first cleared the land. But a majority is a hard thing to maintain in a slum where almost no one has permanent work. People came and went, selling or renting their huts in a thriving underground trade, and by early 2008, the North Indian migrants against whom Shiv Sena campaigned had become a plurality. What was clear to Asha was also clear to the Corporator of Ward 76, the elected official of the precinct in which Annawadi sat: Robert now belonged to his zebras. He'd lost interest in Shiv Sena and the slum.

The Corporator, Subhash Sawant, was a man of pancake makeup, hair dye, aviator sunglasses, and perspicacity. While the obvious choice to succeed Robert as slumlord would have been a well-spoken Shiv Sena activist named Avinash, Avinash was too distracted to serve the Corporator's interests. He was fixing hotel septic systems day and night to afford private schooling for his son.

Asha, on the other hand, had time. Her temp work, teaching kindergartners at a large municipal school for modest pay, was a sinecure the Corporator had helped her obtain, overlooking the fact that her formal schooling had stopped at seventh grade. In return, she spent a good deal of class time on her cellphone, conducting Shiv Sena business. She could deliver her neighbors to the polls. She could mobilize a hundred women for a last-minute protest march. The Corporator thought she could do more. He asked her to handle a petty Annawadi problem, and then another, somewhat less petty, and yet another, not petty at all, at which point he gave her a bouquet of flowers and his fat wife started giving her the fish eye.

Asha took these things to be signs of an imminent triumph. Eight years after arriving in Annawadi and investing her hopes for economic betterment in political work, she had an influential patron. In time, she imagined, even the men of Annawadi would have to admit she was becoming the most powerful person in this stinking place.

Many of the men had preyed on her, early on. Assaying her large breasts and her small, drunken husband, they had suggested diversions that might allay her children's poverty. The menacing Robert had made his own blunt proposal one evening as she was filling a pot of water at the tap. Asha had set down the pot and replied coolly, "Whatever you want. Tell me, bastard. Shall I strip naked and dance for you now?" No other woman, then or since, had spoken to the slumlord that way.

Asha had developed her sharp tongue as a child, working the fields of an impoverished village in northeastern Maharashtra. Pointed expression had been a useful defense when laboring among lecherous men. Discretion and subtlety, qualities useful in controlling a slum, were things she had learned since coming to the city.

She had by now seen past the obvious truth—that Mumbai was a hive of hope and ambition—to a profitable corollary. Mumbai was a place of festering grievance and ambient envy. Was there a soul in this enriching, unequal city who didn't blame his dissatisfaction on someone else? Wealthy citizens accused the slumdwellers of making the city filthy and unlivable, even as an oversupply of human capital kept the wages of their maids and chauffeurs low. Slumdwellers complained about the obstacles the rich and powerful erected to prevent them from sharing in new profit. Everyone, everywhere, complained about their neighbors. But in the twenty-first-century city, fewer people joined up to take their disputes to the streets. As group identities based on caste, ethnicity, and religion gradually attenuated, anger and hope were being privatized, like so much else in Mumbai. This development increased the demand for canny mediators—human shock absorbers for the colliding, narrowly construed interests of one of the world's largest cities.

Over time, of course, many shock absorbers lost their spring. But who was to say that a woman, a relative novelty, wouldn't prove to have a longer life? Asha had a gift for solving the problems of her neighbors. Now that she had the Corporator's ear, she could fix more such problems, on commission. And when she had real control over the slum, she could create problems in order to fix them—a profitable sequence she'd learned by studying the Corporator.

Guilt of the sort that had overcome Robert was an impediment to effective work in the city's back channels, and Asha considered it a luxury emotion. "Corruption, it's all corruption," she told her children, fluttering her hands like two birds taking flight.

AS ASHA ARRIVED HOME from her teaching job one afternoon, her step didn't quicken when she saw supplicants lined up against the wall of her hut. From the Corporator she had learned the psychological advantage of making people wait and stew. With barely a nod to her visitors, she stepped behind a lacy curtain at the back of her hut and unraveled the deep red sari she'd worn to work.

Now that she was older, her eyes drew more attention than her breasts. She could weaponize them in an instant, and boys caught gaping at her magnificent nineteen-year-old daughter, Manju, would reel backward as if they'd been struck. When Asha thought about money, her eyes narrowed. She thought about money most of the time; Annawadians called her Squint behind her back. But the real distinction of her eyes was their brightness. Most eyes dulled with age and disappointment. Hers looked far more radiant now than they did in the photograph she possessed of her youth. A tall, stooped, emaciated farm girl with sun-darkened skin, freshly embarked on a disastrous marriage: When Asha looked at that photo, she laughed.

She emerged from behind the curtain in a shapeless housedress, another strategy picked up from the Corporator. He often presided over his lavender-walled, lavender-furnished living room in an undershirt, legs barely covered by his lungi, while his petitioners flop-sweated in polyester suits. He might as well have said it aloud: *Your concerns are so unimportant to me that I haven't bothered to dress.*

Settling on the floor, Asha accepted the cup of tea brought by Manju and nodded for the first of her neighbors to speak. An old woman with a creased, beautiful face and matted coils of silver hair, she hadn't arrived with a problem. She was weeping in gratitude, because on this date, three years earlier, Asha had helped her secure a temp job with the city government, extricating trash from clogged sewers for ninety rupees a day. Before Asha had learned better, she had performed many such kindnesses for free.

From her pay, the older woman had bought Asha a cheap green sari. Asha didn't care for the color. Still, it was good for the other visitors to hear the old woman's blessings, see the way she pressed her forehead to Asha's bare feet.

Another weeper spoke next: an overweight exotic dancer who had lost her job in a bar and was now getting by as the concubine of a married policeman. She had to service the officer in the hut she shared with her mother and her children, which was prompting family hysterics. "He says he's going to stop coming, because of the drama. Then what will we eat?"

Asha clucked. A morals campaign had driven most of the sex trade out of the airport area, and Annawadi's "outline women," as they were known, now had three bad options for satisfying their clients: in their family huts; behind a line of trucks parked nightly outside of Annawadi; or in the goaty, one-room brothel.

Briskly, Asha issued her advice: Explain more clearly to your family the long-term advantages of the liaison. "Maybe the officer doesn't give you too much now, but later, he might fix your house. So tell them to stay quiet and wait and see."

As she spoke, she ran her fingertips over her new orange ceramic floor tiles. Eight years back, when Annawadi was a flimsy encampment, her three children had jumped truckbeds to steal the wood and aluminum scrap from which the family had hammered up a shack. Now the hut had plaster walls, a ceiling fan, a wooden shrine with an electric candle, and a high-status, if nonfunctioning, refrigerator. The place was narrow and cramped, though. That had been the trade-off. To finance the improvements that might persuade her neighbors of her rising status, she'd rented bits of her living space to some of the continual stream of newcomers to Mumbai. Migrant tenants were holed up in a side room, a back room, and on the roof.

Although Shiv Sena was hostile to such migrants, Asha had always been more practical than ideological, and considered no financial opportunity too small. "Why do you care if other people call us misers?" she asked her children. As they said in her village, drops of rain fill the lake.

"Be quick, I have people waiting," Asha said into her cellphone. It was her younger sister, of whom she was jealous. Her sister's husband was a hardworking chauffeur, and their hut in a nearby slum had a stereo system and four fluffy white dogs, just for fun. Asha's consolation was that her sister's daughter was plain and slow and nothing like Manju, the only college-going girl in Annawadi, who was now kneading bread dough for dinner and pretending she wasn't eavesdropping on her mother's conversations.

Asha's sister had been trying to enter the fixing business, and saw an opening in the fact that a Hindu girl in her slum had run off with a Muslim boy. Asha stepped outside her house and lowered her voice. "The main thing," she advised her sister, "is that you take money from the family of the girl, but never say it's you who is asking for money. Tell them the police are asking for it. I have to go."

An old friend, Raja Kamble, stiffened when Asha came back in, for his turn to speak had come. Asha and Mr. Kamble had come to Annawadi at the same time; their children had grown up together. Now Mr. Kamble was painful to look at, kneeknobs and eyesockets mainly. He was counting on Asha to save his life.

Mr. Kamble had grown up even poorer than Asha: abandoned infant; dweller on pavement; doer of hopeless jobs, among them trudging office to office trying to sell scented cloths to slip into the earpieces of telephones, on the tiniest of commissions. "A perfumed phone cloth, sa'ab? To hide the hot-season stink?" In his thirties, though, he'd had a bolt of fortune. While he was working at a train-station food kiosk, a regular customer, a maintenance worker for the city government, had come to like and pity him. In short order, the man offered Mr. Kamble his own surname, a bride, and the grail of every poor person in Mumbai: a permanent job, like his own.

That job had been to clean public toilets and falsify the time sheets of his benefactor and other sanitation workers, so that they could take other jobs while collecting their municipal pay. Mr. Kamble felt honored by this responsibility. He and his wife had three children, bricked the walls of their hut, and on one wall installed a cage for two pet pigeons. (In his pavement-dwelling years, he'd developed a fondness for birds.) Mr. Kamble had been one of Annawadi's great successes—a man deemed worthy of titles like *ji* or *mister*—until the day he collapsed while cleaning a shitter.

His heart was bad. The sanitation department laid him off, saying that if he got a new heart valve and a doctor's clearance, he could return. Mumbai's public hospitals were supposed to do such operations for next to nothing, but the hospital surgeons wanted under-the-table money. Sixty thousand rupees, said the surgeon at Sion Hospital. The doctor at Cooper Hospital wanted more.

For every two people in Annawadi inching up, there was one in a catastrophic plunge. But Mr. Kamble still had hope. For the last two months, he'd been dragging his betrayal of a body out on the streets, asking politicians, charities, and corporations to donate to his heart-valve fund. The Corporator had pledged three hundred rupees. An executive at a paint factory had pledged a thousand. After hundreds of pleas, he was still forty thousand rupees short.

Now he clenched a smile at Asha—ten square yellow teeth that appeared huge in his wasted face. "I don't want a handout," he said. "I want to fix my heart so I can keep working and see my children married. So could you fix one of the government loans for me?"

He had learned that Asha was a minor player in a scam involving one of the many anti-poverty schemes the central government in

New Delhi had enacted in order to bring more citizens into its growth story. The government was lending money at subsidized rates to help poor entrepreneurs start employment-generating businesses. These new companies could be fictions, though. A slumdweller would request a loan for an imaginary business; a local government official would certify how many jobs it would bring to a needy community; and an executive of the state-owned Dena Bank would approve it. Then the official and the bank manager would take a hunk of the loan money. Asha, having befriended the bank manager, was helping him select the Annawadians who would get loans—for her own cut of the loan money, she hoped.

Mr. Kamble had decided his imaginary business would be a food stall like the one where he'd been working when his luck changed. If he got a loan of fifty thousand rupees, and from that paid five thousand each to Asha, the bank manager, and the government official, he would be only five thousand rupees short of the heart valve, and could go to a loan shark for the rest.

"You can see my situation, Asha," he said. "No work, no income, until I have the operation. And if I don't have the operation—you understand."

She looked him over, made the *ch-ch* sound she often made when she was thinking. "Yes, I can see you are in a bad state," she said after a minute. "What you should do, I think, is go to the temple. No, go to my godman, Gajanan Maharaj, and pray."

He looked stunned. "Pray?"

"Yes. You should pray for what you want every day. A loan, good health—pray to this godman. Keep hope, tell him to help you, and you might get it."

Asha's daughter Manju inhaled sharply. Growing up, she had sometimes wished that the gentle Mr. Kamble had been her father.

And she knew, as Mr. Kamble did, that when Asha said go to the temple and the godman, it meant to come back with a better financial proposal.

"But we are friends—you have known me, so I thought . . ." Mr. Kamble sounded as if he'd swallowed sand.

"Fixing a loan is not a simple thing. It is because we are friends that I want the gods to help you. So you live a long good life."

As Mr. Kamble limped away, Asha felt confident that he'd come back to her before he would go to any temple. A dying man should pay a lot to live.

Lately, Asha had been shirking the temple herself. She considered herself a religious woman, but in recent weeks she'd noticed that she got what she wanted from the gods regardless of whether she prayed or fasted. For some time she'd been meaning to pray for the downfall of a neighbor woman who said rude things about the nature of Asha's relationship to the Corporator, but before Asha had gotten around to it, the woman's husband fell ill, her elder son got hit by a car, and her younger son fell off a motorcycle. Asha concluded from this and other evidence that she had fallen into a cosmic groove of fortune. Perhaps the very groove that Mr. Kamble had recently vacated.

Across the room, her daughter was throwing a tantrum—the quiet kind, the only kind Manju ever threw. She was flinging the chopped onions into the frying pan with such force that some bounced out and onto the floor. Asha raised an eyebrow. Later tonight, the girl would sneak out to meet her friend Meena in the eye-watering public toilet, no doubt to cry over her mother's rejection of a dying neighbor. Asha wasn't supposed to know about those toilet tell-all sessions, but little happened in Annawadi that didn't get back to her eventually.

Asha was pleased with Manju's obedience, her locally heralded beauty, and the college studies that brought strange names like "Titania" and "Desdemona" to the household. But Asha considered it a failure of her parenting that Manju was sentimental. The girl spent her afternoons teaching English to some of the poorest Annawadi children—a job that had been Asha's idea, since it brought in three hundred rupees a month—but now Manju was always talking about this or that hungry child whose stepmother beat her.

Asha grasped many of her own contradictions, among them that you could be proud of having spared your offspring hardship while also resenting them for having been spared. When food was short in Asha's childhood, the girls of the family went without. Although most people talked of hunger as a matter of the stomach, what Asha recalled was the taste—a foul thing that burrowed into your tongue and was sometimes still there when you swallowed, decades later. Manju looked at her mother with compassion, not comprehension, when Asha tried to describe it.

As habitually as Asha sought a financial angle in her neighbors' complaints, so far most were merely tedious—for instance, the bickering between the Muslim breeder, Zehrunisa Husain, and Fatima the One Leg over whose small child had pinched whose. Asha didn't care for either woman. Fatima beat her children with her crutches. And Asha found Zehrunisa intolerably smug. Just three years back, in a killing monsoon, the Husains had no roof over their heads, at which time Rahul had perfected a wicked imitation of Zehrunisa, weeping. But now she and her morose son Abdul were rumored to be making money. "Dirty Muslim money, *haram ka paisa,*" was how Asha put it. Her own aspirations centered on anti-poverty initiatives, not garbage.

A government-sponsored women's self-help group looked somewhat promising, now that she knew how to game it. The program was supposed to encourage financially vulnerable women to pool their savings and make low-interest loans to one another in times of need. But Asha's self-help group preferred to lend the pooled money at high interest to poorer women whom they'd excluded from the collective — the old sewer cleaner who had brought her a sari, for instance.

Still, when foreign journalists came to Mumbai to see whether self-help groups were empowering women, government officials sometimes took them to Asha. Her job was to gather random female neighbors to smile demurely while the officials went on about how their collective had lifted them from poverty. Manju would then be paraded in as Asha delivered the clinching line: "And now my girl will be a college graduate, not dependent on any man." The foreign women always got emotional when she said this.

"The big people think that because we are poor we don't understand much," she said to her children. Asha understood plenty. She was a chit in a national game of make-believe, in which many of India's old problems—poverty, disease, illiteracy, child labor—were being aggressively addressed. Meanwhile the other old problems, corruption and exploitation of the weak by the less weak, continued with minimal interference.

In the West, and among some in the Indian elite, this word, *corruption,* had purely negative connotations; it was seen as blocking India's modern, global ambitions. But for the poor of a country where corruption thieved a great deal of opportunity, corruption was one of the genuine opportunities that remained.

AS MANJU FINISHED COOKING, Asha flipped on her TV, which had been the first in Annawadi, though something had since gone wrong with the color. The newscaster was hot pink as he provided an update on the famous Baby Lakshmi, a toddler born with eight limbs and duly named after the multi-limbed Hindu goddess. A few months back, a crack team of Bangalore surgeons had undertaken her de-limbing. The news story followed the usual script: the marvel of medical technology, the heroism of the surgeons, a video clip of the two-year-old girl at home, supposedly happy and normal. But even on a bad TV screen, it was obvious that the girl was not fine. Asha thought the family could have done better, financially, if they'd left Lakshmi alone and run her as a circus act. Still, it was the kind of medical-transformation report that would get Mr. Kamble, who watched the same Marathi-language channel, further riled up.

Everyone in Annawadi wanted one of the life-changing miracles that were said to happen in the New India. They wanted to go from zero to hero, as the saying went, and they wanted to go there fast. Asha believed in New Indian miracles but thought they happened only gradually, as incremental advantages over one's neighbors were parlayed into larger ones.

Her long-term goal was to become not just slumlord but the Corporator of Ward 76—a dream made plausible by progressive, internationally acclaimed legislation. In an effort to ensure that women had a significant role in the governance of India, the political parties were required to put up only female candidates for certain elections. The last time Ward 76 had an all-female ballot, Corporator Subhash Sawant had put up his housemaid. The maid had won, and he had kept running the ward. Asha thought that he might just pick her to run in the next all-female election, since his new maid was a deaf-mute—ideal for keeping his secrets, less so for campaigning.

Ward 76 contained many slums larger than her own, but Asha had just made her first move to develop a reputation beyond Annawadi's boundaries: investing in a large plastic banner with her name, color photo, and a list of her accomplishments as a representative of Shiv Sena's women's wing. The banner was now strung up at an open-air market half a mile away. Unfortunately, she'd had to include the photos of three other Shiv Sena women. The Corporator had warned her more than once about hogging credit.

"But I had to pay the whole whack," she complained to her husband, who had appeared for dinner cheerful-drunk instead of fighty-drunk, a relieving change. "These other women, they still have the village mentality," she told him. "They don't understand that if you spend a little up front, you get more later."

Rahul and her youngest son, Ganesh, came in, too. Asha stood, laughing, to yank Rahul's cargo shorts up from his hips. "I know, it's the *style*, your *style*, American *style*," she said. "All that, and it's still foolish." They each took a plate of lentils, soggy vegetables, and lopsided wheat-flour rotis, a meal whose tastelessness seemed intentional, and perhaps the product of Manju's silent rage about Mr. Kamble.

Asha knew her daughter judged her for her plots and side deals, and for the nighttime meetings with the Corporator, policemen, and government bureaucrats that these schemes always seemed to entail. But the politics for which Manju had contempt had bought her a college education, and might someday lift them all into the middle class.

"So do I have to teach you all over again how to make the rotis round?" Asha teased her daughter, merrily holding one of them up. "Come on! Who will marry you when you make such ridiculous bread?"

The roti dangling in Asha's fingertips was such a forlorn specimen that even Manju had to laugh, and Asha decided, wrongly, that her daughter had forgotten Mr. Kamble.

3.

Sunil

ABDUL WAS ALWAYS TWITCHY, but by February 2008 the scavengers saw he was more so: jingling coins in his pocket, shaking his legs as if preparing to sprint, chewing a wooden matchstick while his tongue did something weird behind his teeth. Across the city, gangs of young Maharashtrians had begun beating up migrants from the North — *bhaiyas*, as they were called — in hope of driving them out of the city and easing the scramble for jobs.

Though Abdul had been born in Mumbai, the fact that his father had come from the North qualified the family as targets, and not abstractly. Rioters chanting "Beat the bhaiyas!" were moving through the airport slums, ransacking small North Indian businesses, torching the taxis of North Indian drivers, confiscating the wares that migrant hawkers displayed on blankets.

These poor-against-poor riots were not spontaneous, grassroots protests against the city's shortage of work. Riots seldom were, in modern Mumbai. Rather, the anti-migrant campaign had been orches trated in the overcity by an aspiring politician—a nephew of the founder of Shiv Sena. The upstart nephew wanted to show voters that a new political party he had started disliked bhaiyas like Abdul even more than Shiv Sena did.

Abdul quit working and stayed inside to avoid the violence, about which roaming scavengers brought lurid reports. Ribs broken, heads stomped, two men on fire—"Enough," Abdul cried out one night. "Can you please stop talking about it! The riots are just a show, a few bastards making noise and intimidating people."

Abdul was repeating the reassurances of his father, Karam, who sought to keep his children incurious about aspects of Indian life beyond their control. Though Karam and Zehrunisa occasionally spoke in whispers of the city's 1992–1993 Hindu–Muslim riots and the 2002 Hindu–Muslim riots in the bordering state of Gujarat, they raised their children on a diet of patriotic songs about India, where tolerant citizens of a thousand ethnicities, faiths, languages, and castes all got along.

Better than the entire world is our Hindustan
We are its nightingales, and it our garden abode

This song, based on verses by the great Urdu poet Iqbal, played every time Karam's cellphone rang. "First these children have to learn to run after bread and rice," he told his wife. "When they're older, they can worry about the other things."

But Sunil Sharma, a perceptive twelve-year-old scavenger, could read the frantic matchstick in Abdul's mouth. The garbage sorter was already worried.

Sunil, a Hindu bhaiya, wondered about Abdul, who he thought worked harder than anyone else in Annawadi—"keeps his head down night and day." Sunil was startled once when he saw the garbage sorter's face in full sunlight. Except for the child-eyes, black as keyholes, Abdul looked to him like a broken old man.

Sunil was a seed of a boy, smaller even than Abdul, but he considered himself more sophisticated than the other scavengers. He was especially good for his age at discerning motives. It was a skill he had acquired during his on-and-off stays at the Handmaids of the Blessed Trinity orphanage.

Though Sunil was not an orphan, he understood that phrases like *AIDS orphan* and *When I was the second-hand woman to Mother Teresa* helped Sister Paulette, the nun who ran the Handmaids of the Blessed Trinity children's home, get money from foreigners. He knew why he and the other children received ice cream only when newspaper photographers came to visit, and why food and clothing donated for the children got furtively resold outside the orphanage gate. Sunil rarely got angry when he discovered the secret reasons behind the ways people behaved. Having a sense of how the world operated, beyond its pretenses, seemed to him an armoring thing. And when Sister Paulette decided that boys over eleven years old were too much to handle and Sunil was turned out onto the street, he tried to concentrate on what he had gained in her care. He'd learned how to read in the Marathi language as well as his native Hindi, and to count to a hundred in English. How to find India on a map of the world. How to multiply, sort of. How nuns weren't as different from regular people as nuns were commonly said to be.

His sister Sunita, two years younger, didn't want to stay in the orphanage without him, so together they'd walked back to Annawadi, where their mother had died of TB long ago. Their father still rented a hut on Annawadi's stenchiest lane, where the feral pigs gorged on rotten hotel food. The house was ten feet long, six feet wide, filthy, lightless, and crammed with firewood for cooking, and Sunil felt nearly as ashamed of it as he did of his father.

When the man was drunk, he smelled like a stove. When not drunk, he did road work in order to smell like a stove again, rarely setting aside money for food. Sunil alone watched out for Sunita. Once, when he was five or six, he'd lost her for a week, but he'd been careful not to misplace her after that.

Losing Sunita was one of Sunil's few clear memories of early childhood—how upset Rahul's mother, Asha, had become. Suddenly his ally, she'd tracked down Sunita in the south of the city, then barreled into his father's hut to say his children were going to die, the way he was drinking. Not long after, Sunil and Sunita ran across Airport Road, each holding one of Asha's hands, as if they were any old family. When they reached the black iron gate of the orphanage, though, Asha had dropped their hands and left.

In the years since, Sunil had come back to Annawadi frequently— whenever he'd had chicken pox or jaundice or some other goddess-in-the-body situation that threatened the health of Sister Paulette's other wards. He was therefore used to the transition: reaccustoming himself to scavenging work, to rats that emerged from the woodpile to bite him as he slept, and to a state of almost constant hunger.

In the old days, Sunil and Sunita had stood silently outside the huts of their neighbors at dinnertime. Sooner or later, some pitying woman would emerge with a plate. Sunita could still work this angle, but Sunil had now crossed an age line over which charity did not reliably extend. He looked closer to nine years old than to twelve, a fact that pained him on a masculine level, and might at least have been a practical help. But no one felt sorry for him anymore.

He minded being unpitiable only at mealtime. At the orphanage, when rich white women visited, Sunil had refused to beg for rupees. Instead he'd harbored the idea that one of the women might single him out, reward his dignified restraint. For years, he had waited for this discriminating visitor to meet his eye; he planned to introduce himself as "Sunny," a name a foreigner might like. Eventually, he'd come to realize the improbability of his hope, and his general indistinction in the mass of need. But by then, the habit of not asking anyone for anything had become a part of who he was.

In his first weeks back home, scavenging skills rusty, he took the sandals from the feet of his sleeping father and sold them to Abdul for food. He had consumed five vada pav by the time his father woke to thrash him. Another day, he'd sold his father's cooking pot. His own sandals he'd exchanged for rice, after which there was little left to sell. The hunger cramps could be treated by hits off discarded cigarettes. Lying down also helped. But nothing soothed his apprehension that the hunger was stunting his growth.

Sunil had inherited his father's full lips, wide-set eyes, and the pelt of hair that swooshed up from his forehead. (One distinction of his father was that his hair looked good even when his head was in a ditch.) But Sunil feared he'd also inherited his father's puniness.

A year earlier, at the orphanage, he'd stopped growing. He'd tried to believe that his body was just pausing, gathering strength in advance of some strenuous enlargement. But Sunita had since grown taller than he.

To jumpstart his system, he saw he'd have to become a better scavenger. This entailed not dwelling on the obvious: that his profession could wreck a body in a very short time. Scrapes from dumpster-diving pocked and became infected. Where skin broke, maggots got in. Lice colonized hair, gangrene inched up fingers, calves swelled into tree trunks, and Abdul and his younger brothers kept a running wager about which of the scavengers would be the next to die.

Sunil had his own guess: the deranged guy who talked to the hotels and believed the Hyatt was trying to kill him. "I think his guarantee is over," he told Abdul. But Abdul said it would be a Tamil guy whose eyes had gone from yellow to orange, and Abdul turned out to be right.

LIKE MOST SCAVENGERS, Sunil knew how he appeared to the people who frequented the airport: shoeless, unclean, pathetic. By winter's end, he had defended against this imagined contempt by developing a rangy, loose-hipped stride for exclusive use on Airport Road. It was the walk of a boy on his way to school, taking his time, eating air. His trash sack was empty on this first leg of his daily route, so it could be tucked under his arm or worn over his shoulders like a superhero cape. When Sister Paulette passed by in her chauffeured white van, it could be draped over his head. Sister Paulette-Toilet was how he thought of her now. He imagined her riding down Airport Road looking for children more promising than he.

On this road in the early morning, well-dressed young women hustled from the bus stop to their jobs inside the hotels, carrying handbags as big as household shrines. He hated meeting those purses on a crowded sidewalk. They could knock a kid into the street. But at dawn, the city felt roomy enough for everyone. Instead of being pushed along by the pedestrian stream, he could poke around the gardens that the airport's new management had installed on the roadsides. He was an expert climber and intended to make use of the coconut trees when they fruited. He took care not to step on the emaciated junkies who nodded out behind the lilies.

It interested him that from Airport Road, only the smoke plumes of Annawadi's cooking fires could now be seen. The airport people had erected tall, gleaming aluminum fences on the side of the slum that most drivers passed before turning into the international terminal. Drivers approaching the terminal from the other direction would see only a concrete wall covered with sunshine-yellow advertisements. The ads were for Italianate floor tiles, and the corporate slogan ran the wall's length: BEAUTIFUL FOREVER BEAUTIFUL FOREVER BEAUTIFUL FOREVER. Sunil regularly walked atop the Beautiful Forever wall, surveying for trash, but Airport Road was unhelpfully clean.

For waste-pickers, the road where air cargo was loaded and unloaded was the most profitable, and therefore competitive, part of the airport. Crammed with trucks, truck bays, overflowing dumpsters, and small food joints, the place was every week more overrun by scavengers. Some of the men flashed knives to keep Sunil out of promising dumpsters; more often, they waited until he had filled his bag, then kicked his ass and stole it. Women from the Matang caste, traditional waste-pickers, hurled stones. The Matangs worked in red and green saris, dowry jewels in their noses, and were nice to him back at Annawadi, where everyone waited in line to put their bags on a scale. But people of other castes were encroaching on the Matangs' historical livelihood, because steady work was hard to come by, and trash was always there. To the Matangs, people like Sunil, who belonged to an Uttar Pradesh carpenter caste, were invaders on Cargo Road.

Worse for the Matangs, and for Sunil, was the increased professional competition for trash. An army of uniformed workers kept the environs of the international terminal free of rubbish. Big recycling concerns took most of the luxury-hotel garbage—"a fortune beyond counting," as Abdul put it, in a whisper. And on the streets, new municipal garbage trucks were rolling around, as a civic campaign fronted by Bollywood heroines attempted to combat Mumbai's reputation as a dirty city. Stylish orange signs above dumpsters were commanding, CLEAN UP! Some freelance scavengers worried that, soon, they would have no work at all.

At the end of Sunil's brutal days, he sold to Abdul what hadn't been stolen from him. While the Matangs averaged forty rupees a day, his take was rarely more than fifteen—about thirty-three U.S. cents. Sunil felt he would never grow unless he discovered scrounging places that other people hadn't thought of, and to that end, started paying less attention to the other scavengers and more attention to the people who threw things away. It was what Annawadi crows did, circling and observing before trying to seize.

Rich travelers surely dropped fantastic garbage outside the international terminal, but airport security guards chased off the scavengers who came near it, even small ones who just wanted to hear if the signboard listing incoming flights went *chuck-a-chuck-a-whirrr* when updated, as Annawadi old-timers insisted. The construction workers building the new terminal would also leave trash, but their site was enclosed by blue-and-white aluminum fencing, which provided no traction for climbing. The officers at the Sahar Police Station, which was located on airport grounds, would have a trash flow, too, but like most people in Annawadi, Sunil was afraid of the police. He focused instead on a stand of yellow-and-black taxis next to the station.

A food stall at the taxi stand served the drivers who awaited arrivals. Most of the drivers quaffed their plastic cups of tea, ate their samosas, and dropped their trash where they stood. This choice territory belonged to other scavengers, but Sunil noticed that not all of the drivers behaved the same.

Some of the taximen tossed their cups and bottles over a low stone wall behind the food stand. On the other side of the wall, seventy feet down, was the Mithi River—actually, a concrete sluice where the river had been redirected as the airport enlarged. The drivers probably liked to imagine their garbage hitting the water and floating away, but Sunil had climbed the wall and discovered a narrow ledge on the other side, five feet down. By some trick of wind in the sluice, trash tossed over the wall tended to blow back and settle on this sliver of concrete. It was a space on which a small boy could balance.

Of course, if he stumbled, jumping down, he'd be in the river. Sunil knew how to swim, having learned in Naupada, a slum next to the Intercontinental hotel that went underwater each monsoon. He'd never heard of anyone drowning in Naupada, though. Naupada was the local definition of fun. The Mithi River, with its unnatural currents, was the place with the body count. After a few jumps, he trusted his feet.

The ledge stretched four hundred feet from the taxi stand to a traffic ramp, and people driving up the ramp sometimes slowed and pointed at him as he crouched there, high above the water. He liked the idea that the ledge work looked dramatic from a distance. In truth, it was less scary than working Cargo Road or scavenging during the riots, with the "Beat the bhaiyas!" men running around. And he was willing to take risks in order not to be a runt and a stub. His sack grew bulky and awkward as he moved down the ledge, and he learned to concentrate only on the trash immediately in front of him, looking neither down nor ahead.

BY MARCH, THE RIOTS OVER, their deepest effect began to surface in slums like Annawadi. Many North Indians had been afraid to work for two weeks. Unable to recover from the loss of wages, some migrants were belatedly fulfilling the hopes of the new political party, Maharashtra Navnirman Sena, which sought to uproot them from Mumbai.

Abdul's parents rented a forty-five-square-foot room in the back of their hut to the extended family of a Hindu autorickshaw driver from the northern state of Bihar. One afternoon in mid-March, the driver's distressed wife came to see Abdul's mother. Zehrunisa took her two-year-old son, Lallu, to her breast as she heard her tenant out.

The woman's husband and his brother rented their autorickshaw for two hundred rupees a day. Although they hadn't worked during the riots, they'd still had to pay the rent on the three-wheeled taxi. Now they didn't have money to buy gas for it, nor the rent they owed the Husains. The Bihari woman asked Zehrunisa's forbearance. "What can I do? Please don't chuck us out!"

"Ah, but the riots hurt us all," said Zehrunisa. "Abdul had to stop working, too. What do I hide from you? You know what the health of my children's father is like. We are four days away from sleeping on the footpath ourselves." It was her habit to exaggerate her poverty to her neighbors, the scavengers, and the policemen who came for bribes.

"But your business will keep you going," the Bihari woman said, fiddling with the ends of the sheer green pallu that covered her head. "Your house will not go away. You know the way we live—we earn to eat. You see my husband works hard, that my children are good." Her middle son was the best student in the small school run by Asha's daughter, Manju. He knew an English word for every letter of the alphabet: *jog kite lion marigold night owl pot queen rose.*

Zehrunisa tried to steer the conversation to politics. "Allah, those fucking Shiv Sena people, and whatever this new party is. For so many years they've tried to run us off. We work hard. Who is relying on their charity? Do they come to put food on our plates? All they do is create a useless *tamasha*—"

The ends of the Bihari woman's pallu were now balled in her fists. She didn't want to talk about politics, especially with Zehrunisa, who could run on like a train without brakes. She studied a lizard on the wall as it fanned out its throat. Finally, she interrupted her land-lady. "What does your heart say? I won't complain about taking the children back to the village, looking like a fool in front of my people. At least I can grow food there. But my husband and his brother—what? To leave them on the pavement?" She searched Zehrunisa's face until the Muslim woman looked away.

It was as the scavengers always said of Abdul's mother: Ten men pulling couldn't get her purse out of her pocket. As tears filled the Bihari woman's eyes, Zehrunisa cradled Lallu and began to sing to him. The scavengers said this, too: She wore that big, spoiled baby like a shield. And so the Bihari men were on the pavement, and the wife and children were on the three-day train ride back home.

"She said listen to your heart, and I did," Zehrunisa told Abdul a few days later. "My heart said if we let the money go, how will we pay the next installment on this land in Vasai? What if your father goes back to hospital? Finally we are making a little money, but once we start to think we're safe, we'll be stuck in Annawadi forever, swatting flies."

"New people will come after the monsoon," Abdul told Sunil and the other scavengers, because that is what his father told him. "Where else are they going to go?" The city was rough on migrants, terrible sometimes, and also better than anywhere else.

FOR DECADES, THE AIRPORT on which Annawadi livelihoods depended was a realm of duct tape, convulsing toilets, and disorganization. Now, in the name of global competitiveness, the government had privatized the place. The new management consortium, led by an image-conscious conglomerate called GVK, was charged with building a beautiful, hyperefficient new terminal—a piece of architecture that might impress on travelers Mumbai's rising status as a global city. The new management was also deputized to raze Annawadi and thirty other squatter settlements that had sprouted on vacant airport land. Though the airport-slum clearance had been proposed and postponed for decades, GVK and the government seemed poised to get it done.

Securing the airport perimeter was one reason to reclaim the land from the roughly ninety thousand families squatting there. The value of the land was another, since the huts sprawled across space that could be developed vertically at enormous profit. The third reason, in an airport branded "the New Gateway of India," with a peacock-feather logo, was national pride. For among the things that breakneck globalization had changed about India was its sensitivity about its slums.

As big banks in America and Britain failed, restless capital was looking eastward. Singapore and Shanghai were thriving, but Mumbai had profited less handsomely. Though it, too, had an abundance of young, cheap, trainable labor, there were opportunity costs attached to the fact that the Indian financial capital was alternatively known as Slumbai. Despite economic growth, more than half of Greater Mumbai's citizenry lived in makeshift housing. And while some international businessmen descending into the Mumbai airport eyed the vista of slums with disgust, and others regarded it with pity, few took the sight as evidence of a high-functioning, well-managed city.

Annawadians understood that their settlement was widely perceived as a blight, and that their homes, like their work, were provisional. Still they clung to this half-acre, which to them was three distinct places. Abdul and Rahul lived in Tamil Sai Nagar, the oldest and most salubrious section, which was anchored by the public toilets. Sunil's stretch of Annawadi, poorer and cruder, had been built by Dalits from rural Maharashtra. (In the Indian caste system, the most artfully oppressive division of labor ever devised, Dalits—once termed untouchables—were at the bottom of the heap.) Annawadi's Dalits had christened their slumlanes Gautam Nagar, after an eight-year-old boy who had died of pneumonia during one of the airport authority's periodic demolitions.

The third side of Annawadi was a cratered road at the slum's entrance where many scavengers lived. This side had no huts. Scavengers slept on top of their garbage bags to prevent other scavengers from stealing them.

Petty thieves slept on the rut-road, too. Their main targets were construction sites around the airport, where builders were sometimes careless with screws, rods, and nails. Before the airport was privatized, many of the thieves had worked there, carrying travelers' luggage to cars in exchange for tips. But as part of the makeover that had made the grounds of the international terminal nearly as lush as those of the luxury hotels, the ragtag loaders had been banished, along with the mothers who held up babies and begged for milk money, and the children hawking pocket gods.

The luggage-loaders-turned-thieves made a bit more money than waste-pickers like Sunil, and spent most of it on chicken-chili rice from a Chinese woman's Airport Road stall. They typically topped off their dinners with Eraz-ex, the Indian equivalent of Wite-Out. People in the office buildings threw out the bottles prematurely. Annawadi road boys knew the value of the dregs. Dilute with spit, daub onto a rag, inhale: an infusion of daring for after-midnight work.

Sniffing Eraz-ex was problematic in the long run, though. As Abdul pointed out to Sunil, the addicts were either thin as matchsticks or had big, troubling balls in their bellies.

Abdul felt vaguely protective of the undersized scavenger. The boy got excited about unusual things, like a map of the city he'd recently seen outside an airport workers' canteen. Back at Annawadi, Sunil talked about that map as if it were a gold brick he'd found in the gutter, and seemed surprised when other scavengers took no interest. Abdul recognized this tendency to get punchy about discoveries to which other people were indifferent. He no longer tried to explain his private enthusiasms, and figured Sunil would learn his own aloneness, in time.

As for Sunil, he couldn't help noting that the stoned thieves were having more fun than sober, drudgy Abdul. When spring came, they amassed raucously at Annawadi's first entertainment center, a shack on the road with two hulking red video-game consoles inside.

The game parlor was a loss leader for an old Tamil man who had begun competing with Abdul for the scavengers' goods. The Tamil was nearly as clever as Asha. He lent the scavengers the one rupee it cost to play Bomberman or Metal Slug 3. He lent them bars of soap and money for food. To the thieves, he lent tools for cutting concertina wire or wedging off hubcaps. Indebted, the scavengers and thieves had to sell their goods to him.

The Husains considered this unfair competition, and one night, seeking revenge, Mirchi broke into the game shed and cleaned out the consoles' coin boxes. When the Tamil discovered the culprit, he laughed. The game-shed profits were negligible against his larger return from stolen goods.

To Sunil, one road boy stood apart from the others: an antic fifteen-year-old named Kalu, who was the closest thing Abdul had to a friend. Kalu mocked the game-parlor man for wearing his lungis too short, and disputed his contention that Muslims like Abdul were cheats with magnets hidden under their scales. Kalu's specialty as a thief was airport recycling bins, which often contained aluminum scrap. Though the bins were in compounds secured by barbed-wire fences, his tolerance for pain was a thing of legend. Thanks to Eraz-ex, which was also the local balm for concertina-wire wounds, he could make three round-trips over the fences in a night. After selling his metal to Abdul, he sometimes slipped Sunil a few rupees for food.

Like Sunil, Kalu had lost his mother when he was young, and he'd been working since age ten. One of his jobs had been polishing diamonds in a heavily guarded local factory, contemplation of which drove the other boys batshit.

"Why didn't you put a diamond in your ear?"

"Or ten diamonds up your asshole!"

They weren't convinced by Kalu's description of the diamond-detecting machines he'd had to pass through at the end of each day.

What Sunil loved about Kalu were his inspired enactments of movies he'd seen, for the benefit of kids who'd never been to a theater. With a high-pitched approximation of Bengali, Kalu would become the possessed woman in the Bollywood thriller *Bhool Bhulaiya*. With a guttural approximation of Chinese, he'd be Bruce Lee in *Enter the Dragon*. He refused to do *King Kong* anymore, despite popular requests. Becoming Deepika in *Om Shanti Om* pleased him more. "*Arre kya item hai!*" he'd say, sashaying. "Only she can pull off those old-style outfits!"

Kalu himself was plain, if you broke the face down to features: small eyes, flat nose, pointy chin, dark skin. When other road boys gave him his nickname—*Kalu*, meaning "black boy"—they hadn't meant it as a compliment. But he had status, not just for the pain tolerance but for his ability to manufacture fun. When bored with mimicking film stars, he'd act out the leading freaks of Annawadi, including the lipsticky One Leg who walked with her butt stuck out and who was lately screwing a heroin-addicted road boy when her husband went to work. That a road boy was getting sex, even with a defective like the One Leg, was immense.

Sunil often eavesdropped on Kalu's conversations after dark, and in this way learned that policemen sometimes advised the road boys about nearby warehouses and construction sites where they might steal building materials. The cops then took a share of the proceeds. One midnight, Sunil overheard Kalu, uncharacteristically serious, tell Abdul about a thieving expedition he'd botched near the airport.

A police officer had turned him on to an industrial site with metal lying on the ground and no barbed-wire fences—a place Kalu called "the workshops." He went at 11 P.M. and found some pieces of iron, but a security guard had come after him. Ditching the metal in high weeds, he'd run back home.

"If I don't get the iron before morning, another boy will find it," Kalu told Abdul. "But I'm too tired to go back now."

"So ask one of these boys out here to wake you later," Abdul suggested.

The other boys were high, though, and anyway had a loose sense of time.

"I could wake you," Sunil offered. The rats in his hut left him sleepless.

"Good," said Kalu. "Come at three A.M., and if you don't, I'll be finished."

Kalu said *finished* lightly, the way he said most things, but Sunil took it hard. He lay down on the maidan, a few feet from Abdul, and tracked the time by the movement of the moon. At his best guess of 3 A.M., he found Kalu curled up asleep in the backseat of an autorickshaw. Rising, the fifteen-year-old wiped his lips and said, "The boy who was going to go with me is too stoned. Will you come?"

Sunil was startled, then honored.

"Are you afraid of water?" Kalu asked.

"I can swim. I swim at Naupada."

"Do you have a bedsheet?"

A bedsheet was one thing Sunil had. He ran to fetch it, then followed Kalu out onto Airport Road. As the boys crossed the street, Sunil wrapped the sheet around himself. He felt shivery, though this was not a cool night. Kalu turned and laughed. "You'll scare people like that! They'll think you're a walking ghost!" Reluctantly, Sunil gobbed his sheet under his arm as they gained the road leading up to the international terminal.

Cars were still coming out of the airport. Arrivals from Europe and America, Kalu said; he'd learned the flight schedules and the names of many world cities while loading luggage. He said the best tippers were Saudis, Americans, and Germans, in that order.

Past a glittery DEPARTURES sign and some security barricades that read HAPPY JOURNEY, the boys sprinted down a half-paved road used by construction vehicles, then veered onto a narrower, pitch-dark lane. Sunil could navigate it blind. After some high fences behind which airplane meals got made was an open-air toilet where he'd often found empty water bottles. The boys skipped quickly over this wasteland. Now they were standing at the edge of a wide gully that took runoff from the Mithi River. Sunil came here from time to time to catch mangoor fish to sell back at the slum. When he was young, the water had been blue—"like swimming-pool water," he said. It had since turned black and reeking, but the fish still tasted sweet.

Across the gully to his right were towering security fences, protecting floodlit hangars. Jets were rolling in for the night. The far left side of the gully, where Kalu said they were going, was dim and still. Sunil could make out one spindly Ashoka tree, and behind it, indistinct, several large, shedlike buildings. Kalu jumped into the fetid water and paddled toward them. Sunil swam too, then waded when he saw Kalu wading. The current in the trench was gentle, the monsoon being nine months past. Still, Sunil's stomach felt liquid as he scrambled up the opposite bank.

What Kalu called "the workshops" was a large new industrial estate. Smelting. Plasticizers. Lubricants. A concern called Gold-I-Am Jewels Unlimited. Bluish lights in front of a few of the warehouses illuminated the figures of uniformed guards, whose shadows seemed thirty feet long.

Sunil wanted to dive back into the water. But Kalu had planned a circuitous route to the weeds where he'd hidden the iron. "The guards won't see," he said. "It will be easy." Which was how it turned out. The iron in the weeds looked like barbells to Sunil, and felt like barbells when lifted. This posed the sole dilemma of the night: How much weight could the two boys manage, swimming? Making their bedsheets into slings, they decided to carry three irons apiece.

They staggered away with their loads, and fifteen minutes later they were back in Annawadi, sopping. When Abdul woke at dawn, he bought the iron for 380 rupees, and Sunil got a cut of one-third. What the police officers got, Sunil couldn't say. Kalu seemed quietly satisfied with his profit. For Sunil, it was the first disposable income of his life.

To Pinky Talkie Town, then. Kalu led the way to the movie theater, where Sunil was mesmerized by the carpet and the clean. The noon film was an American one, its lead actor a man named Will Smith who, on the screen, seemed to be the lone human survivor of a plague in New York City. A she-dog had also survived this plague, and became the hero's friend. The dog was yellow with a large spot like a saddle on her back, and the man spoke to her as if she could understand everything. Then, near the end, the man strangled her.

Sunil figured the hero had a motive for murdering his only friend. In addition to the plague, there had been a ghost and an explosion, and while these events no doubt contributed to the hero's decision, Sunil couldn't work out the chain of logic. When he emerged from the dark theater into the sunblast of a spring afternoon, he felt sickened by the betrayal of the she-dog. He partially recovered after eating until his belly was full.

A few weeks later, Kalu asked for his help again, and as Sunil considered other thieves devouring plates of chicken-chili rice, he began to weigh this potential career path against the waste-picking that led to maggots, boils, and orange eyes. But for now, he thought, he'd stick with his dumpsters and his ledge.

Abdul seemed relieved at this choice, though Sunil could never read all of what that old man of a boy was thinking. Kalu didn't press him either, which was good, because Sunil wasn't sure that his reasoning would make sense to anyone else. It had something to do with the fact that, on the most profitable day of his life, he'd failed to reach the state of exhilaration that other boys called "the full enjoy." The strangled she-dog had been only part of it. He sometimes said of being a scavenger, "I don't like myself, doing this work. It's like being an insult." He thought he might like himself even less, being a thief. Moreover, Kalu's dealings with the Sahar Police made him uneasy.

Later, Sunil would come to understand the extent of the power that Mumbai police officers had over Annawadi road boys. But now, as good as he was at divining motives, he could only conclude that the workings behind Kalu's night jobs were beyond a twelve-year-old's ability to grasp.

4.

Manju

THE PLOT OF THIS NOVEL *Mrs. Dalloway* made no sense whatsoever to Manju. Doing her college reading, Asha's daughter felt so sluggish that she feared she'd caught dengue fever or malaria again—hazards of living thirty feet from a buzzing sewage lake. No, she decided. It was simply the weather: Only spring and already the sun was scorching, a knifing white force that made the eyes ache and sent Annawadi water buffalo prematurely into heat. Manju thought her mother looked wan, too, but this was possibly because Corporator Subhash Sawant—the man Asha hoped would make her slum boss—had been accused in court of electoral fraud.

When Manju first asked about the rumor, Asha had shrugged it off. Her patron had previously made two murder charges disappear. "Court cases can be managed in Mumbai," as the Corporator put it. So why did his bulk seem to be slipping from his chest to his belly? The clamminess around his collar seemed imperfectly correlated to the weather.

Just as the Indian government allowed only women to stand for certain elections, it reserved other elections strictly for low-caste candidates, to increase the presence of historically excluded populations in the country's political leadership. In the previous year's elections, restricted in Ward 76 to low-caste candidates, the Corporator had won handily. Subhash Sawant wasn't low-caste, though. He'd simply manufactured a new caste certificate, a new birthplace, and a new set of ancestors to qualify for the ballot. At least ten candidates in other city wards, mostly Shiv Sena, had done the same.

But the Congress Party candidate for Ward 76, a genuine low-caste who had finished second, was now papering the High Court with evidence of Subhash Sawant's falsifications, asking the judge to overturn the election. Suddenly, the Corporator felt the need for citizen homage. He'd been running this ward for more than a decade, could barely recall the autorickshaw-driving and petty thuggery that came before. So he'd begun visiting the ward's slums to receive the love of his constituents, in hopes that it might somehow trump a paperwork discrepancy.

Annawadi's turn next. Asha and Manju would assemble the slum-dwellers in a pink temple by the sewage lake in order to pray with him for a victory in court.

Asha winced when he gave the order. It was the season of school exams, and parents were reluctant to leave their huts and risk having their children abandon their textbooks. She had to bring all her influence to bear to ensure a respectable attendance.

At sunset on the designated night, Subhash Sawant strode into Annawadi in an impeccable white safari suit, accompanied by an entourage. Sunil and the other scavengers gaped from a distance. The Corporator had one of those spread-leg policeman strides—as if his thighs were too muscled for normal walking. And there was enough oil in his hair to fry garlic.

The Corporator approved of the poori bhaji that Manju and her friend Meena were cooking for the ceremony. He was pleased, too, with the decorations in the tiny temple, which was furnished with an old metal school desk. The Tamil construction workers who'd settled Annawadi, Meena's parents among them, had erected this hut and consecrated it to Mariamma, the goddess who protects against plagues. With Subhash Sawant's approval, Asha had helped wrest control of it for the Maharashtrians, after which the pink temple sat locked most days. But this afternoon, Meena and Manju had given it a proper scrubbing. The dead flies and rat turds were gone, the new idols shining.

"Call people, and I'll come after dinner to speak," the Corporator told Asha before he and his entourage departed in their SUVs. Asha rang the temple bell at 8 P.M., and soon the place was packed. As a tabla player drummed quietly, Asha arranged herself by the school desk, the gold border of her best sari catching the light of a dozen votive candles.

Almost every person in the temple, Asha included, was genuinely low-caste. Most were the migrants Shiv Sena wanted to banish from Mumbai. But the residents had come not just out of fear of angering Asha, but out of belief in the Corporator himself.

They understood Subhash Sawant to be corrupt. They assumed he'd faked his caste certificate. "But he alone comes here, shows his face," Annawadians said. Before each election, he'd used city money or tapped the largesse of a prominent American Christian charity, World Vision, to give Annawadi an amenity: a public toilet; a flagpole; gutters; a concrete platform by the sewage lake, where he usually stood when he came. And each time he visited, he told residents how hard he'd been fighting to hold off the bulldozers of the airport authority, which had razed huts here in 2001 and 2004. In the scheme of the airport modernization project, and of the governance of Mumbai, the Corporator was a bit player, a pothole-filler of a politician. But he loomed larger than the Indian prime minister in the political imaginations of Annawadians. He needed their votes; they needed to believe in his power to protect them.

"When does he come?" people asked.

"Soon," Asha promised. The packed temple grew ripe with sweat. Slum dwellings, temples included, sucked in the heat of the city and held it, but in the first hour the misery went unexpressed. The next hour, the temple was teeming with sighs.

Time was precious to Annawadians, even those not tense about their children's exams. They had work at dawn, homes to clean, children to bathe, and above all water to get from the slum's trickle-taps before they went dry, which involved standing in line for hours. The municipality sent water through six Annawadi faucets for ninety minutes in the morning and ninety minutes at night. Shiv Sena men had appropriated the taps, charging usage fees to their neighbors. These water-brokers were resented, but not as much as the renegade World Vision social worker who had collected money from Annawadians for a new tap, then run away with it.

At 10 P.M., Asha's sari blouse was soaked at the throat and armpits, but she'd finally reached Subhash Sawant's chauffeur on the phone. "He's on his way," she told the crowd, then struck up a group prayer, so that when the Corporator arrived he would find the residents hard at their devotions.

At 11 P.M., he still hadn't come. Asha gestured to her daughter. "Get the food." The dishes Manju had prepared were to be consumed after the ceremony, but people were starting to leave, and neither the Corporator nor the chauffeur was answering his phone.

The would-be celebrants ate and went home, leaving only a dozen people, mostly sad-sack drunks, in the temple. Asha could not compose her face.

The departees would say that Asha had promised to deliver the Corporator and failed. Worse, Subhash Sawant, a late-night type, would arrive to find an empty temple. It was a catastrophe for which she alone would be blamed. He would give her that smile that could not be read but as an insult. He would say that she didn't have the respect of the residents, that Annawadi wasn't ready for a female slumlord. No doubt he would mention how many people had gathered for how successful an evening at how many other slums.

As Asha bitterly laid out these probabilities to her daughter, a beautiful young eunuch wandered into Annawadi. Seeing a drummer sitting idle in an empty temple glowing with light, he went inside and started to dance.

The eunuch had long thick curls, lashes that touched his eyebrows, cheap metal bangles on his wrists, and hips that swiveled slowly, at first. He held his arms out, statue-still, while his legs became slithery things. The drummer came to life. Manju's mouth fell open. It was as if the eunuch's upper and lower body were being operated by separate controls. He paused to take a votive candle in his teeth, then launched into a spin that extinguished the flame.

The eunuchs, or *hijras*, of Mumbai were feared and fetishized both. They had so much bad luck, being sexually ambiguous, that the bad luck was understood to be contagious. When eunuchs came to your doorstep, you had to pay them to go away. You paid a little more if you wanted them to throw a coconut in front of your enemy. But once the coconut was thrown, the evil eye would stick, even if your enemy hired a *baba* to burn three incense sticks in a glass of rice with a sprinkle of vermilion powder on top.

Six eunuchs lived in Annawadi and wore hardship on their makeup-smeared faces. Some of them had come into the temple behind the young one. But this young eunuch, a stranger, was unblemished, his femaleness not a matter of dress and lip paint but of something in his face beyond naming. He did not want money to go away. He was now spinning so fast his locks were perpendicular to the ground, his sweat splattering the faces of the slumdwellers who had come back inside the temple, ensorcelled.

Dropping down on all fours, he bucked, butt high in the air, then sang a clear, high note that reverberated with his jerking. His name was Suraj, and he was eighteen years old. Asha's son Rahul guessed at once what others did not: Under his tight jeans, Suraj was intact. He had simply felt, for as long as he could remember, and to the heartbreak of his mother and sisters, that he was three parts girl, one part boy. Now he lived on the tips he earned going slum to slum, dancing so hard it gave him intestinal afflictions. Like Asha, he was trying to make his name in Ward 76.

Two women pushed forward to spin with the eunuch, becoming sinuous red-and-green blurs. Then the eunuch collapsed on the floor. People gasped, suspecting a seizure, until he announced that a goddess inside him had something to say. "Yellamma says bring her a neem leaf, and she will answer your questions of the future!"

Asha frowned. What if Subhash Sawant arrived to witness this performance? She decided it was better than his finding an empty temple. People were still arriving, jumping up to try to catch a glimpse of the eunuch over all the other heads. The road boys came out, as did the brothelkeeper and his customers. The sons of the zebra-tending Robert set two tires on fire in the maidan, compounding the excitement, while inside the temple, questions were put to the goddess lodged in the eunuch's soul.

"Should I take a loan to fix my house?" "Should I pay this man who says he can get me a job?" "How will I afford my daughter's wedding?" "What will my son become?" There were several questions about whether children would pass their exams, one question about a heart valve, and many questions about the airport authority. "When are these airport people going to break our houses?" The goddess might know even more than Corporator Subhash Sawant.

It mattered little that the eunuch's responses were gibberish, or some goddess-tongue that no one understood. The voice, whether the goddess's or the eunuch's, was hypnotic and felt like a blessing in itself.

People were now screaming their questions. Inside the Husain house, across the maidan, screaming could also be heard.

"What *is* this! When will they shut up?" Abdul's brother Mirchi cried, placing his forehead on his math book. How could he study for his ninth-grade exams? His father paced back and forth, cursing the Corporator and the Hindus of Annawadi. "These work-shirking idolators inflict their noise on us on a hundred holidays a year, and now, not even a holiday, they've lost their heads over this dancing . . . freak."

The most advanced student in Annawadi, a twenty-one-year-old named Prakash, lived four doors down from the temple. He sat at home with an economics book in his lap and his head in his hands. Two teardrops rolled between his fingers. His all-important final exams before college graduation, sabotaged by a spinning eunuch. He would flee to Bangalore, a city he considered more respectful of scholars, the first chance he got.

At 1 A.M., the Corporator answered his phone. He wasn't coming, was tied up with more important people. But he was pleased with Asha, for he assumed the glorious din he heard over the phone was all of Annawadi rallying in his honor.

Asha's lucky streak was continuing. "Inside now," she said to Manju.

"Coming," Manju said vacantly, her eyes still fixed on the sweat-wet eunuch. "But, Mother? Never have I seen such a thing in my life."

———

ANNAWADIANS AGREED THAT Manju was nicer than she had to be, given her looks, her mother's political connections, and her punishing schedule. Mornings, she went to college. Afternoons, in the family hut, she ran the slum's only school. In the other hours, she provided cooking, cleaning, water-collection, and laundry services to her household of five. These obligations were fulfilled by sleeping only four hours a night, and rarely impinged on her temperament. But this spring, her composure was being tested by a series of mysterious infections and fevers.

Asha worried that her daughter's body ran hot, which increased the risk that she'd lose her virtue. Manju was hardly in danger. She had spent her teenaged years turning herself into a model of proper and gentle deportment—deportment she thought her own mother lacked.

One afternoon, her brother Rahul stood at a small mirror tacked on the wall of their hut. As he massaged his face with Manju's Fair and Lovely skin-lightening lotion, he considered her through the brown freckled glass. She was kneeling on the floor, glossy braid flung over her shoulder, murmuring English words with an escalating desperation.

"What a face you're making," Rahul said. Manju looked up.

"Rahul, not so much cream!"

The Fair and Lovely lotion was crucial to maintaining her light complexion, and thereby her status in the marriage market, but Rahul and their younger brother, Ganesh, applied it more liberally than she did.

Rahul turned on the TV, where the cartoon mouse Jerry, disguised in shoe polish, was convincing Tom that he'd swallowed enough explosives to blow up a city. Manju watched for a minute, then sighed again. "I don't know what I am doing," she said. "My students will come in an hour, and I'm behind on my own work. My computer teacher said, 'Ask your mother what she wants you to do—your Photoshop assignment or your housework?' Else he will fail me. And did I tell you what happened yesterday in psychology class? I left my purse under the desk to go to the toilet and someone took my money. What sort of people! And the other girls have more money than I do. But why do I bother telling you? Your eyes are inside the TV—not even listening."

"I *am* listening," Rahul protested. "You're just sitting on so many tensions I don't know which one to think about."

Rahul had his own tensions, balancing ninth-grade exams and late-night hotel temp work. By now he could expertly mimic the way the Intercontinental waiters fixed their faces when they got near a guest. There had to be both an upward tilt, saying *I am alert and obliging,* and a chin-down servile thing: *I am invisible to you, sir, if you'd prefer that.* His own face was open, with amusement-seeking eyes. Annawadi girls came around to it quickly. But he thought that a better-managed face might have spared him the humiliation he had suffered at a recent hotel party.

The trouble had begun with a deejay who, after midnight, seemed to be reading his telepathic requests. A Christina Aguilera belter—*I am beautiful, no matter what they say*—segued into "Rise Up," a dance song that was Rahul's current favorite.

Rise up! Don't be falling down again
Rise up! Long time I broke the chains.

The lyrics, in English, were meaningless to him, the bass line irresistible. Every time he heard it, he vibrated inside. When the first echoing chords came through the hotel speakers, he might have smiled, or tapped a foot. Suddenly two young hotel guests were tugging his arm, asking him to demonstrate some "Mumbai moves."

Sozzled white people were known to be generous tippers. He began, discreetly he thought, to demonstrate a few steps—no shoulders and hands, just head and feet.

"Have you gone mad, asshole?"

A hotel superior grabbed him. Other managers came running from across the room. It was if he'd stabbed a Bollywood star with a fork. The permanent waiters sniggered as he was dragged on his heels into the trash room. Only later, recovering at home, did he find the line of argument he might have used to defend himself. If the first law of hotel work was not to stare at the guests, wasn't the second law to give them whatever they asked for?

As cartoon Tom blew a house to smithereens, Rahul turned back to the mirror, and Manju began her reading for her major, English literature. Today's assignment was eighteenth-century Restoration drama and Congreve's *The Way of the World*.

Manju hadn't read *The Way of the World*, nor did her professors expect her to. Except in the best colleges, dominated by high-caste, affluent students, Indian liberal arts education was taught by rote. At her mediocre all-girls college, founded by the Lions Club, she was simply required to memorize a summary the teacher provided for each literary work on the syllabus, then restate it on the test and, later, on state board exams. Manju had a gift for memorization— she called it "my by-hearting." But she found the characters in *The Way of the World* hard to keep straight.

"Millament, Mirabell, Petulant—have you ever heard such names? And there are so many more," she told Rahul after a while. "Everyone is telling lies and tricking people to get money, but where my teacher wrote what the story means, I don't understand."

"Love is subordinated" was the trouble spot. Although she had never held the hand of a boy her own age, *love* was an English word about which she felt confident. *Subordinated*, though, evoked only irritation at her mother, who hadn't kept her promise to buy Manju an English-Marathi dictionary. Neither Rahul nor her mother knew English, and both took umbrage that the language of India's former colonizers was considered requisite for decent jobs in offices and hotels, when Marathi was just as venerable a language.

To Manju, the new importance of English was a by-product of something she generally welcomed: a more globalized, meritocratic India. It didn't much matter whether a person learned the language by studying Congreve or by practicing Chase Manhattan Visa Card dialogue at Personaliteez Spoken English or one of the training courses for international call-center work. Competence in English—a credential bespeaking worldliness and superior education—was a potential springboard out of the slums. Her own English was still slow and wooden, though good enough to be the second-best in Annawadi.

The best English was spoken by Prakash, the economics student who lived near the temple. In the intricate social hierarchy of Annawadi's young people—something now based less on caste than on future economic prospects—Prakash was the guy at the top. He had once been middle class, studying in a good private school, before his father got hit by a train. In his spare time, he sold mutual funds for ICICI Bank, making cold calls for a paltry commission.

Manju figured that Prakash would know the meaning of the word *subordinated*, but she had never spoken to him. A young woman in the slum had to weigh the value of each potential interaction with a male against the rumors it would inspire. Already people were gossiping about a cricket player who had secured her photo and laminated it in the shape of a heart. So as she went outside to scrub the laundry, she didn't even glance at the fellow college student who was reading outside his hut, a few yards away.

"Mirabell—beau. Millament—gallant. Mr. Fainall—cuckold." She murmured bits of plot summary as she applied the stone to her mother's large panties, her father's small shirt.

"No, *Mirabell* is the gallant." She took the wrung-out clothes inside and hung them on a string against the wall. Part of the wall stopped two feet from the roof, and her father had been promising to close the gap for ages, but that was as likely as her mother arriving home with an English-Marathi dictionary.

As she cleaned the two-burner stove, she repeated, "Themes are love affairs, social position, and money." Roaches, a hundred of them, scattered. Stepping over Rahul, now asleep on the floor, she took some food scraps outside and dumped them in the sewage lake, which the hot season had magicked into a thick mat of water-hyacinth weed.

"Mirabell seeks social advantage through marriage to the beauty, Millament."

When Manju by-hearted, she often pictured herself in the role of the heroine, but this girl, Millament, left her cold—whining when she was rich and independent enough to be negotiating her own marriage. Manju wanted to be a teacher when she finished college, and her great fear was that, in a fit of pique, her mother would wed her to a village boy who didn't think that a woman should work. That she'd die doing the things she was doing now: sweeping the dirt that had blown in from outside, mopping, then sweeping the new dirt that had blown in while she mopped.

"In Congreve's drama, money is more important than love."

This was her mother's position, obviously. Manju's younger brother Ganesh was at the front of the house, manning a small grocery that represented Asha's latest entrepreneurial scheme, a failing one. To start the store, she had secured for herself one of the government loans that Mr. Kamble hoped would finance his heart valve. Asha had intended for her husband to run the store, but he'd been using the proceeds to get drunk while he worked. He was currently passed out at Ganesh's feet.

Manju wasn't too interested in money. She hungered for virtue, a desire that was partly a fear. When studying, she sometimes fingered the scar on her neck from a night, years ago, when she'd stolen money from her mother to buy chocolates. Asha had responded with an axe. But Manju's desire to be good was also rebellion—a way of chastising a mother who was said to have acquired the television set and other advantages by behaving badly.

Manju's instrument for demonstrating her decency was the school she ran out of her hut every afternoon. The school was financed by central government money, funneled through a Catholic charity, and Asha was the teacher, officially. But her mother was busy with Shiv Sena, so Manju had been running the class since she was in seventh grade, displaying a commitment her mother found annoying. Although Asha was pleased with the small stipend the school brought to the household, she thought Manju should conduct the class only on days when the supervisor came to check, the way a lot of other hut-school teachers did.

The central government called schools like Manju's "bridge schools." Her brief was to provide two hours of daily lessons to child laborers or girls kept home by household responsibilities, in order to get them acclimated to, and excited about, formal education. Sparking enthusiasm wasn't hard. As every slumdweller knew, there were three main ways out of poverty: finding an entrepreneurial niche, as the Husains had found in garbage; politics and corruption, in which Asha placed her hopes; and education. Several dozen parents in the slum were getting by on roti and salt in order to pay private school tuition.

In the last five years, more than one hundred schools had opened around the airport—some excellent and expensive; some fraudulent; some, like Manju's, taught by unqualified teenagers. But all were understood to be better than the free schools like Marol Municipal, where Asha was a contract teacher. Nearly 60 percent of the state's public school teachers hadn't finished college, and many of the permanent teachers had paid large under-the-table sums to school officials to secure their positions. The Corporator was among the politicians who preferred to capitalize on these abysmal schools instead of reforming them. He'd opened his own private school, using a front man.

"At Marol, we play, take recess, play again, then have lunch," was how the Nepali boy, Adarsh, described the municipal school curriculum. The free lunches were the big draw. Adarsh came to Manju's school after his regular school day, since she was always teaching something—often, the plot summaries she was trying to memorize for college. Her students didn't understand the plot of *Mrs. Dalloway* any better than Manju did, but they got that Othello was distrusted because of his dark skin.

Now one of the other students flew into her hut with such velocity that a poster of Bal Thackeray, Shiv Sena's aging founder, fluttered off its tack on the wall. "Devo! You're early!" Manju protested. "And you forgot to take off your shoes!"

Her eyes then moved from the mud tracks on the floor to his face, which was covered in blood.

"Oh," the boy said, holding his head. "A taxi . . ."

Annawadi kids were always getting hit on the chaotic roads—usually, while crossing a treacherous intersection to get to Marol Municipal School. New drivers talking on new cellphones could be a lethal combination. Manju leaped up, grabbed the turmeric by the stove, and poured the yellow powder over Devo's head. Turmeric, as good for wounds as for brides before weddings. She rubbed the spice until it blended with the blood into a bright orange paste, then pressed down hard. She was checking to see if she'd stanched the bleeding when Devo's one-eyed, widowed mother came through the door, brandishing a foot-long piece of metal.

"No car will kill you! No god will save you! You went in the road, roaming loose like that, and now you will die at my hands!"

Devo darted under a wooden cupboard where Manju's family stored their possessions, and emitted a stricken, anticipatory howl. Pulling him out, his mother began to beat him with the strip of metal.

"No!" Manju said. "Not the head! Not where he's hurt!"

"I'll break your teeth! I will turn your flesh red," Devo's mother shouted. The fastest way to financial ruin in Annawadi was injury or illness, and the woman was already in debt to the loan shark who had financed the final hospital stay of her late husband. "If the driver had hurt you worse, how would I have paid the doctor? Tell me, Devo. Do I have one rupee to spend to save your life?"

"Stop," Manju cried, trying and failing to catch the woman's hand. Rahul, awake now, rolled his eyes; he considered the hut school a magnet for family histrionics. In calmer moments, Manju could argue that parents were terrified of losing control of their children in a city where dangers seemed to be multiplying—a city they didn't fully understand. And as much as Manju hated violence of any stripe, the odd thrashing, like the odd axe blow, could be effective in keeping a child close to home.

Devo's mother had now moved past the point of constructive teaching, however. Manju lunged between mother and son, managing to capture Devo's mother in a hug.

"Promise," Manju said to Devo, panting. "You will not go in the road again."

"Will not," he got out between heaving sobs. "Now I won't make such a mistake."

Fixing her one eye on Manju before departing, his mother said, "Tomorrow if he does not sit with you and study, I will break his legs and pour kerosene on his face."

Manju was stanching the boy's wound for a second time when a little girl said accusingly, "Teacher. You're late for school."

Manju untied her dupatta, which was streaked with blood and spice. "Come, let's get the others." Left unattended in the house, her students could be as extravagant as her brothers with the Fair and Lovely.

Manju always looked angry when emerging from her hut. Everyone who left her house got tight in the lip unless they wanted a mouthful of flies, the only creatures in the slum enthusiastic about the stale goods in her mother's new store. "Class, come," she called out as she crossed the maidan, stepping lightly around the piles of trash being sorted by Abdul. She knew who he was because Rahul hung out with his brother, Mirchi, but of course she didn't speak to him. The garbage boy didn't speak to anyone, as far as she could tell.

"Children, quickly now," she called, clapping her hands as she turned into one of the slumlanes. "Phut-a-phut! It's late!" Her official position was that having to round up her students was a bother. Shouldn't they show up voluntarily?

In fact she liked being outside, peering into doors and collecting snatches of neighborhood gossip, in these minutes when the mantle of teacher protected her from rumor. Today's raging controversy involved clipboards that advertised Honda motorcycles, from a dealership in Siloam Springs, Arkansas. The World Vision charity had intended them as gifts to three dozen children it sponsored in Annawadi, but the clipboards were being hoarded by the social workers assigned to hand them out. Manju was always relieved to hear of local scandals in which her mother played no pivotal role.

One by one her students, mostly girls under age twelve, emerged from their huts. Several of their sun-bleached dresses had broken zippers, exposing bony backs. Manju didn't worry about little Sharda. The girl was born spiny, like her mother, who'd broken rocks on the road before her lungs went. Lakshmi was the painful case. Her stepmother reserved the food of the house for her own children. The brothelkeeper's eleven-year-old daughter, kitted in tight black bicycle shorts and dangling earrings, had her brother in tow. Both children liked to be out of their hut when visitors came to have sex, especially when the sex was with their mother. For many of these children, Manju's little school was no bridge. It was all the education they would get.

The troupe then marched to the hut of Manju's secret pupil, her friend Meena. Meena's parents kept the old ways about girls and education: Too much learning reduced a girl's compliancy. Manju had been teaching Meena English on the sly.

Meena, fifteen, had been the first girl born in Annawadi, arriving two years after her parents helped turn the swamp into a slum. She was a Dalit; Manju belonged to the Kunbi farming caste, a backward caste but higher. Like most young Annawadians, the girls considered the caste obsession of their elders to be an irrelevant artifact. Manju and Meena had become friends because they both loved to dance, and stayed friends because they could keep each other's secrets.

Now, seeing Manju in her doorway, Meena flashed a smile that was not her wide, thrilling film-star smile—the one that other girls tried unsuccessfully to emulate. Today's smile was the go-away version, which indicated that she was on lockdown, allowed out only to fetch water or use the toilet. Her crime, as usual, was a failure to hold her tongue with her brothers and parents. Why couldn't she listen to the boys in the maidan when they were talking about the hotels? Why couldn't she go to school? During the day, she did her household duty, but at night fury sometimes overcame her, and her mother and brothers would feel compelled to beat it out of her. Such behavior could sabotage the marriage being arranged for her in their Tamil Nadu village.

Manju routinely advised Meena to keep her discontents to herself, as Manju did. Still, the Tamil girl's defiance spoke to something inside Manju. This morning as Manju was getting ready for college, the small silvery bindi she was putting on her forehead slipped and caught in the small of her neck. It glinted prettily there. Asha had already left for work. Manju let it stay. A girl could be virtuous without being perfect.

Back in the hut, her students arranged themselves on the bloody floor.

"Good afternoon, students," she said in English.

"Good afternoon, teacher," the children called back at deafening volume.

She paused, uncertain of what to do next. She didn't grasp enough of *The Way of the World* to practice its plot with her students. That would have to be internalized later, while she cooked dinner, and before her mother started fighting with her father about being drunk. The day's official class assignment was the English names of fruits — apples, bananas, mangoes, papayas. She'd work to it gradually, after a review of a previous lesson on cars, trains, and planes. But first, since the children were poking each other, there would be ten energy-depleting minutes of "Head-Shoulders-Knees-and-Toes."

Her students' singing rang out across the maidan, as it always did at this hour. Sunil, the young scavenger, liked to eavesdrop when he brought his goods to sell to Abdul. He'd sat in on Manju's class for a few days in January, mastering the English twinkle-star song, before deciding that his time was better spent working for food. He was now taking the position that Manju's school was two-bit games in a hut.

Abdul, who considered Manju the most-everything girl in Annawadi, could only wonder at the small boy's sense of superiority. One of Abdul's own arrogances, in these weeks before the One Leg burned and everything changed, was that he could predict the fates of other people, especially scavengers. But Sunil's future was hard to make out. Although contempt was a force that changed a person, being a waste-picker hadn't yet infected Sunil's mind, if he still thought memorizing "A Is for Apple" might make some difference in his life.

PART TWO

the business of burning

Rich people fight about stupid things.

Why shouldn't poor people do the same?

— AN ANNAWADI MOTHER,
RAMBHA JHA

5.

Ghost House

AT FIRST, FATIMA THE ONE LEG loved her poor, older husband in the brother-sister way. She learned other ways of love after marriage. This taste of affection was too much a revelation to be hidden. At thirty-five, more or less, she had become known in Annawadi for a sexual need as blatant as her lipstick. Had she been another sort of woman, her affairs might have been a scandal; that she was disabled made them a joke. As were her spectacular rages, which enlivened many an Annawadi evening.

Fatima had refined her verbal arsenal early, given the insults about the leg she was born with, which turned into a flipper past the knee. By thirty, she could out-curse even Zehrunisa. When a government program provided her with metal crutches, she was doubly armed. Strong in the shoulders, she brought the crutches down hard on neighbors she considered disrespectful. She threw the crutches, too, with uncanny aim. Desi liquor, some people whispered, by way of explaining her fits, though there wasn't enough liquor in all of Annawadi to keep Fatima as mad as she was.

She was damaged, and acknowledged it freely. She was illiterate — acknowledged that, too. But when others spoke of her fury as an ignorant, animal thing, that was *bukwaas*, utter nonsense. Much of her outrage derived from a belated recognition that she was as human as anyone else.

Sometimes, the afternoon men left her money; most were too poor to do so. But even the poorest of them helped her grasp what her parents had taken from her — those ashamed and shaming parents who'd hidden an imperfect daughter in their hut.

It had been daily punishment, watching her siblings run off to school and return to suck up their parents' affection. "I had such hate for myself, back then," Fatima told Zehrunisa, whom she alternately relied on and resented. "All I heard was that I had been born wrong." Nowadays, when her mother took the train across the city to visit, she couldn't help but pass around a glamour photo of Fatima's younger sister — that two-legged marvel with a sparkling jewel in her nose. "*This* one is a good girl," the mother liked to say. "See how nice she looks, and fair?"

"The One Leg could say worse, be worse, the way she grew up," Zehrunisa told Abdul, though she privately considered it self-indulgent for a grown woman to complain about her childhood. Zehrunisa could barely stand to speak of her own early years of water-and-wheat-husk soup in Pakistan, before an arranged marriage sent her across the border. Few women in Annawadi could look back on a honeyed youth. But Fatima thought wretched early years should be rounded out by a few good ones, which she had yet to have.

She had no interest in playing the shuffling, grateful role that the charitable types expected of the disabled. It was hard enough maintaining her pride in a slum where even hardy women grew exhausted running a household. In the monsoon, Fatima's mornings sometimes started like this: one leg, two crutches, twelve-pound vessel of pump-water, mudslick, splat. Add to this young daughters whom she couldn't chase after—needy, rambunctious creatures who laid her deficiencies bare. Only in the hours when the men came—husband at work, daughters at school—did the part of her body she had to offer feel more important than the part of it she lacked.

JUNE, THE BEGINNING of the four-month monsoon season, made every sensible Annawadian pensive. The slum was a floodbowl, surrounded as it was by high walls and mounds of illegally dumped construction rubble. In a 2005 deluge that brought the whole city to a standstill, Fatima's family had lost most of what they owned, as had the Husains and many other Annawadians. Two residents had drowned, and more would have, had not a construction crew building an addition to the Intercontinental hotel supplied ropes and pulled slumdwellers through the floodwaters to safety.

This year, the clouds broke early, and for a week the rain came down like nails. Outside Annawadi, construction projects stopped, and daily-wage workers braced for hunger. Hut walls grew green and black with mold, the contents of the public toilet spewed out onto the maidan, and fungi protruded from feet like tiny sculptures—a special torment to those whose native customs involved toe rings.

"I'm going to die of these feet," said a woman whose fungus fanned out like butterfly wings as she lined up in the rain for water. "The way my children eat, the rice I've stored won't last two weeks," said the woman behind her, as the seasonal complaints gathered momentum. "I don't want to be stuck inside with my husband for all these months." "At least you're not married to Mr. Kamble—heart valve day and night." But just as the women settled into the rhythm of monsoon grievance, the rains ceased, replaced by a syrupy yellow sun. Then the women wished the rains would start again; it seemed unnatural for them to quit for so many days.

The children saw the break in the rains differently. While the school year would soon resume, a clear sky permitted a final orgy of play. Abdul's brother Mirchi started a giant game of ring toss in the maidan, using the flagpole and busted bicycle tubes from Abdul's storeroom.

"It's a fluke," Mirchi said to Rahul, whose inner tube had juddered down the flagpole.

"What fluke?" protested Rahul, as other boys cheered and thumped his back. "Watch me—I can do it again!"

Zehrunisa came out to watch the game, wiping away tears as she considered her exuberant son. Mirchi seemed to have forgotten the pall he'd brought over the household by failing ninth grade. She considered him her brightest child, had even imagined him becoming a doctor. Now his unexpected failure brought the tally of Husain household crises to three. Her husband was in the hospital, struggling to breathe, and her eldest daughter, Kehkashan, had run away from her husband of a year.

Mirchi's cheerfulness had much to do with the return of his sister. All of the Husain children had been elated to see her. It wasn't just that she could cook and clean in place of their mother, who spent most of her days at the hospital. To her younger brothers and sisters, Kehkashan had been a second mother—a more organized, less exhausted version of the original. But she'd returned home with heartbreak in her eyes.

Kehkashan's husband was also her cousin; Zehrunisa and one of her sisters had arranged the marriage when their children were two. But Kehkashan felt that the intimate photos in her husband's cellphone—of a woman not more beautiful than she—resolved a question that had troubled her since the wedding. Why didn't her new husband want to make love? "He told me once, 'It's because you go off to sleep too early,' so I would stay up late," she told her mother. "Then he stopped coming home at night. He says, 'Don't correct me, you don't have any rights over me.' What kind of life is this?" The women in her husband's family kept strict purdah—stayed inside the house unless accompanied by a man. "So I sit at home, entirely dependent on this man," she said, "and then it turns out his heart was never with me."

Zehrunisa hoped that her sister would be able to bring the husband back in line. But to her daughter's urgent question—"How is it possible to force someone to love me?"—she had no answer, because the faults of her own husband did not include a lack of love.

The Hindu cricketers took note of Kehkashan's return, deciding that the Muslim girl's resplendent looks trumped the taint of her goat-eating and dwelling amid garbage, especially now that she was presumed not to be a virgin. Boys stared into her hut. Kehkashan averted her eyes. She sometimes wished, for peace's sake, that she was plainer.

Zehrunisa blamed Fatima for drawing such dogs in heat to the family doorstep. She'd managed to beat away one of Fatima's lovers, who kept drifting over to leer at her daughter, but he was frail from a heroin habit. Other men might fight back. Fatima would sit on her neck, too. With Kehkashan crushed, Mirchi a failure, toddlers to chase after, her husband in the hospital, and a fever she couldn't get rid of, Zehrunisa lacked the energy for a fight with the One Leg.

Zehrunisa tried not to judge the private morality that Fatima had developed; she knew the woman craved affection and respect. But especially when Zehrunisa considered Fatima's children, her own respect drained away. Recently, Fatima had gone at her eight-year-old, Noori, so hard with the crutches that Zehrunisa and another woman had had to tackle her. And then there was Fatima's two-year-old, Medina. After the little girl got TB, Fatima had become obsessed about catching the disease herself. Then Medina had drowned in a pail.

"I was in the toilet when it happened," Fatima had claimed to Zehrunisa. But shared walls leak secrets, one of which was that when Medina drowned in a very small hut, Fatima and her mother were there. Fatima's six-year-old daughter, Heena, had also been on hand, and said afterward, "Medina was a very nice sister until that day."

Zehrunisa had paid for the funeral shroud and the burial plot, and tried to convince herself that Medina's death had in fact been an accident. She thought about her own children, and how she didn't know what they were up to half the time.

The police came to Annawadi one day to ask about Medina's death, an inquiry quickly closed. Young girls in the slums died all the time under dubious circumstances, since most slum families couldn't afford the sonograms that allowed wealthier families to dispose of their female liabilities before birth. Sickly children of both sexes were sometimes done away with, because of the ruinous cost of their care.

One-year-old Danush, who lived two lanes over from the Husains, had gotten an infection in the filthy public hospital where he was born. His skin peeled off, and the touch of a sheet made him scream. His family took loan after loan at usurious interest, spending fifteen thousand rupees trying to cure him. Then one night in March, his father had beaten back his wife and emptied a pot of boiling lentils on the baby in his sari-sling cradle. Asha's son Rahul had jumped smack into the middle of that horror show—had run to get the police. Zehrunisa admired the hell out of Rahul for that. Danush reached a hospital and survived. Now Zehrunisa ached every time she saw him: that grave, unblinking eye in a burn-mapped face.

After Medina drowned, Fatima seemed oddly liberated. Other

women said the worst of her, and she found that she didn't much care. She drew on dramatic black eyebrows, shellacked her cheeks with powder—"spent fifty rupees to turn into a white lady," the Husain boys whispered—and picked up a fresh set of lovers. "Did you see how that guy and his friend are looking at me?" she would say to Zehrunisa. "Are you jealous? No man looks at you." The men she invited inside found her beautiful, she told her neighbor. Said there was no woman like her in all of India. Said she deserved a nicer life than she had.

The Husains felt for Fatima's husband, who sorted garbage in another slum, earning a hundred rupees for a fourteen-hour day. Mirchi put it bluntly: "She treats that old man like a shoe." The shoe often came over to complain about his wayward wife, and one night Zehrunisa had teased him. "Idiot, you should have asked me before you married. I could have picked you a nice Muslim woman with two legs who would raise your children and run your household properly."

Mistake. Thin walls. Fatima was in her face, crutches waving. "Who are you to call me a bad wife!"

Still, when Fatima and her husband fought, she would call out Zehrunisa's name. And Zehrunisa would go, sighing, to separate the miserable couple, just as she sighed on Eid and other Muslim holidays before inviting them to share her mutton korma. The family of the child-abusing Fatima, the family of the skeezy brothel owner: This was the Muslim fellowship she had in Annawadi.

"It's easy to break a single bamboo stick, but when you bundle the sticks, you can't even bend them," she told her children. "It's the same with family and with the people of our faith. Despite the petty differences, Muslims have to join up in big sufferings, and for Eid."

BLACK CLOUDS HUNCHED over the hills west of the city, but didn't break. Annawadi children kept flinging their inner tubes toward the flagpole, and one July morning, Abdul's father watched the game from his doorway, beaming. His shirt hung as loosely as ever off his shoulders, but Fatima and the other neighbors marveled when they saw his face. Garbage proceeds had financed a two-week stay in a small private hospital, where he'd breathed oxygen instead of foul slum air. Karam was shining. He looked *naya tak-a-tak,* brand new.

"I can't believe it," the Tamil woman who ran the liquor still told Zehrunisa. "Ten years gone from his face, like that. He looks like some Bollywood hero—Salman Khan."

"He ought to look good," said Zehrunisa. "We paid twenty thousand rupees to that hospital. But it's true, he got so young—like a boy! I see him from the corner of my eye and I think, oh shit, I forgot that I had another child. Now I will have to arrange another marriage! Allah knows I have enough marriages to do already."

The next marriage would be Abdul's. Though the financials remained to be worked out, she and her husband had settled on a likely girl, the sixteen-year-old daughter of a scrap dealer in Saki Naka, the industrial slum where Abdul sold his goods. The girl was pretty, no moles evident. Crucially, she was habituated to filthy men. She had come to the house three times, demure in a burqa, her younger sister in tow. From what Mirchi could make out, this younger sister was extremely hot, and in her honor, he painted a large red heart on the front of the family hut.

Mirchi claimed to be eager for marriage. One day, well out of his father's earshot, he said, "Mother, I want a wife just like you—she'll do all the work, and I'll do nothing." But Abdul was as cautious about marrying as he was about everything else.

"I hear of this love so often that I think I know it, but I don't feel it, and I myself don't know why," he fretted. "These people who love and then the girlfriend goes away—they cut their arms with a blade, they put a cigarette butt out in their hand, they won't sleep, they won't eat, they'll sing—they must have different hearts than mine."

He told his parents, "You don't hold a hot iron in your palm, do you? You let it cool. You think on it slowly."

"No, I think we should marry him quickly," Zehrunisa told her husband as she cooked lunch a few days after his homecoming. He'd asked for meat to build his strength, and she was crouched on the floor breast-feeding Lallu while stirring a cartilaginous stew. "A marriage would make him happy, I think. So much turmoil inside him— I don't think he's been happy for a single day in Annawadi."

"Who is happy, living here?" her husband replied, fishing a silver-foil packet of prednisolone from a plastic bag of medicines he'd tacked on the wall. "Am I happy? All around us, third-class people and no one with whom I can relate. Does anyone here even know of the American war in Iraq? All they know of is each other's business. But I don't complain to you. Why is Abdul complaining?"

"Do you know your own son? He says nothing—just does his work, does what we ask him. But why is it only his mother who sees that he is sad?"

"He will be happier when we go to Vasai," he replied.

"Happier in Vasai," she quietly repeated, with a sarcasm he chose to ignore.

The small plot of land on which they'd made a deposit in January was an hour and a half farther outside the city, in a community of construction suppliers and industrial recyclers. Many of its residents were Muslims from the Uttar Pradesh district in which Karam had been raised, on the Nepal border. He'd learned of the Vasai community from a Muslim developer so given to religious disquisition that Mirchi and Abdul called him the imam, rolling their eyes.

The first time Karam visited the place, he'd been struck by a group of men clutching newspapers and speaking animatedly at a tea stall. He imagined they were discussing the black man in the United States who was trying to become the country's president. Karam had heard that this Obama was secretly a Muslim, and was rooting for him.

The dirt roads twisting upward from the tea stall had been giddy with chickens, which reminded him of his native village. He wasn't sentimental about that village, in a district where there was little work except in sugarcane fields and children died at one of the highest rates in India. But he felt that urban slums surrounded by affluence turned children contemptuous of their parents—"because we can't give the brand-name clothes, the car." He considered it fortunate that Mirchi was merely lazy, not a defiant consumer of Eraz-ex, but there were six other children after Mirchi. To Karam, Vasai was the ideal village-city hybrid: a place where opportunity and parental respect weren't mutually exclusive.

"And at least there they would not be insulted for their religion," he told his wife.

Zehrunisa felt it premature to invest their dreams for their children in a part-owned bit of dirt that lacked even four bamboo poles and a tarp under which to sleep. "Our ghost house," she'd taken to calling the property. She'd given him permission to make the deposit. He always consulted her on financial decisions, since the results had been dire the two times he ignored her advice. But it irritated her that he hadn't yet taken her to see the land.

"How can I take you, with all these children to care for?" he'd been saying all year. But Kehkashan was now here to help, and she still hadn't seen the place. She wondered if the community was so like his native village that it had gotten him to thinking like the conservative Muslim men who lived there.

Before her husband's hospitalization, the developer had visited to discuss the property payments. She'd worn her burqa, served tea, then crouched in a corner, as her mother had done in Pakistan. Covered and unseen by men outside her family was the way Zehrunisa had expected to live out her adult life. But shortly after marriage brought her to Uttar Pradesh, she was working the sugarcane fields— at night, among men. She had prayed constantly for her husband's TB to relent so that she could go back into purdah. "I couldn't even speak in those days," she told her children. "I was scared of the whole world." Having a man to deal with that world on her behalf had seemed to her a fine thing.

She had stopped praying for a return to purdah after Kehkashan was born. She believed in focusing her requests to Allah, troubling Him with only one matter at a time. So she prayed for the health of Kehkashan and then for the health of Abdul, who entered the world in a pile of dirt by the Intercontinental hotel. Her husband had brought the family to Mumbai in hopes of finding work less strenuous than farming. Renting a pushcart to transport waste to recyclers was the work he could find.

Abdul had been a sulky infant—refused his mother's breast as often as he took it. But he had survived, unlike the next boy. Then Mirchi came, fat and pretty, followed by six more, also healthy. Nothing in Zehrunisa's life had brought her more satisfaction than the fact that her children took after her, not her husband, in their haleness. Not an undersized one in the lot, after Abdul.

Soon, one of the younger boys would prove clever enough to take over her role in Abdul's business—negotiating with scavengers, thieves, and police. Then she would gladly stay in the house. But to go back to purdah? It had belatedly dawned on her that this might be expected in Vasai. It would exacerbate her husband's condescension, a quality sufficiently annoying that she had to snap at him from time to time.

"Just because I can't read, you pretend to everyone that you're the hero in this family and I am the nothing," she'd said to him recently. "Like I would have been stuck in my mother's womb without you to get me out! Go, act like this big-time shareef, but it is I who have been managing everything!"

Annawadi's lack of censorious, conservative Muslims allowed her to call out her husband when necessary, just as it had allowed her to work to feed her children. Such freedoms would be painful to give up.

"In your mind, you've already moved to Vasai," she told her husband, ladling out the stew and handing it over with the economy of motion people develop when living in small, overpopulated huts. "Maybe you should pack up and go. And then go to Saudi—oh, there you can really relax! But this house is where your wife and children live. Look at it. You also felt ashamed when that imam came over."

Walls bloated and watermarked from flooding. Uneven stone floor with a hoard of recyclables in every corner, and more recyclables beneath an iron bed they'd recently purchased because Karam's breathing improved when he slept a foot higher than the trash. But had he slept like a bat on the ceiling, there would be no escaping the smell: trash, stale cooking smoke, and the olfactory traces of eleven human beings who lacked sufficient water to get clean.

"I'd like to leave this place, too," Zehrunisa said. "But where do your children grow up? In the ghost house?"

He looked at her, confused. All last night, all morning, she had been affection itself.

But Zehrunisa had had an idea, and sensed an auspicious moment when her husband came out of the hospital. It had nothing to do with the position of the moon and the stars. It had to do with the shortness of life and a break in the rains.

"Do you remember how anxious you were in the hospital?" she

said. "Thinking, what if you were to leave this family?" He had told her, then, "I fear God is inviting me in."

Karam nodded, frowning. "So?"

"He let you out this time." She paused. "Do I work hard for this family? Do I ask for jewelry?"

"No," he admitted. "You don't ask."

She was less and less sure she wanted to go to Vasai, less and less sure her husband would live to get there. She wanted a more hygienic home here, in the name of her children's vitality. She wanted a shelf on which to cook without rat intrusions—a stone shelf, not some cast-off piece of plywood. She wanted a small window to vent the cooking smoke that caused the little ones to cough like their father. On the floor she wanted ceramic tiles like the ones advertised on the Beautiful Forever wall—tiles that could be scrubbed clean, instead of broken concrete that harbored filth in each striation. With these small improvements, she thought her children might stay as healthy as children in Annawadi could be.

Before she'd even finished making her petition, her husband had assented, setting into motion the chain of contingency that would damage two families forever. The Husains would spend some of their savings to make a decent home. The next day, typically, Karam was acting as if the renovation had been his own idea. In this instance, a happy wife let her husband's nonsense go.

6.

The Hole She Called
a Window

THE LITTLE HUSAINS grasped the seriousness of the house renovation when their parents kept them home from school, now back in session. For the next three days, even six-year-old hands would have assignments, the first of which was to drag everything in their hut onto the maidan. The rusty bed came out first, and Karam and Zehrunisa settled in, guarding their possessions from passersby while watching Abdul direct his sibling labor crew.

"Finally, my kitchen!" Zehrunisa said, leaning into her husband, her head scarf slipping down to her shoulders.

"Look at Atahar," said Karam after a while. Their third son was furiously stirring cement to keep it from hardening in the day's oppressive heat. "I despair because he has no brains—eighth grade and can't write the number 8. But he works hard. Like Abdul, not afraid of labor."

"He'll be okay," Zehrunisa agreed. Her fifth son, Safdar, was the child she worried about. He was dreamy and impractical, like her husband. He loved frogs, and in pursuit of them sometimes swam the sewage lake. No one liked to sleep next to him after he did that.

Asha's husband, Mahadeo, materialized at the bedside. Slight and weathered, he was monosyllabic when sober, as he'd been since Asha found a cleverer hiding place for her purse. In hopes of relieving this painful condition, he offered his construction skills to the Husains for a hundred rupees.

Abdul, who didn't quite know what he was doing, was glad for Mahadeo's help. Asha was the only one in that family who unnerved him. "I think she's mad in her ambitions," Abdul's father had said a few nights earlier. "She wants a shining public life, wants to be some big politician, when her private life is so shameful. Does she think other people can't hear her fight with her husband at night?" Their fights were indeed as loud as the ones between Fatima the One Leg and her husband. Asha, it was rumored, always won.

As Mahadeo and the Husain children worked, some of Manju's students wandered over, curious. Manju would soon be calling them to class, but in the meantime they perused the Husain possessions, piled up on the maidan. Adults also came to look. Only a handful of neighbors had been inside the Husains' hut, but to judge by the piles, the Muslim garbage people were less poor than had been assumed.

Many Annawadians recalled how much the Husains had lost in the 2005 deluge. Their youngest daughter had nearly drowned, and their clothing, rice stores, and savings of five thousand rupees had washed away. Now they had a roughly carpentered wooden cupboard for their clothing—a cupboard twice as large as Asha's. A small television, bought on an installment plan. Two thick cotton quilts, one blue-and-white checked, one chocolate brown. Eleven stainless steel plates, five cooking pots. Fresh cardamom and cinnamon, superior to the spices most Annawadians used. A cracked mirror, a tube of Bryl-creem, a big bag of medicines. The rusty bed. Most people in the slum, Asha included, slept on the floor.

"Everyone is jealous of us, fixing our house," Kehkashan explained to an older cousin who'd just arrived from the countryside.

"So let them be jealous," Zehrunisa exclaimed. "Why shouldn't we live in a better room now that we are doing a little better?" Still, she decided to entrust the television to the brothelkeeper for the duration of the repair work.

No onlooker asked, *Why fix a house when the airport authority might demolish it?* Almost everyone here improved his hut when he was able, in pursuit not just of better hygiene and protection from the monsoon but of protection from the airport authority. If the bulldozers came to flatten the slum, a decent hut was seen as a kind of insurance. The state of Maharashtra had promised to relocate those families who had squatted at the airport since 2000 to tiny apartments in high-rises. To Annawadians, a difficult-to-raze house increased the odds that a family's tenure on airport land would be acknowledged by the relocation authorities. And so they put their money into what would be destroyed.

To Abdul, fixing the family hut seemed unwise for reasons that had nothing to do with the airport authority. To him, it was like standing on the roof bragging that a Muslim family was out-earning the Hindus. Why throw ghee on an open flame? His mother's new tile floor would in any case get carpeted in garbage.

Had the family funds been at his disposal, he would have bought an iPod. Mirchi had told him about this iPod, and while Abdul knew little of music, he had been enchanted by the concept: a small machine that let you hear only what you wanted to hear. A machine to drown out your neighbors.

The window that would let out the cooking smoke was finished the first day, and on the second day the children turned to breaking the cracked stone floor and leveling it in preparation for tiles. "*Ceramic* tiles," Zehrunisa instructed her husband, who felt well enough to go and shop for them. Two-year-old Lallu, unhappy at being excluded from the construction work, applied a rag to his father's shoes for the momentous outing. Shortly after noon, Karam put two thousand rupees in his pocket and left for a small tile shop in Saki Naka. Abdul was glad to see him go. Delay was a specialty of his father, and Abdul hoped to finish the work by nightfall.

"You're all hammering too loud! I can't hear my radio!" Fatima yelled through the wall after a while. The younger Husain boys looked at one another, amused. Each of the last three times they'd made small repairs to their house, she'd thrown one of her famous fits.

"We're breaking the floor, putting in a kitchen," Zehrunisa called back. "I wish the tiles and shelf would magically jump into place, but they won't, so there will be some noise today."

Abdul ignored the exchange, intent on his own problem. His mother's cooking shelf was driving him mad. The four-foot gray slab was uneven, as was the floor, so the shelf wobbled perilously on two supports he'd built to hold it up. Nothing in this idiot house was straight. The only way to stabilize the shelf, and make it level, would be to cut into the brick wall, itself uneven, and cement the slab in place.

Asha's husband being too hungover to work today, another neighbor had offered to help, for money up front. This man seemed wobbly, too, but Abdul put it out of his head as the two of them began chipping away at the brick. Zehrunisa said, "We'll really hear from the One Leg now." Thirty seconds later, Fatima began to shout.

"What's happening to my wall?"

"Don't take tension, Fatima," Zehrunisa called back. "We're doing the shelf now. Just give us this day—we also want it done fast, before the rains come."

Abdul kept working. He was a categorizer of people as well as garbage, and as distinctive as Fatima looked, he considered her a common type. At the heart of her bad nature, like many bad natures, was probably envy. And at the heart of envy was possibly hope—that the good fortune of others might one day be hers. His mother claimed that back when every life at Annawadi was roughly equal in its misery, neighborly resentments didn't get out of hand, though Zehrunisa was known to be sentimental about history.

"You bastards! You're going to break down my wall!"

Fatima, again.

"*Your* wall?" said Zehrunisa, irritated. "We built this wall and never took a paisa from you. Shouldn't we be allowed to put a nail in it from time to time? Be patient. If anything happens, we'll repair it once the shelf is in."

Fatima went quiet, until bricks began crumbling on her side. "There is rubble in my rice!" she shouted. "My dinner is ruined! Sand is spraying everywhere!"

Abdul was dismayed. The readiness of the bricks to disintegrate, long suspected, was now confirmed. They'd been made with too much sand, and the mortar between them had deteriorated. Crap bricks that weren't even glued to one another—less a wall than a tremulous stack. As he considered how to install the kitchen ledge without toppling the whole house, Zehrunisa went outside. So did Fatima, and the two women started shoving each other. Neighbors came out to watch, the children debating which of the two women was more like the Great Khali, an Indian fighter in the World Wrestling Entertainment franchise.

"If you don't stop breaking my house, motherfucker, I will put you in a trap," shouted Fatima.

"It's my wall to break, prostitute," Zehrunisa shouted back. "If we'd waited for you to build a wall, we'd all still be seeing each other naked!"

Abdul ran outside and pushed the two women apart. Taking his mother by the neck, he dragged her back home.

"Don't you have children?" he said, disgusted. "You're no better than the One Leg, fighting outside in front of everyone!" Such scenes violated his first principle of Annawadi: Don't call attention to yourself.

"But she used bad language first," his mother protested.

"This woman talks badly to her own man," Abdul said. "Would she hesitate to throw bad words at you? But you didn't have to throw them back at her. She has a crack in her—she's cracked, you know this."

Fatima was still swearing when she crossed the maidan and departed Annawadi. Abdul heard female neighbors laughing at her as she went, but the things that females laughed at did not interest him. He registered only that Fatima's absence gave him a chance to finish installing the ledge in peace. Except that the neighbor he'd hired to help him had now collapsed, taking the slab down with him.

"You *are* drunk!" Abdul accused his neighbor, who was pinned to the floor by the stone. The man could not deny it. He had advanced TB and explained, "Lately, if I don't drink, I don't have the strength to lift anything."

Abdul felt like crying when he saw the wall's fresh degradation. Fortunately, the stone hadn't broken when it fell, and the neighbor seemed sobered by the accident. He assured Abdul that they could finish the job in an hour. Abdul calmed himself by imagining that it his mother had a nicer house, she might start practicing a nicer way of speaking.

But now a neighbor arrived to report an extraordinary sight. Fatima, a woman with few rupees to spare, had been seen riding off in an autorickshaw.

Another report, fifteen minutes later: Fatima was in the Sahar Police Station, accusing Zehrunisa of violent assault.

"Allah," said Zehrunisa. "When did she become such a liar?"

"Go quickly," Kehkashan told her mother. "If you don't get to the station fast, they will have only her story to judge by."

Karam returned home as his wife was departing. Tiles were more expensive than he'd realized, and he'd been two hundred rupees short. She told him, "Stop delaying. Get the money, buy the tiles. If the police come and see all that we have outside, they'll clean us out." The younger boys were already picking up the family possessions and tossing them into the storeroom.

"Don't worry about me," Zehrunisa told Abdul. "Just don't stop working, get it done."

When Zehrunisa reached the station, winded from the half-mile run, Fatima was sitting at a desk telling her story to a tall female officer named Kulkarni.

"This is the one who beat me, and you see I am a cripple, with only one leg," Fatima said.

"I did not beat her!" Zehrunisa protested. "So many people were outside watching, and not one would say I did. She came and started a fight."

"They broke my wall! Got sand in my rice!"

"She said she wanted to put us in a trap! When all we do is work and mind our own business—"

Fatima was crying, so Zehrunisa turned on her own waterworks.

The officer put up her palms. "Are you women mad, bothering us like this? You think the police have nothing better to do than listen to you fighting about some small thing? We are protecting the airport. You go home and cook your dinner and mind your children," she told Fatima. To Zehrunisa, she said, "You sit over there."

Zehrunisa took a seat on a row of bucket chairs and doubled over. Now her tears were real. Fatima had put her in a trap, as threatened. She would soon be back at Annawadi telling everyone that the police were holding Zehrunisa like a common criminal.

When she recovered from her bout of sobbing, Asha was in the seat beside her.

Asha had been helping some police officers find a government-subsidized apartment in which to conduct a side business—brokering work for which she hoped to earn real money. The potential profit to be made by patching up a dispute between two Muslims would be small. However, if she didn't handle the petty conflicts at Annawadi, people would start turning to a woman from the Congress Party whom everyone called "white sari," and Corporator Subhash Sawant would hear about it.

Asha met Zehrunisa's eye. For a thousand rupees, Asha said, she'd convince Fatima to make no further trouble. The money wouldn't be for Asha herself. She would put it—some of it—in Fatima's hand.

Asha wasn't always this explicit about money, but she felt she had to be with Zehrunisa. Mirchi had once been picked up by the police for buying stolen goods, and Zehrunisa had begged for Asha's help. Asha had impressed on the officers that Mirchi was a child and unwell—which happened to be true, for he had six badly infected rat bites on his butt. When Asha brought Mirchi home, Zehrunisa had *thanked* her, as if she didn't know that Asha's help had become a business.

But Zehrunisa distrusted Asha as much as Asha distrusted her. Asha was Shiv Sena, anti-Muslim, like many of the officers in the station.

"We'll work it out with Fatima's husband," Zehrunisa told Asha, concluding the conversation. "Thank you, but it will be fine."

An hour later, she started to believe it *would* be fine when Officer Kulkarni offered her a cup of tea and advice: "You need to really beat the crap out of this One Leg, finish the matter once and for all."

"Oh, but how can I beat her when she is a cripple?"

"But if you don't beat people like that, you will have to deal with them over and over again. Just whack her, and I will handle it if she complains. Don't worry."

Zehrunisa thought the officer's friendliness might also be a request for payment. A male officer named Thokale was less subtle. He regularly demanded bribes from the family, since people squatting on airport land were not allowed to run businesses. "You owe me for so many months," he said when he saw her. "Have you been hiding from me? Now that you're here, we can settle your account."

Zehrunisa had more money than Fatima. Extracting some of that money was probably why she, not Fatima, had been kept in the station. She would have to pay Thokale; he would shut down their business otherwise. But she decided to give Officer Kulkarni a wet-eyed look that conveyed enormous gratitude for the advice about beating her neighbor. Then she turned her attention to a cup of milky tea.

IT WAS DUSK, and, in Annawadi, Kehkashan was fuming. Sitting in the clearing guarding the family's things, she could see her panicked brothers spading cement, trying to finish before the police showed up and asked for money. Kehkashan could also see through Fatima's open door, where she was swaying on crutches to a cassette tape of

Hindi film songs, turned up loud. Upon returning from the police station, Fatima had painted her face more extravagantly than usual: a shining bindi on her forehead, black kajal around her eyes, red lipstick. She looked as if she were about to step onto a stage.

Kehkashan couldn't hold her tongue. "The police are keeping my mother because of the lies that you told, and you're dressing up and dancing like some film heroine?"

A fresh fight began on the maidan.

"Bitch, I can put you in the police station, too," Fatima shouted. "I won't leave it—I will put your family in a trap!"

"Isn't what you've done enough? Getting my mother arrested! I should twist off your other leg for that!"

The audience of neighbors re-formed for this lively *tamasha*. No one had ever seen Kehkashan angry; she was usually a mediator among Annawadi women. Now, with her flashing, tear-spangled eyes, she looked like Parvati in that soap opera, *Kahaani Ghar Ghar Ki.*

"You may twist my leg, but I'll do worse to you," Fatima said. "You say you are married, but where's your husband? Did he find out you prostitute yourself to other men?"

Hearing his daughter's virtue disparaged, Karam came outside. Being called a whore was not Kehkashan's central worry. She said to her father, "Have you lost track of the hour? It's almost night, and Mother is still in the station."

"Run and see if your mother is okay," Karam instructed Mirchi. To Fatima he said, "Listen, beggar. We'll finish this work, then we stay out of each other's business forever."

Inside the hut, Abdul was bagging up shards of brick; the cooking shelf was now installed. For some days, Abdul had imagined his mother's pleasure at seeing it done. Instead, she was being held by the police. The floor was half rubble, half wet cement, awaiting tiles his father had not yet bought. The installment-plan television, stored in the brothelkeeper's house, had been broken by the man's son. Abdul's little brothers and sisters had been frightened by all the shouting, and his father, surveying the wreck of his home, appeared to be losing his mind.

Suddenly Karam stormed back to Fatima's doorway. "Half-wit," he shouted, "you lied and said my wife beat you, so now I'm going to make you recall what a real beating feels like!"

On second thought, he wouldn't do the hitting himself.

"Abdul," he called to his son. "Come and beat her!"

Abdul froze. Though he had obeyed his father all his life, he wasn't about to hit a disabled woman. Fortunately, his older sister intervened. "Father, calm down," she ordered. "Mother will handle this when she gets home!" Kehkashan understood where the family authority resided in a crisis.

As she led Karam home, he called over his shoulder, "One Leg, tell your husband that if this is how you treat our years of kindness, I want half of what we spent to make this wall."

"Yes, you will need your small change for your own funeral," Fatima replied. "I am going to hurt you all."

Mirchi soon returned from his police-station reconnaissance: His mother, apparently unharmed, was sitting quietly with a female officer. Relieved, Kehkashan started dinner.

At this hour, cooking fires were being lit all over Annawadi, the spumes converging to form a great smoke column over the slum. In the Hyatt, people staying on the top floors would soon start calling the lobby. "A big fire is coming toward the hotel!" Or, "I think there's been an explosion!" The complaints about the cow-dung ash settling in the hotel swimming pool would start half an hour later.

And now came one more fire, in Fatima's hut.

Fatima's eight-year-old daughter, Noori, had come home for dinner, but the wooden door wouldn't open when she pushed. Inside, a love song was blasting, and she thought her mother was so busy dancing she'd forgotten the hour. Noori ran to get her mother's friend Cynthia. Cynthia couldn't open the door, either, so she lifted Noori up to a hole near the roof of the hut—a hole that Noori proudly called their window.

"What do you see, Noori?"

"She's pouring kerosene on her head."

"Don't, Fatima," Cynthia yelled, trying to make her voice heard over the music. Seconds later, the film song was overwhelmed by a *whoosh*, a small boom, and an eight-year-old screaming, "My mother! On fire!"

Kehkashan shrieked. The brothelkeeper was the first across the maidan, three boys fast behind, throwing their weight against the door until it broke. They found Fatima thrashing on the floor, smoke pouring off her skin. At her side was a yellow plastic jug of kerosene, overturned, along with a vessel of water. She had poured cooking fuel over her head, lit a match, then doused the flames with water.

"Save me!" she shouted.

The brothelkeeper tensed. Something low on Fatima's back was still burning. He grabbed a blanket and smothered the flame, as a vast crowd formed outside the hut.

"All day these Muslim garbage people have been fighting so loudly."

"Didn't she think of her daughters before she did this?"

"She's okay now," the brothelkeeper announced, rolling away some cooking pots he'd knocked on top of her in his haste to extinguish the fire. "Alive, no problem!"

He pulled Fatima up. When he let go, she flopped back down, howling.

People took note of the upturned vessel of water.

"She's a fool then," said an old man. "She wanted to burn herself a little, create a drama, and instead she burned herself a lot."

"It is because of these people that I have done this," Fatima cried out, her voice astonishingly clear. Everyone knew which people she meant.

Kehkashan stopped sobbing long enough to issue a command to her brothers and father. "Run! Go! She said she was going to trap us. She might say we have set her on fire!"

"A police case now—they're finished," a neighbor said, watching the Husain boys tear past the public toilet in the general direction of the Hotel Leela, with its eight-hundred-dollar suites.

"Water!" Fatima was pleading. Her face was red and black.

"But if she dies while you give her water, the ghost will get inside you," someone said.

"Ghosts of women are the worst. Years go by and they don't leave you be."

A luckless teenaged girl named Priya finally brought the water. Priya, one of the poorest girls in Annawadi, sometimes helped Fatima cook and care for her children in exchange for food. She was said to have two ghosts inside her already.

"Stupid people. They say it's bad to give water after a burn."

This was a new voice, crisper than the others: Asha's voice. She was standing at the back of the crowd.

People turned. "Then tell her not to drink, Asha! Stop her!"

"But how do I snatch it away?" Asha said. "If it's her last moment, I don't want to take a dying woman's curse. What if she passed right then?"

Manju came out. Her mother ordered her away. Manju's best friend, Meena, came closer. It was unspeakable, what she saw. Fatima writhing in a brown two-piece outfit with pink flowers on the front and back, most of the flowers now burned away. Where the flowers had been, strips of skin were hanging. Meena ran away to be sick, felt she'd be sick her whole life, what she'd seen.

"How will I get to the hospital?" Fatima was saying. "My husband isn't here!"

"Someone should get an autorickshaw and take her to Cooper Hospital. All these idiots are just staring—she's going to die before our eyes."

"But if you take her to Cooper, the police will say you were the one to set her on fire."

"Asha should take the One Leg to the hospital," someone said. "She's Shiv Sena. The police won't fuck with her."

Fatima's eyes zeroed in on Asha. "Teacher," she cried. "How can I walk and go, when I am like this?"

"I will pay for the autorickshaw," Asha replied. "But I have people waiting for me. I am too busy to go myself."

The other Annawadians watched as Asha strode back to her hut.

"I offered to pay for the rickshaw, but why should I have gone?" Asha told her husband later, at home. "It was a fight between these garbage people and who knows what happens when you get involved. Anyway, Zehrunisa should have taken my offer of help at the police station. She doesn't understand the basic thing: You pay early, it costs less later on. You put money in the One Leg's hand like she's a beggar. You stop it before it gets to the hysterical level. Now it will be a police case and she'll need a lawyer. Does she think the lawyer will do the work first, before taking the money? Does the midwife wait to get paid? Even when the baby dies, the midwife collects her fee. But I wash my hands of her, that family and their dirty money. *Haram ka paisa.*"

She smiled. "What the One Leg should do is tell the police, 'I was born Hindu and these Muslims taunted me and set me on fire because I'm Hindu.' Then these guys would be inside the prison forever."

It was 8 P.M. now, the sky above the maidan purple as a bruise. Everyone had decided that when Fatima's husband returned from his garbage-sorting work, he could take his wife to the hospital.

The adults drifted back to their dinners, while a few boys waited to see if Fatima's face would come off. That had happened to a woman who had rented a room from Asha. The woman's husband had left her, and she, unlike Fatima, had torched herself thoroughly. The woman's charred face-skin had stuck to the floor, and Rahul claimed that her chest had sort of exploded and that you could see straight through to her heart.

7.

The Come-Apart

FATIMA'S HAIR, WHAT WAS LEFT OF IT, had pulled free of the coil into which she'd put it before striking the match. Her face was now black and shiny, as if an artist commissioned to lacquer the eyes of a statue of Kali had gotten carried away and done the whole face. There was no mirror in Burn Ward Number 10, Cooper Hospital, the large hospital serving the poor of Mumbai's western suburbs, but she didn't need to see herself to know that she was bigger. The swelling was part of it, but there were other ways in which the fire had increased her.

Leaving Annawadi, her spindly husband carrying her on his back, she'd started to be treated as a mattering person. "What have I done to myself!" she had cried out to sympathetic bystanders near the Hyatt. "But it is done now, and I will make them pay!"

No autorickshaw driver had wanted to transport a woman in such a state as she, given the potential damage to seat covers. But three young men had intervened, getting her to the hospital by threatening a driver with his life.

And here at Cooper, where fluorescent lights buzzed like horse-flies, she continued to feel like a person who counted. Though the small burn ward stank of fetid gauze, it was a fine place compared to the general wards, where many patients lay on the floor. She was sharing a room with only one other woman, whose husband swore he hadn't lit the fateful match. She had her first foam mattress, now sopping with urine. She had a plastic tube in her nostrils, attached to nothing. She had an IV bag with a used syringe sticking out of it, since the nurse said it was a waste to use a fresh syringe every time. She had a rusty metal contraption over her torso, to keep the stained sheet from sticking to her skin. But of all the new experiences Fatima was having in the burn ward, the most unexpected was the stream of respectable female visitors from Annawadi.

The first to come had been her former best friend, Cynthia, whom Fatima blamed for her current situation. Cynthia's husband had run a garbage-trading business that failed as the Husains' business prospered, and Cynthia had encouraged Fatima to do something dramatic to prompt a police case against the family that had bested her own. This had been terrible advice, Fatima saw belatedly, though the banana lassi Cynthia brought had been good.

Zehrunisa came, too; Fatima caught a glimpse of her one morning, cowering just outside the room. Then four other neighbors appeared, led by Asha. Fatima felt honored that Asha had come. At Annawadi, the Shiv Sena woman looked right through her. Now, proffering sweet lime juice and coconut water, Asha whispered into Fatima's blackened ear.

She reminded Fatima that what had happened between her and the Husains had been seen by hundreds of people on the maidan, and that Fatima ought not to tell lies about being beaten or set on fire. "What's the point of having such *ghamand*, such ego?" Asha wanted to know. "Your skin is burned, you've done this stupid thing, and still your heart is full of vengeance?"

Asha was trying to broker a truce that would avoid a police case. If Fatima would admit that the Husains hadn't attacked her, Zehrunisa would pay for a bed in a private hospital and settle some money on Fatima's daughters. Fatima understood that Asha intended to take a commission from Zehrunisa for this settlement. She was burned, not mental. But it was too late to tell the truth. She's already made her accusations to the police.

On arrival at Cooper, Fatima had said that Karam, Abdul, and Kehkashan had set her on fire—the account that had propelled officers into Annawadi after midnight to arrest Karam, as Abdul hid in his garbage. But by the next morning, the Sahar police had learned that Fatima's statement was untrue. Her eight-year-old daughter, Noori, had been especially clear in her account: that she'd watched through a hole in the family hut as her mother set herself on fire.

If a charge against the Husains was going to stick, and money from the family extracted, a more plausible victim statement was required. In order to help Fatima make such a statement, the police had dispatched a pretty, plump government official to Cooper—a woman with gold-rimmed designer eyeglasses who had left Fatima's bedside shortly before Asha arrived.

Poornima Paikrao, a special executive officer of the government of Maharashtra, was commissioned to take the hospital-bed statements of victims. Gently, she helped Fatima construct a new account of the events that led to her burning. Even when Fatima had admitted that she couldn't read over what the officer had written, nor sign her own name at the bottom, the woman in the gold-rimmed glasses had remained respectful. A thumbprint would be fine.

As the special executive officer understood, inciting a person to attempt suicide is a serious crime in India. The British had written the criminal code, and their strict anti-suicide provisions were designed to end a historical practice of families encouraging widows onto the funeral pyres of their dead husbands—a practice that relieved the families of the expense of feeding the widows.

In the new account, Fatima admitted to burning herself, then carefully apportioned the blame for this self-immolation. She accurately reported Kehkashan's curse at sundown about twisting off her other leg. She accurately reported Karam's threat about beating her, and his demand that her husband pay for half the wall that divided their huts. She didn't mention Zehrunisa, who had the best possible alibi, having been in the police station when Fatima burned. Instead, Fatima put the weight of her accusation on Abdul.

Abdul Husain had threatened and throttled her, she said in her statement. Abdul Husain had beaten her up.

How could you bring down a family you envied if you failed to name the boy in that family who did most of the work?

"As my left leg is handicapped, I could not retaliate at them. In anger, I put the kerosene lying in my house on myself, and set myself on fire," her statement concluded.

Special Executive Officer Poornima Paikrao added to her account, "Record made under clear light of tubelight," and departed the hospital room to begin her real work. With this improved witness statement, and several other witness statements she hoped to influence at Annawadi, she thought she could make a handsome profit from the Husains.

BY FATIMA'S THIRD DAY at the public hospital, the blackened skin on her face had puckered, turning her almond-shaped eyes into rounds. She looked surprised, as if she hadn't known, lighting the match, what would happen. "The more I talk, the more I hurt," she said to her husband, who stood at her bedside. Despite the pain, she felt compelled to yell at him from time to time, though her voice was lower-pitched than it had been.

Her husband had always been shovel-faced, but now his face seemed to lengthen by the day. And while he had a garbage sorter's superior coordination, his stricken state turned him into a bumbler. Grinding Fatima's pills into powder, he seemed overwhelmed by the complexity of the physical task. He broke the bread he'd brought to feed her down to crumbs.

She wasn't very hungry, which was fortunate. Food wasn't one of the amenities at Cooper, the five-hundred-bed hospital on which millions of poor people depended. Nor was medicine. "Out of stock today" was the nurses' official explanation. Plundered and resold out of supply cabinets was an unofficial one. What patients needed, families had to buy on the street and bring in. A small tub of silver sulfadiazine, the burn cream recommended by the doctor, cost 211 rupees and was finished in two days; Fatima's husband had to borrow money to replace it. As he applied the cream, he feared hurting his wife, especially when touching the part of her belly stripped of pigment. He had thought the nurses might help, but they avoided physical contact with the patients.

The tall young doctor didn't mind touching patients. He came one night and stretched out one of Fatima's arms, and then the other, and when he did so, her bandages, which had turned yellow and black, came loose.

"Something's wrong," she told him. "I'm so cold."

"Drink three bottles of water a day," he said, and put the filthy bandages back in place. Fatima's husband had no money to buy bottled water after buying the burn cream. The doctor called the old man irresponsible behind his back, for failing to give his wife what she needed.

As the husband returned to work to afford medical supplies, Fatima's mother took over the hospital care. "The neighbor family set me on fire," Fatima told her mother, and then she told a different story of what had happened, and the mother became confused. Fatima was confused herself by now, and didn't want to explain it all over again. Her job was to heal. The police could take care of the fine points of her accusation, now that they had Abdul and Karam Husain in the station.

THE FIRST TIME the officer with the fish lips brought down the leather strap, Abdul screamed before it landed—a howl that had built in him since early morning, when he had raced to the police station to surrender.

Running through the airport, he had hoped he might be able to explain what had happened the previous evening with Fatima, or at least offer up his own body to protect his father from violence. Maybe, bent over a wooden table, he was taking blows that would otherwise have landed on his father. He wasn't sure. The only clear thing was that the officers were not listening. They didn't want a story of hot tempers and a crappy brick wall. They seemed to want Abdul to confess to pouring kerosene on a disabled woman and lighting a match.

"She's going to die, and it will be a 302," an officer told Abdul, with what sounded to the boy like delight. Abdul knew that a 302, in the Indian penal code, was murder.

Later in the beating—how much later, he couldn't say—he was pulled back into sentience by the sound of his mother's voice. She seemed to be just outside what the officers called the reception room of the station. "Don't hurt him," she was begging at considerable volume. "Do this peacefully! Show kindness!"

Abdul didn't want his mother to hear him scream. He tried to gather his self-discipline. No point looking at his handcuffs. No point looking at the fat-lipped officer or those sharp creases in his regulation khaki pants. He closed his eyes and tried to recall some key words from the last time he had prayed.

His efforts did not help him maintain his silence. His screaming, then his sobbing, rang out onto the road. But afterward, watching the shiny brown shoes move away, he tried to tell himself that he hadn't uttered a sound. Although his mother's wails had become deafening as he was being beaten, that in itself was not conclusive. Given his mother's tendencies, she'd probably been wailing all day.

The good thing was that her distress was now coming from farther away. Maybe the officers had dragged her off for being so loud. The airport management had improved the grounds of the old bungalow that housed the police station—fronted it with pink flowers and tropical plants, their leaves as shiny as the new police jeeps parked nearby. Abdul hoped his mother was retreating fast past this strip of garden. He wanted to think of her at home.

The large cell in which he was being kept housed seven other prisoners, including his father, who had taken his own beating in front of Abdul. The place was nothing like the sparse jail cells in movies Abdul had seen in the Saki Naka video shed. Rather, it contained metal chairs, a large, handsome wooden table with a laminated top, and four new steel cabinets—the nicest cabinets Abdul had ever seen. Godrej brand. Painted bronze and sky blue and smoke blue. Two cabinets had shiny mirrors embedded in their doors. It was like being in a cabinet showroom, except for the tension and the screaming.

The Sahar Police had a more typical holding pen elsewhere in

the station. The room where Abdul and his father were kept was
what repeat inhabitants called the "unofficial cell"—a large office
where police paperwork was supposed to get done. As a matter of official record, the Husains had not been arrested, were not in custody.
What happened in this office was off the books. The room's best feature, those being held agreed, was a small window through which
friends or relatives could relay cigarettes and consolations.

Abdul kept waiting for Sunil or Kalu the garbage thief or some
other boy to look in, ask if he was okay. He imagined his answer. Not
okay. He imagined reassuring replies. No one but his mother came to
see him, though. By the third day, he had stopped expecting that
anyone else would.

"Why did you do such a thing to a cripple?" The officers asked
him the same question again and again.

Abdul had his pathetic answer. "Sir, I am such a weakling I would
have told you, after so many slaps, but I haven't done it. We only all
threw insults at each other."

He had his other pathetic answer: "Please, go to Annawadi and
ask. So many people were there. I didn't touch her. Why would I
fight with a woman? A one-legged woman? Ask anyone, have I teased
a girl? I don't fight. I don't talk to anyone. My brother Mirchi is the
only guy I tease. Even earlier I never hit him—my own little brother,
who I knew I could hit."

He feared the police weren't going to Annawadi to ask, though.
This inspired his resigned answer: "She has set herself on fire in a fit
of rage. She has taken a small quarrel with my mother and stretched
the thing like rubber. But what is the use? Now that she has done
that, said that, you will listen to her because she is burned. You aren't
going to listen to me."

The officers asked his father more interesting questions, like,
"Why did you give birth to so many children, Mussulman? You are

not going to be able to feed and educate them now. You'll be in jail for so many years that your wife won't remember your face."

"I'd rather be beaten than see them beat you," Abdul said to his father, who said the same back to him when they were handcuffed together on the floor one sleepless night. The salutary effect of the oxygen Karam had received two weeks earlier at the private hospital had been negated.

As they lay on the tiles, Karam attempted to convince his son that the police didn't really believe they'd tried to murder Fatima. By now, he whispered, the officers would have at least some sense of what had actually happened, given the hundreds of witnesses. But the specifics of what had or had not been done to a disabled woman were not the officers' animating concern. The concern, he told his son, was the money that might be made off of the tragedy. "So you've made big bucks there at Annawadi," one officer kept saying to Karam.

The idea was to get terrified prisoners to pay everything they had, and everything they could secure from a moneylender, to stop a false criminal charge from being recorded. Beatings, though outlawed in the human rights code, were practical, as they increased the price that detainees would pay for their release.

The Indian criminal justice system was a market like garbage, Abdul now understood. Innocence and guilt could be bought and sold like a kilo of polyurethane bags.

Abdul wasn't sure how much money his family had left after fixing the house and paying his father's hospital bill. But he thought that whatever remained should be paid, in order to be innocent. He wanted to go home to the place that he hated.

"But what if Fatima dies tomorrow," Karam said. Abdul knew his father was talking to himself, not asking for advice. If they paid now, and Fatima died, their savings would be gone, and the police might still register a criminal case against them. Then how would they afford a lawyer? His father's voice changed every time he said this bankrupting word, *lawyer*. Another man being held unofficially had been on trial before, and warned that if they used one of the city's public defenders, they'd get sent away forever.

As the days in detention went on, Abdul and his father stopped talking, which Abdul felt was just as well. What did he have to say, anyway? That if his parents had been as paranoid and alert as he was, they would have kept their mouths shut with the crazy One Leg? It was better to pretend that he and his father were too tired for talk, having answered all the questions of the lead investigator, Subinspector Shankar Yeram, whose lips Abdul had by now decided looked more like a monkey's than a fish's.

Every day, sometimes twice a day, a haggard Zehrunisa appeared at the cell window to explain the compounding price of their freedom. Asha was saying it would cost fifty thousand rupees to make the police case go away. Not that she'd pocket the money herself, of course. She would pay the police and placate Fatima's husband with a more modest sum.

Zehrunisa had felt grateful to Asha in the first days after the burning. Despite her political antipathy toward Muslims and migrants, Asha had worked hard on behalf of the Husains, and for free. In addition to asking Fatima to retract her false statement, she'd accompanied Zehrunisa to the police station in order to impress upon the officers that Fatima had set herself on fire. This attempted intervention had gone badly. An officer had shouted, "What? Do you women think you are the police? Go away! We will do our own investigation!" For all Asha's power in Annawadi, it was inconsistent beyond the slum's boundaries.

At the cell window, Zehrunisa told her husband, "The point is, for a few days Asha helped for free, but now she says I'm sitting on money and I have to open the purse strings. I would, to get you both out of here, but I'm not sure that paying her will do it."

Zehrunisa had already paid Officer Thokale, the man who'd asked her to settle her "account" with him while she was in the station after her own fight with Fatima. After the burning, he'd told her he could help ensure that the investigation was "fair" and that her husband and son wouldn't be badly hurt during interrogations. "I told him I'd pay anything for that, and I think he feels terrible for us, really," she told her husband. "He knows it is a frame-up. He could have taken so much more money than he did."

The special executive officer who took Fatima's statement in the hospital also wanted money. She'd visited Zehrunisa to report that that statement, and the statements of other Annawadi witnesses, were under her control. She was as gentle with Zehrunisa as she'd been with Fatima, saying, palms open, "What do you want me to do? Good statements or bad statements? I am working for the government, so what I say will decide the matter. It is in your hands, and you will have to decide very soon."

Zehrunisa told her husband, "She's like Asha. She says that whatever we pay won't be for herself—that she would give the money to Fatima's husband. But I've already told him directly that I'll help his girls and get Fatima into a private hospital—pay for everything, bed, medicine, food. I'm scared to pay this witness-statement woman. What if she steals the money from the husband, and Fatima stays there at Cooper?"

"What does the husband say when you ask about the private hospital?"

"Not a word. He's upset and can't take a decision. It's crazy. Does he want her to die, so he can get a new wife? Cooper is going to kill her, and then everything we have—"

There was a rhyme that Zehrunisa had heard Mirchi sing: "People who go to Cooper, they go *upar.*" They go above, to heaven. If Fatima went upar, Zehrunisa's husband, son, and daughter would face a decade or more in prison.

Karam agreed that his wife should ignore the special executive officer and keep pressing Fatima's husband about a private hospital.

"I will," she said, starting to cry. "But now you see what will happen. This government woman will be angry and get the investigators to take the statements of the people who want us to be fucked. If it were our own village, with our own people, we might hope the witnesses would care for us and tell the truth. But we are so alone in this city."

A light rain began to fall, and hearing it on the station roof one night, Abdul remembered an action movie he and Kalu had seen. *Zinda.* Alive. The hero had been imprisoned for years, not knowing why and going mad in his not-knowing.

Kalu had liked the part at the end when the guy escaped, discovered why he'd been imprisoned, and hammered to death all responsible parties, despite the knife sticking out of his back. In the part Abdul remembered now, the man was still trapped in his cell, but after years of chipping away at a brick wall that was apparently sturdier than the one between the Husains and Fatima, he had managed to make a small hole. The prisoner stuck his hand through, cherishing the rain on his skin.

At home, Abdul had never given his future much thought, beyond vague fantasies about living in Vasai and more concrete, health-related worries. Were his lungs going bad like his father's? Did his right shoulder hunch forward? That tended to happen after a decade of squatting over scrap.

Having accepted a life of sorting early on, he considered himself a separate species from Mirchi or the most-everything girl, Manju, or the other young people at Annawadi who believed they might become something different. Abdul had been aiming for a future like the past, but with more money. The rage of a neighbor with less money had played no part in his calculations.

He didn't know if his mother was right about an earlier, peaceful age in which poor people had accepted the fates that their respective gods had written on their foreheads, and in turn treated one another more kindly. He just knew that she didn't really long for companionable misery. She'd known abjectness, loathed its recollection, and raised her son for a modern age of ruthless competition. In this age, some people rose and some people fell, and ever since he was little, she'd made him understand that he had to rise. They'd lost a lot in the 2005 floods, but many other Annawadians had, too. He felt his mother hadn't prepared him for what it felt like, falling alone.

Which day was this? How long had he been here? He was being beaten and phones were ringing in a room next door, which Abdul had concluded was some kind of control room, because of the radio squawks. The officers all spoke in Marathi, which he made the effort to follow. Trying to figure out what the officers were saying gave him something to do besides worrying the obvious problem of being innocent and beaten in a jail cell.

The officers had been going after his hands, the body part on which his livelihood depended. Small hands, with the prominent veins, orange rust stains, and healed cuts that were standard in his profession, they had been seriously injured only once—a bicycle spoke that went deep.

His mind broke a little. The phone conversations in the other room faded out. Only later, when the voices reestablished themselves, did he realize that one officer was speaking about him.

"The ones who attacked the cripple . . . Not the father, the boy . . . But no one's beating anyone, Asha. . . . No, nothing like that."

Annawadi's Asha was on the phone. Abdul was terrified then. She was probably calling to make the beatings worse, so that his mother would change her mind about paying her off.

Suddenly, Officer Thokale was standing in the unofficial cell. "Asha says this boy didn't set anyone on fire, doesn't cause any trouble in Annawadi, so there's no point in hitting him," he told his colleagues with the straps. Abdul was let up, and neither he nor his father was beaten again. Abdul's shackles came off, too.

Abdul tried to make sense of this reprieve. Asha's son Rahul was Mirchi's best friend. Maybe Rahul had convinced his mother to protect Abdul. Or maybe Asha had noticed Abdul over the years, sorting his trash on the maidan—seen he was a hardworking kid, a quiet loser who didn't deserve to be brutalized.

Abdul's father had a better guess. The call was probably a show conducted for father and son, who could be counted on to report it to Zehrunisa. Asha and Thokale often worked together. Now Thokale was demonstrating his power to ensure that Abdul and his father would not be severely injured in police custody—what he'd assured Zehrunisa in exchange for money. For Asha, the show would prove to the Husains that she *did* have influence at Sahar Police Station, and increase the likelihood that she would get a payoff, too.

But Karam wasn't about to explain the economics of reprieve to his traumatized son. He thought it better for the boy to believe that someone had noticed his frantic labor on behalf of his family and decided to defend him out of kindness.

AT SUNDOWN, FOUR DAYS AFTER the burning, a Muslim fakir came to Annawadi with a peacock-feather broom to offer blessings and drive away evil spirits. Fakirs rarely came to Annawadi because the slum contained so few Muslims, the constituency most likely to pay for their extraworldly services. Abdul's sister Kehkashan jumped up when she saw the old man. Her mother, fearing what might happen to a beautiful young woman in the police station, had pleaded with Officer Thokale to keep her out of custody as long as possible, but Kehkashan had now been ordered to turn herself in. She felt desperate for a fakir's blessing.

Taking a ten-rupee note from her bra, she closed her eyes as the fakir touched the top of her head with the broom. She was relieved he didn't beat her with the broom, as some fakirs did when they performed the *jhaad-phoonk*. She hoped it was because he sensed no diabolical spirits hovering over her, and not just that he had adopted some modern, client-pleasing technique. As Kehkashan sat still, the better to allow his blessing to seep through her body, the fakir moved on to Fatima's door.

Fatima's husband stormed out of the hut, wild-eyed. "Are you without hands? Are you without legs? You have come to *me* to beg? In the name of God! Go earn your living, go get a job!"

The fakir looked at the sky, fingered the golden zari threads in the pocket of his kurta, and backed away.

Now Kehkashan was distraught. "Allah! To turn away a fakir, to take his curse?" Fatima's husband had set himself up for bad luck, the way he'd spoken to the fakir, and the bad luck most likely to befall him would be a ruination of the Husains as well.

"What has happened to that man," the fakir wanted to know.

"His wife burned herself," Kehkashan said in a low voice.

"So when did she die?"

"No! No!" Kehkashan cried out. "Pray that she lives, else we will be in a grave situation."

Fatima's daughter Noori leaned against Kehkashan. The girl had been clinging to Kehkashan ever since she'd seen her mother burning. "I am playing a boy today," Noori said. "Talking like a boy, too."

"Like my sister Tabu," Kehkashan replied, distracted. "She only wants to wear boy clothes or she'll cry." Kehkashan was resolved not to cry herself.

"Get the rice so I can clean it," she said to Mirchi, rising and brushing herself off. "And whose turn is it at the tap?"

Her youngest brother, Lallu, was now old enough to curse like his mother: "Give dinner to me fast or I will put your eyes out!" Her youngest sister was having a come-apart, having not received her rightful share of a packet of Parle-G biscuits.

When the fakir completed his ministries and departed Annawadi, the scene through the door of the Husain hut was little different from those unfolding behind the other doors he passed. As night dropped its hood over the slum, dinners were being scrabbled together, abuses were being hurled, tears were getting kissed away. The next morning, Fatima came home in a white metal box.

AN INFECTION HAD KILLED HER. A doctor adjusted the record in the name of hospital deniability. Burns that covered 35 percent of Fatima's body upon admission to Cooper became 95 percent at her death—a certain fatality, an unsalvageable case. "Greenish yellowish sloughs formation all over burn injuries with foul smell," read the postmortem. "Brain congested, lungs congested. Heart pale." Fatima's file was tied up in red string and sent to the records room of the morgue, where feral dogs slept among the towering stacks of folders on the floor, and birdsong came through the window. A flock of spotted doves had colonized a palm tree outside, the *croo-croo-croo* of one bird overlapping the call of another.

Fatima had gotten small again, dying—took up less than half of the box. All of Annawadi came outside, as it had when she burned, but this time the onlookers kept their distance. The slum grew quiet, and quieter still when Zehrunisa and Kehkashan emerged from their hut, heads covered, to wash the corpse.

Only other Muslim women could perform this crucial ritual, the washing away of Fatima's sins. No matter what, Zehrunisa always said, Muslims had to join up for festivals and sufferings. It was the tradition to tell Fatima she was dead now and going to be buried, so the Husain women murmured the words while dipping cotton rags into a vessel of water and camphor oil. Lifting a sheet of white muslin, they began to clean Fatima's body. They moved up the length of her long leg, then the half leg, working slowly toward the shiny black face. "Close the mouth," someone said. "Flies are getting in."

When Fatima was clean and sinless, Kehkashan closed the box and covered the bier with the Husains' best cotton quilt, the one with tiny blue checks. Fatima would now be taken to a Muslim burial ground a mile away, and Kehkashan would go to jail. A charge would be filed, likely based on Fatima's second statement that the Husains had beaten her and driven her to self-immolation, which named Abdul as the most violent actor. At the police station, an officer had told Zehrunisa she'd have to pay another five thousand rupees to see the chargesheet.

Zehrunisa returned to her hut and sobbed, still clutching the rag with which she'd cleaned her neighbor. She didn't cry for the fate of her husband, son, and daughter, or for the great web of corruption she was now forced to navigate, or for a system in which the most wretched tried to punish the slightly less wretched by turning to a justice system so malign it sank them all. She cried for the manageable thing—the loss of that beautiful quilt, a parting gift to a woman who had used her own body as a weapon against her neighbors.

Only men could go to the Muslim burial ground. Mirchi stood beside Fatima's husband, who held one of the bier's four poles. It was rush hour as the camphor-scented metal box moved out onto Airport Road.

The procession of dolorous slumdwellers seemed even smaller against the outsized enthusiasms of the airport city. Giant billboards announced the forthcoming launch of an Indian version of *People* magazine. Chauffeur-driven black sedans rolled out of the Hyatt—attendees of a pharmaceutical convention, taking a break to check out the town. At the Hotel Leela, Americans representing Universal theme parks were feeling optimistic about their plan for entering the Indian market. "The percentage of rich people is small in India, but look at the absolute numbers. Enough of them that we can make this work. Don't talk to me about Disney—we're the best brand. Spider-Man, Revenge of the Mummy, and now we're seeing good results out of Harry Potter. I know, people say I should go to Disney World, check out the rival, but I can't do it. I'm too competitive—not going to give the opposition a dime—"

The white box proceeded across a hectic intersection, past Marol Municipal School, through the narrow lanes of one slum and then another, until it reached a water-stained green mosque, a papaya tree, and a burial ground filled with pigeons.

Fatima went into the same earth that held her drowned two-year-old daughter. In a matter of days, her other two daughters were entrusted to Sister Paulette.

Fatima's husband loved his daughters, and grieved as he sent them off. But he worked fourteen hours a day sorting garbage, and local drunks sometimes despoiled little girls left home alone in Annawadi.

8.

The Master

NOW IT POURED, a stinging rain. On the high grounds of the liquid city, rich people spoke of the romance of monsoon: the languorous sex, retail therapy, and hot jalebis that eased July into August. At Annawadi, the sewage lake crept forward like a living thing. Sick water buffalo nosed for food through mounds of wet, devalued garbage, shitting out the consequences of bad choices with a velocity Annawadi water taps had never equaled. People, also sick, stamped the mud from their feet and said, "My stomach is on fire, my chest." "All up and down this leg, all night." The sewage lake's frogs sang sympathetically, but you couldn't hear the frogsong indoors. Rain banged on the metal rooftops as if slum zebras were stampeding overhead.

Someone had once told Sunil that the rains washed the mean out of people. They certainly washed the stripes off the zebras. For weeks the animals stood revealed as poke-bone, yellow-hide nags, until the slumlord-in-decline, Robert, refreshed the black stripes with Garnier Nutrisse hair dye.

The trail of garbage was sparser in the monsoon than in other seasons, since traffic at the airport declined and construction projects stalled. Sunil's concrete ledge above the Mithi River was wiped clean by the wind and the rain. He found a little consolation behind one of the walls lining Airport Road. In this wet, jungly spot, six purple lotuses bloomed. He kept the discovery to himself, fearing other boys might pluck the blooms and try to sell them.

As Sunil moved through the streets around his secret lotuses, chasing busted flip-flops, plastic bottles, and other floaters, he sometimes passed Zehrunisa Husain, who was uncharacteristically garbed in a burqa. She kept losing her footing, trying to move too fast through muddy ponds that had formed on the roads.

Other scavengers whispered that she'd sold the room in the back of the family hut to pay for a lawyer. Sunil hoped that whatever she was doing for Abdul would spring him from custody, since Mirchi was useless as Abdul's replacement at the weighing scales. The younger Husain boy didn't know the value of anything, and when Sunil and the other waste-pickers tried to help him, he made fun of their boils.

Scavengers were sensitive about their boils, and the worth of their goods. The business of the Husains' competitor, the Tamil man with the video-game parlor, surged accordingly.

Zehrunisa saw that Mirchi's inexperience was hurting the business, but she was too busy with the criminal case to negotiate with the scavengers herself. She was too busy to bathe or feed her young children. Those children, too, became Mirchi's responsibility, since the relatives before whom Zehrunisa needed to prostrate herself were scattered in slums across a rain-wrecked city. "Please, will you put up bail to get my sick husband, son, and daughter out of jail?"

In each hut, she'd had to sit through an hour of clucking sympathy and excuses before moving on to the next humiliating visit. Only one begging session had been brief. She'd practically had to swim through Saki Naka slum in the damned burqa in order to reach the hut of Abdul's soon-to-be-former fiancée. The girl's father looked at her as if she'd spent the morning at the local liquor still, and that was that.

Her problem was that she lacked collateral to secure the jail bonds. Since she couldn't read, Mirchi had reviewed the official documents that her husband had stored in a gray plastic case along with some Iqbal poems and a racy Urdu paperback thriller. Mirchi had unearthed a document for each of the five possessions that had changed the family fortunes. A pushcart that had allowed his father to carry garbage to the recycling plants, and thus to become a buyer of scavengers' goods. The family hut, purchased from a migrant who'd given up on Mumbai. The storeroom next to the hut, which allowed the family to forestall selling their goods when market prices were low. The three-wheeled jalopy with a truckbed that could transport more than the pushcart. The deposit on the land in Vasai. Only Karam Husain's name was on these papers.

"Mother, be calm. I'm fine here," lied Kehkashan when her mother came to the women's wing of the Byculla Jail to explain why she couldn't post bail.

Karam was less understanding when she arrived at Arthur Road Jail, the city's largest, most infamous detention center. She'd had to queue for four hours in order to see him, paying off guards and officers long before she'd gotten through the gates. Behind those gates, there were four times as many inmates as official capacity.

"I am desperate," her husband told her. His cell had so many bodies that no one could lie flat. He couldn't breathe because of the crowding. He couldn't choke down the food. He yelled at her for starting the fight with Fatima, then yelled at her to get him out. As if she hadn't been trying. As if he hadn't been the idiot who had threatened to beat Fatima. As if he hadn't been the one to leave his wife's name off the family papers.

She'd been furious at her husband as she left the jail, but she couldn't sustain it. Arthur Road Jail was a name that terrified every sentient Mumbaikar, and also Zehrunisa, who was not strictly sentient at this time. That her sick husband would have a fight and become an Arthur Road inmate, facing a ten-year felony sentence, was an eventuality for which neither of them had prepared.

One morning, she was outside prison gates in a turbid downpour, Lallu cursing because the burqa impeded his access to her breast. She switched him to her other arm in order to answer her husband's cellphone, now in her care: Officer Thokale, her only ally in the Sahar police station, more furious than Lallu. How had other people at Annawadi come to hear that he'd taken money from her to help with the case?

And what could Zehrunisa say? She had been babbling everything to anyone, waddling around half mad in the weeks since the arrests. Hearing her eldest son screaming as he got beaten at the police station. Seeing her gentle daughter escorted by officers into jail—a moment in which the single word in Zehrunisa's head was *qayamat*, the end of the world.

She couldn't sleep after that. She couldn't sleep before that. She barely knew which jail she stood in front of this morning. With the rain had come a snaking white fog. Lallu was saying, "I will have that dog bite your body!" Bicycle boys were whirring past, delivering tiffin lunches to office workers. The Saifee Ambulance Day and Night seemed to have a flat tire.

The officer on the phone was still shouting.

"Yes but no, sa'ab," she told Thokale, frantic. "I am outside. I am in the hospital. Who said all that? No, sa'ab, no. They're just giving you this false story, instigating all this, making you angry at me. I am in the hospital and my health is very bad. Please listen to me: Such tension about my son, about my daughter. No sir, I am indebted to you. Whoever is saying all this must be crazy. No sir, I said nothing at all."

At sunset, clouds distended, the monsoon sky corded red, she would be on her knees outside the station, begging the officer's forgiveness. Allah only knew what an angry officer might do to further hurt her family.

The trial might be years away, and what she'd made from selling the back room of the hut was gone. Mirchi's earnings from garbage covered food and little else. Should she sell the storeroom next? With the imprisonment of her husband, she was the decision-maker, and every choice she'd made thus far seemed to be the wrong one. Maybe she *was* the zero she'd insisted to her husband she was not.

She should have paid Asha to calm Fatima down, that day at the police station. She should have paid the special executive officer who claimed to control the witness statements. She should have kept silent about paying Thokale to stop the beatings and postpone her daughter's arrest. There was only one decision about which she felt confident, which was the decision that she had made for Abdul.

THE POLICE WERE GOING to charge Abdul as an adult, because he looked like one, and because Zehrunisa lacked any proof of his age. Hence he would be sent to Arthur Road Jail along with his father.

Zehrunisa didn't know Abdul's age herself. Seventeen was what she'd said before the burning, when people asked her, but he could have been twenty-seven, for all she knew. You didn't keep track of a child's years when you were fighting daily to keep him from starving, as she and many other Annawadi mothers had been doing when their teenagers were young.

Asha had invented her children's birthdays and now marked them with parties and cake. In January, Manju had celebrated her eighteenth for the second year running—one of Asha's tricks to preserve her daughter's value as a bride. Abdul had never asked for a birthday party. What he'd wanted was a date and a year. His mother could tell him only what she knew:

"Before you were born, Saddam Hussein had been killing a lot of people somewhere. Maybe a year before, or two, I don't know. Oh, you beat me up when you were inside me, worse than any of your brothers and sisters afterward, and I cried out so often that people started saying I had another Saddam in my belly. When you came out, you were so small, like a rat's son, not any Saddam. Still we picked a peaceful name for you, because we worried that what people had said might be true. Abdul Hakim, a person who cures others just by his own understanding. I was relieved when you were a little older and there was nothing in you like Saddam."

Had Abdul been more Saddam-like, she would have been less repulsed by the idea of his being in Arthur Road Jail with contract killers, pedophiles, and mafia dons. But she feared that for an argument she had begun, he would be victimized, perhaps raped, in Arthur Road. The only way she could think to prevent this was to pay someone to manufacture a record of his age, to ensure he would be charged as a juvenile.

She went across the maidan to see the brothelkeeper, who had been accused of drug dealing, pimping, robbery, and who knew what else over the years, but had been imprisoned only twice. She thought he would know about efficacious bribery.

The brothelkeeper acknowledged that this was one of his expertises, and was eager to help in exchange for financial consideration. However, age-related records weren't part of his repertoire.

Who else might know whom and how to bribe for such a record? Of course: the Sahar police. Belatedly, she realized that one constable had been dropping hints for days.

Upon receiving his advice, she sent her money flowing through Marol Municipal School, and into the pocket of the constable. She returned home with just what she'd wanted: a fake school record showing that Abdul Hakim Husain, former student, was sixteen years old. Her son, who had hardly been a child, would at least now be treated like one by the criminal justice system.

MUMBAI'S DETENTION CENTER for juveniles was in Dongri, a neighborhood thirteen miles south of Annawadi. For the first leg of the journey there, Abdul had been smushed against two dozen others inside the back of a police van. But after a stop at a courthouse in Bandra, where his status as a juvenile was recorded, he'd come to Dongri in a taxi, a bored female civilian as his only escort. Past her shoulder, he could track the evening street life of a thriving middle-class Muslim neighborhood.

On either side of a dark green mosque, storefronts were humming with commerce despite the rain. Halal butcher. Muslim furniture-wallah. Nazir chemist. Habib hospital. Kitchen shops with ladles dangling from hooks. A restaurant with a bright yellow door. Tattered pennants on poles advertising exam-prep courses and aspiring Muslim politicians. A man in a stall selling pinwheels, right before the street life blanked out.

Immense and mossy stone walls encircled one city block. The front wall was broken by a single iron gate. The gate to Dongri detention center was a strangely small one—child-sized, Abdul supposed.

He could have run instead of ducking through it; the mind of his escort seemed to be elsewhere, her hand barely gripping his own. But through the door he went, and down a dim passage with a wooden Hindu shrine built into the wall. At its end, he was surprised to find a pleasant courtyard with a palm tree.

The juvenile facility was a congregation of handsome sandstone buildings erected by the British early in the nineteenth century, supplemented by newer constructions that were half bungalow, half shed. Indian and British criminals had been hanged here in colonial days, and their bloody bones were piled in the basements, or so other juvenile detainees informed Abdul upon his arrival. The ghosts of the hanged men were said to come out every night. Though Abdul had been as afraid of ghosts as most Annawadi boys, these reports did not disturb him. Being terrorized by living people seemed to have diminished his fear of the dead.

Clothes confiscated, Abdul was handed a too-large uniform and escorted to one of the shedlike buildings, where he was locked in a room crammed with other new arrivals. Its windows were shuttered, breath and body smells fouled the air, and after an hour Abdul felt so suffocated that his mind began to go funny. *If I stay here any longer, I will cut up a small child and eat him.* Afterward, he was astonished that he'd thought this. When the doors finally opened and rotis were passed out, he felt too sick to eat.

To the warden's office, next, to be registered as a juvenile detainee. Here, mercifully, windows were open, and the bald, barrel-chested warden appeared tense, not cruel. A leading newspaper, *The Times of India*, had just run an exposé of the detention facility under the headline "Dongri Home Is a Living Hell." Human rights activists had been making inquiries in regard to children without underpants who'd been forced to drink from toilets. Conditions were being hastily improved.

Abdul sat on the floor in the back of the room with some other boys, waiting for the warden to call his name and enter his particulars into a brown paper file. Along the wall behind the warden were portraits of Indian eminences, and of ten faces Abdul felt certain of the names of three. Gandhi, of course, though his eyes were buggier in the portrait than they were on rupee notes. Abdul knew this Gandhi as the one who cared for poor people, who liked Muslims as well as Hindus, who took on the British and made India free. Abdul also recognized Jawaharlal Nehru, the founder of Independent India, who looked Fair-and-Lovely white and unlike any Indian Abdul had seen in real life. Bhimrao Ambedkar was the man in the red necktie and the black-framed eyeglasses—the one who'd fought for the right of the untouchable castes to be treated as human. At Annawadi, many Dalit families had dust-coated versions of this portrait tacked to the front of their huts.

The other faces on the wall were as mysterious to him as the Hindu gods and goddesses whose statues populated the warden's desk. He figured Mirchi would be able to name all of the Indian eminences. It was the kind of information a boy would have in his head if he were lucky enough to go to school.

Registered, Abdul was taken to a barrack to lie with 122 other boys on a cool tile floor. Through a window came the decisive clatter of steel shutters; in the neighborhood outside the stone walls, shops were being closed for the night. He must have slept, for the next sounds he registered were sonorous calls to prayer—the amplified dawn azan of the neighborhood mosques. *Allah-u Akbar.* God is great.

Abdul's father considered it disrespectful to pray to Allah when you were dirty, so Abdul rarely did namaaz. "And even when I do pray, I am thinking about work," he had confessed to Kehkashan recently. Still, he'd always felt soothed, hearing the muezzins as they summoned believers or announced that lost children in green shirts were at the mosque awaiting reclamation. Under the care of men with such voices, he figured all lost children would be safe.

About Allah himself, Abdul had over time worked up an economics-based proof, since he lacked a strong internal sense of His existence. He put it this way: "It takes me longer than other people to understand things, but many smart people believe in Allah—the imams, the men who call out the azan, the rich Muslims who do all this charity. Would these people be doing this work and spending money for a God who wasn't there? Such big people wouldn't waste their rupees." So there was definitely an Allah, and He would have a reason why Abdul had been locked up for a crime he hadn't committed.

A pockmarked guard was getting everyone up, handing out rags and buckets, ordering the inmates to a long row of taps. There was more water here than at Annawadi, and Abdul felt a little better after washing off the sweating he'd done in the police cell. But on his second morning at Dongri, when ordered to take a bath, he bridled.

He'd seen no reason for a daily washup at Annawadi, since he was only going to get dirty again as soon as he dried himself off. Sometimes he'd get so ripe that his mother would wave a rag in his face: "You fool, it's nice to get fresh!" Perhaps it was nice for other people. He personally found the bathing ritual not just pointless but self-deceiving. Getting fresh for a fresh day, in which something new might happen! He thought it better to start the day by acknowledging that it was going to be just as dull as the days preceding it. That way, you wouldn't be disappointed.

Abdul informed the guard that he would not take a bath. The guard replied, "No bath, no breakfast." That was the rule at Dongri. Abdul decided to go hungry. In retrospect, this tantrum would seem foolhardy. But since Fatima burned, he'd been estranged from all known landmarks. Being dirty was the remnant of a former existence he had to cling to.

On the third morning, the guard said that if he didn't bathe, he'd miss breakfast *and* get put in the airless cell that had made him want to eat small children. He decided to accept the Dongri bathing rules. By the fourth morning, his knees and ears and neck were as clean as they'd ever been. The breakfasts received in exchange for this heroic capitulation were dismal. Stones in the rice. Bread so vile that, had his mother served it, he would have put it in his pocket until he could slip it to the pigs. Most of the other boys in his barrack were Muslim—across India, Muslims were overrepresented in the criminal justice system—and when they sat on the floor to eat, they laughed about the terrible food. They called the Children's Home the *chillar* home, meaning small change, practically worthless.

Mornings, the barrack was unlocked, the chillar extracted. In the courtyard, the boys were ordered to run in a circle, then sing the national anthem, which they did at the top of their lungs. Afterward, they were sent back to the barrack, where they sat on the floor and did nothing at all. In the warden's office, an official schedule of daily educational and vocational activities was posted prominently. Abdul wasn't troubled by this discrepancy. Whatever happened to him at Dongri, or didn't happen, he was safer than at Arthur Road Jail.

The other detainees passed their free time telling stories and offering one another advice about their cases. There was one recurring counsel: "Just say you did what they say you did, and then you'll be let out." The lawyers who came from time to time also said this to their charges. Admit it, the case will be closed, and you can go home.

Abdul wanted to go home so badly that he considered saying he'd beaten up Fatima before her suicide. He still found it strange to think of her as dead, because at Annawadi he hadn't considered her fully alive. Like many of his neighbors, he had assessed her damage, physical and emotional, and casually assigned her to a lesser plane of existence. But as he'd learned in the police station, being damaged was nothing like being dead.

One night in the barrack, a sixteen-year-old confessed to the other boys that he'd stabbed his father to death. It was a matter of honor, he said, after his father strangled his mother. The police were blaming him for both murders, though.

It sounded like a film story to Abdul. To the other inmates, the boy's guilt or innocence was less interesting than his claim that he'd come from a family with money—twenty-five lakhs, or fifty-six thousand dollars, in the bank. "So your parents are dead and you're a rich boy now," one of the other boys pointed out to the father-killer. Even after the boy explained how a double-murder conviction would interfere with the inheritance, the other children couldn't stop talking about the cars and the clothes he could buy.

Many of the children had been detained because they'd been caught working. Most child labor had been outlawed even when Abdul was young, but now, occasionally, the law was enforced.

Two boys who looked to be seven years old had been picked up while sweeping floors in a cheap hotel. They reminded Abdul of his little brothers, and he felt emotional being around them. He couldn't see why the state had taken them from their parents. Being so poor that you had to work so young seemed like punishment enough.

Abdul had kept to himself in his first days at Dongri, aware of his inadequacy in the conversational arts, but the incarceration of the seven-year-olds inflamed him. "What's the use, keeping them here?" he blurted out one day. "You see their faces? So much enthusiasm for life, they are going to break the walls of this jail. The government people should let them work, let them be free."

Only in detention had it occurred to him that drudge labor in an urban armpit like Annawadi might be considered freedom. He was gratified that boys from other urban armpits agreed.

As Abdul was singing the national anthem one morning, a young Tamil woman left her two-year-old son outside the warden's office because she couldn't afford to keep him. Abdul could hardly bear to look at her—the way that grief bagged her face. It was unlike him to be sympathetic. He had seen worse at Annawadi but hadn't felt it, overwhelmed as he had been by his own work and worry.

When he was little, the family hut had collapsed, injuring everyone but Abdul. His mother always said that his selfishness had saved him. She'd fried a fleshy leaf for dinner, and when his father took a bite of his portion, Abdul became alarmed. He'd fled the hut with the rest of his leaf just before the walls caved in.

In captivity, there was nothing to preserve—nothing to buy, sell, or sort. Later he realized it was the first long rest he'd ever had, and that during it, something had happened to his heart.

One morning, he and some other inmates were delivered to a small hospital run by the police department, where a doctor had been assigned to check the ages of suspiciously old-looking juveniles. A forensic examination would settle the matter, and those over eighteen would go to Arthur Road Jail.

In the examination ward, Abdul was weighed by a medical assistant: 108 pounds. He was measured: five foot one. He lay naked on a table as his pubic hair was declared normal, his facial hair categorized as "sub-adult," and a bunchy old scar over his right eyebrow placed in the public record. Then a doctor entered the room with the results of the forensic investigation. Abdul was seventeen years old if he paid two thousand rupees, and twenty years old if he did not.

Abdul sat up, angry. He didn't have two thousand rupees, and what was it with this rich doctor, asking a boy in detention for cash? The doctor held up his hands, rueful. "Yes, it's rubbish, asking poor boys like you, but the government doesn't pay us enough money to raise our children. We're forced to take bribes, to be *kamina*." He smiled at Abdul. "Nowadays, we'd do almost anything for money."

Abdul couldn't help but feel sorry for this friendly doctor, especially when the guy relented and declared him to be 17. A few days later, Abdul would even find himself feeling concern for a Mumbai policeman.

An overweight officer, having delivered a batch of children to the home, started telling one of the guards about his heart problem. "You think you want to be a cop, but you don't, because it kills you," said the officer, mopping his brow. Then he told of another officer with a lung problem, and one who had cancer, and of others who were stress-sick, and of how none of them earned enough to afford decent doctors. Abdul hadn't previously thought of policemen as people with hearts and lungs who worried about money or their health. The world seemed replete with people as bad off as himself, and this made him feel less alone.

One afternoon, the Dongri boys were surprised to learn that they had something to do, possibly because human rights people kept showing up with notepads. Sixty new arrivals were corralled into a concrete-block room with a blackboard and a poster warning of the ills of smoking, and told to wait for a teacher—an individual stirringly referred to as The Master.

When The Master appeared, Abdul felt a little disappointed. The guy wasn't anything as commanding as his title. He was a pudgy, middle-aged Hindu with high-rise hair, watery pink eyes that reminded Abdul of his mother's, and trousers that revealed a great expanse of tube sock. But then The Master started to talk.

He began with a story of a boy who did not listen to his parents and ended up in Arthur Road Jail. As he listed the terrible things that happened to the boy in jail, tears rolled down The Master's face. He could barely get the specifics out, it was so tragic. Then he spoke of other boys: boys who did not respect the law, boys who gave pain to others, boys like those he saw here in this room. "If you were my boys—I will not lie to you. I would have thrown you away long ago," The Master said. Then he cried for their futures, which it seemed he was able to predict.

A few boys in the room, select boys, would reform themselves and live admirably, The Master said. Rewards would come to them. But life would be dire for the other boys, who would continue in their criminal ways. Their disgusted families would cease to visit them in jail, and when they were released as old, broken men, they would die on the pavement, unloved.

The Master cried for parents who beat their children instead of taking time to reason with them. Intriguingly, he also cried about his divorce, and how his wife had been a bitch to his mother, and how in the settlement he'd lost a big car. He cheered up when talking about his pretty new girlfriend.

Whenever the man cried, whether for the loss of his car or for the fates of Dongri inmates, the boys started crying, too. Abdul had never in his life wept as he wept now. The tears weren't the kind he'd shed after being beaten by the Sahar Police. These were tears of inspiration. He'd never encountered a man as refined and honest as this Master.

Abdul was reluctant to name the feeling he had, listening to the man, because it could be taken wrong. But what he felt for The Master was intense. The man had allowed him to become a student.

Not a great student. He didn't quite get the Hindu myth about King Shibi offering up his own flesh to an eagle, which seemed not unlike a story that his father used to tell him when he'd misbehaved, about a different king and his scoundrel sons and a monkey. But his father's king story had left him feeling guilty. The Master's words lit up a virtuous path. Be generous and noble. Offer up your flesh, agree to be eaten by the eagles of the world, and justice will come to you in time. It was a painful way to go through life, but Abdul was drawn to the happy ending.

He assessed himself to have been virtuous in some ways. He had resisted Eraz-ex, desi liquor, brothel visits, or other diversions he felt might impinge on his alertness and ability to work. He refused to encourage other boys to steal things, even if it meant losing out to the Tamil who owned the game shed and maximized his profits by lending out wire-cutting tools. Abdul never fought, lied only sometimes, rarely voiced resentment of his father. But he could have been better and more honorable. He still could be.

He would categorically refuse to buy anything he thought had been stolen, even if it was only stolen garbage. He wouldn't admit to something he hadn't done to Fatima, even if it would get him out of Dongri, even if his family's income suffered in his absence.

To his family, Abdul's physical capability had been the mattering thing. He was the workhorse, his moral judgments irrelevant. He wasn't even sure that he *had* any moral judgments. But when The Master spoke of *taufeez* and *izzat*, respectability and honor, Abdul thought the man's stare had blazed across the rows of heads and come to rest on him alone. It was not too late, at seventeen or whatever age he was, to resist the corrupting influences of his world and his nature. An awkward, uneducated boy might still be capable of righteousness: He intended to remember this and every other truth The Master spoke.

PART THREE

a little wildness

You won't sell anything if you talk about death.

— MANJU WAGHEKAR

9.

Marquee Effect

IN JULY, WHEN ASHA and her family stepped off the train after a thirteen-hour journey north to the Vidarbha region of Maharashtra, their village relatives inspected their faces, finding evidence of how good life was in the Mumbai slums. "You're all fairer than you were when you were little," noted a cousin of Manju, Rahul, and Ganesh. "Smooth-type. *Chikna.* You were very black before, and shy."

To examine Asha properly, the older women had to crane their necks, since their bodies were bent from decades of agricultural labor. Asha's great-grandmother walked on all fours. Looking at the ancient woman, Asha stood mast-straight. She felt like a giantess, coming home.

In Annawadi, she wept buckets when village movies played on the Marathi-language channels. Even the corniest of the flood-and-famine dramas swept her back to her own early years, working Vidarbha's difficult earth. In her occasional recountings to her children, she kept the tone absurdist: a manic teenaged version of Mother

India, dragging the plow after the oxen had died. The women of her village recalled the Asha of that era with respect. She'd been distinguished by her ability to work like a donkey even when she hadn't eaten for days.

"She was one-bone thin, half starving, when we were working the orange groves," one of her relatives whispered to the others. "You wouldn't know it now. She's a double-bone, and the way she talks — you'd think she'd never trod on dirt."

Asha was glad to be the subject of admiring chatter, and to be away from the troubles of Annawadi. She had come home to market her beautiful daughter, and her own relative prosperity, among the people of her farming caste, the Kunbis. Her husband Mahadeo would play sober; she would play deferential wife; Manju would play herself; and marriage offers would by all rights roll in, despite the nominal occasion of the visit.

This occasion was a stripped-down family wedding: no music, no dancing, no jalebis. The groom, one of Mahadeo's nephews, was still in mourning for his elder brother, who had died of AIDS shortly after infecting his wife. The disease was rampant in Vidarbha, and vigorously denied. If word got out that it had claimed one of Manju's relatives, it might diminish her value as a bride. But people in the village weren't terribly interested in the young man's death, or in the widow hidden away for the duration of the festivities, or even in Asha's stories of the city. The farmers' eyes kept turning to the sky.

The break in the rains, as it was called in Annawadi, had a different name in the countryside: drought. Little rain had fallen in June, and millions of cotton seedlings planted the previous month had died. The villagers had paid a steep price for their seeds: genetically modified ones called "hybrids," theoretically designed for Vidarbha's erratic climate. Now more seeds would have to be sown, and new loans arranged to pay for them.

Some Kunbis said that July was the month when the gods slept. Asha's relatives hoped the gods had changed their schedules this year, and were also awake nights, worrying.

In the two decades since Asha and her husband left their respective farming villages, twenty miles apart, much had changed for the better. Some houses had grown larger and sturdier, thanks to the money those who'd left for the city sent back home. Public money had also altered the landscape: Scattered among desiccated farms were new schools, colleges, and handsome government offices with lawns as well tended as those of the Airport Road Hyatt. The government had built more water projects, too, but these had failed to compensate for the decline of Vidarbha's natural water systems. Poor rains and illegal siphoning depleted the water table; streams dried up; rivers reversed course. As fish died and crops failed, moneylenders became unofficial village chiefs.

Ashamed and in debt, some farmers killed themselves—an old story, one of the Marathi-movie staples. But the movie reel was still playing. In the new century, the government counted an average of a thousand farmer suicides a year in Vidarbha; activists counted many more. Whatever the number, the suicides had turned the region into international shorthand for the desperation of rural Indian poverty.

The files accumulating dust in the records rooms of the Vidarbha bureaucracy indicated that modern means of suicide—drinking pesticide, mainly—had supplanted self-immolation. Over thousands of mildewed pages, relatives described their loved ones' distress.

> Last two years we had crop failure. He could not repay his loan. Then came a fire in the hut. All the seeds got burned—sunflower, wheat, destroyed. He couldn't afford to marry his second son, and people would keep asking when the marriage would happen—

His family was so big, and after looking at bank documents he was disturbed and drank insecticide. The loan
was huge, and he didn't see how he could pay.

He was slow-minded, short on his lights, and worked
the fields, then took loans for the daughter's wedding, and
felt trapped.

He said, "Father, I will kill myself if you don't buy me a
cellphone," then he went and drank the poison.

The prime minister, Manmohan Singh, had come down from
Delhi to express his concern for the farmers' hardship, and the central government's determination to relieve it. The families of some
indebted suicides would get government compensation, and a debt-
restructuring and interest-waiver program had begun for the farmers
who had borrowed from banks instead of moneylenders. A massive
national scheme to increase rural incomes was also underway, guaranteeing unemployed villagers a hundred days a year of publicly
subsidized work. One of the government's hopes was to stop villagers
from abandoning their farms and further inundating cities like
Mumbai, but Asha's relatives knew nothing of these celebrated relief
programs.

Among powerful Indians, the distribution of opportunity was typically an insider trade. Elsewhere that summer, public telecom licenses worth the equivalent of tens of billions of dollars were being
sold to the highest under-the-table corporate bidder; public funds
meant to build world-class sports facilities for the 2010 Commonwealth Games were being diverted to private interests; parliamentary
opposition to the future of a landmark India–United States nuclear
treaty was being softened by trunksful of cash; and the combined

wealth of the hundred richest Indians was surging to equal nearly a quarter of the country's GDP.

In a forested stretch of Vidarbha east of where Asha and her husband had grown up, many citizens had stopped believing the government's promises about improving their fortunes. Deprived of their land and historical livelihoods by large-scale corporate and government modernization projects, they'd helped revive a forty-year-old movement of Maoist revolutionaries. Employing land mines, rocket launchers, nail-bombs, and guns against capitalism and the Indian state, the guerrillas were now at work in roughly one-third of India's 627 districts, including an underdeveloped swath of central and eastern India known as the "Red Belt." This summer, the Maoists had been especially productive in the state of Orissa. They'd sunk a boat full of military commandos, killing thirty-eight, and bombed a police van, killing twenty-one more.

In most rural villages, however, people weren't yet talking revolution. They were waiting to see if improvements in infrastructure and agricultural technology might change their prospects. This year, as Manju's seventeen-year-old cousin Anil labored in the cotton and soybean fields, he carried one such advance on his back: a heavy metal canister of Dow pesticide.

The fields on which he worked belonged to a rich politician who paid his laborers a thousand rupees, or twenty-one dollars, a month. While the politician's crop yield and profit increased with the new chemicals, the freight of the canisters and the noxious inhalations made the laborers' work, never easy, blisteringly hard. At the end of a recent workday, one of Anil's co-workers had set down his canister, climbed a tree at the edge of the farm, and hanged himself. His family received no government compensation for the loss.

At night, Anil had many imaginary conversations with the politician for whom he worked, in which he gently argued that more difficult labor be rewarded by slightly higher pay. A complaining worker was easily replaced, though. Anil kept his thoughts, including the suicidal ones, to himself.

Try your luck in Annawadi, Asha had suggested the previous year, and so Anil had become one of the roughly five hundred thousand rural Indians who annually arrived in Mumbai. Each dawn, he stood with other work-seekers at Marol Naka, an intersection near the airport where construction supervisors came in trucks to pick up day laborers. A thousand unemployed men and women came to this crossroads every morning; a few hundred got chosen for work. Anil didn't know that life expectancy in Mumbai was seven years shorter than in the nation as a whole. He just knew that at the intersection, trying unsuccessfully to compete with all the other migrants, he felt as if his chest were stuffed with straw. After a month of rejection, he'd gone home.

"People laughed to see me back," he now told Manju. "I had told them I was going to earn money and see the city, and I didn't do either. Only major thing I saw were airplanes."

The night before the wedding, Manju, in her position as the oldest female of her generation, carried a pot of grains through the village to the temple where prayers would be said for the bride and groom. In a peach-sequined chiffon tunic that her aunt in the city had tired of, she led a parade of family and neighbors along dirt roads full of scavenging donkeys. Past some mud-and-dung houses painted a shade of green no longer known in the fields, she clambered up a steep path to the temple of Hanuman, the monkey god.

Earlier, she'd powdered the groom's face and added glitter around his eyes with a toothbrush. But even in the dark, unelectrified temple she could feel people's eyes following her, not the sparkle-caked groom. An urban, college-going girl was a firework in the village. But which of the Kunbi men would Asha choose to be her husband? Some of them would consider Manju too educated to be docile; others would be too poor to sustain her mother's interest.

Manju failed in her efforts to track Asha's movements at the glum wedding the following day, but soon after, a young soldier appeared at the house where the family was staying. Asha went outside to speak to him privately. From time to time, Manju could hear her mother's hoarse laugh.

Recently in Annawadi, Manju had watched Asha negotiate a marriage between a shy neighbor girl and a boy from another slum. Manju had been excited at the chance to glimpse the sort of negotiations that would one day decide her own future. It had seemed to be going well, until the girl lifted her head. "Not beautiful!" the boy's family had objected, blaming Asha for wasting their time.

The harsh pragmatism of that afternoon had armed Manju, so when Asha called for her to bring out tea, she smoothed her hair, lowered her eyes, and tried to keep her heart ice-cold. Taking his cup, the soldier stared at her for a long moment and said, "Don't stand in the sun—you'll get too black."

He wasn't bad looking, despite the mustache, and Manju's eyes were not so lowered that she failed to note his own eyes sliding down her body. She felt as if she'd been touched. It sometimes disturbed her how strongly she wanted to be wanted; she felt very nearly ready for marriage, for sex. But if Asha arranged any marriage that sentenced her to a life in Vidarbha, Manju had decided that she would run away.

One night before the family returned to Annawadi, Anil told his cousins of a dream he'd had. He was sprinting away from the farm, and Manju, Rahul, and Ganesh were running alongside him. "We were all escaping, and our mothers were angry. They were saying, 'If you go, we won't let you come back.' And we were saying, 'Don't call us back! We don't want to come back! We're going somewhere bet-ter!' We were laughing so hard as we ran."

BACK AT ANNAWADI, Asha shut the sordid Fatima drama out of her mind, and shut her door on the frantic Zehrunisa. She wanted to devote the rest of the monsoon season to self-improvement. For one, she needed to take a college course or two, or she would lose her temp job teaching kindergarten at Marol Municipal School. The government of Maharashtra had been trying to increase the quality of its schools, and some of the teachers were being pressured to show they were trying to get an education themselves. Fortunately, Asha's professor at Yashwantrao Chavan Maharashtra Open University had assured his class of teachers that he would provide answers to the end-of-year papers and exams.

But Asha wanted to be a politician, not a low-paid kindergarten teacher. To achieve this goal, she thought she'd have to shed her slum ways as she'd shed her village ones. It was a second kind of migration—of class. The key, she told Manju, was "to study the first-class people. You see how they're living, how they walk, what they do. And then you do the same."

Asha had raised her daughter to believe that she was different from the other children in Annawadi, superior even to her own broth-ers. At fourteen, Ganesh was gentle and hesitant, while Rahul, for all his confidence, lacked ambition. Having given up on hotel work, he was perfectly content with his new temp job, clearing tables at a can-teen for airport employees. More and more, Asha could see her hus-band in the boys. Having taught them what she thought they could learn—they were now among the fastest male onion-dicers in Annawadi—she let them be. Only she and Manju seemed capable of the intelligent planning that might help carry them into India's expanding middle class.

Asha remembered how it was when her neighbors heard that she'd gotten a kindergarten post with only a seventh-grade education. They called her "Teacher" snidely. Over time, however, the title stuck and the mockery melted away. Similarly, you could pose as a member of the overcity, wait out the heckles, and become one. It was another form of the by-hearting that Manju did at school.

"And don't be afraid to talk to the first-class people directly. Some of them are quite nice, they'll speak back," Asha instructed her daughter. "Inquire of them how to look better, take their advice."

Recently, Asha had asked a Shiv Sena man to make a rigorous critique of her image. "He says, don't wear shoes with heels when you have height, because it cheapens you," she reported to Manju. "Don't wear your housedress outside. Wear a sari instead. Put your mangalsutra on a long chain, not a short one. Don't look as if you're worried, even if you are—no one wants to look at such lines on your face. And don't walk with people who look worse than you."

The Shiv Sena man had been a little blunt, conveying that last tip. She had been walking with him to the Corporator's house one evening, and he'd said, "I am looking nice, and you are looking ugly, and your ugliness takes away from me, too."

Manju brought additional information home from college: dangling earrings, low-class; tiny hoops, high-class. High-class women also wear jeans, she told her mother, who subsequently sanctioned a pair of bell-bottoms. One day, looking in the mirror at how the jeans worked with the peach-sequined secondhand tunic, Manju said aloud to herself, "Marquee Effect." She'd learned the term in computer class, practicing Photoshop.

The Marquee Effect dimmed a bit when Asha's sister gave both mother and daughter haircuts with feathery bangs. In the humidity, the feathers rose in a great cloud of frizz. But it was fun, spending the monsoon getting modern. Sensing her mother suddenly treating her as an equal, Manju broached a new subject: that many first-class people married outside their own caste, to people they, not their parents, had chosen.

"Rich people all have this different mind-set," Manju said.

Asha didn't want to get as first-class as that.

Asha had liked the soldier from Vidarbha, who came from a relatively affluent family, but her husband had objected to the engagement on the unlikely grounds that army men were often drunks like himself. In Annawadi, Sister Paulette had visited Asha twice now to lobby on behalf of another potential groom, a middle-aged man who lived in Mauritius. "He's my brother," the nun said, eyes blinking fast. Asha suspected Sister Paulette was operating on commission. Asha was, too, in a way.

Most Annawadians considered daughters a liability, given the crushing financial burden of the dowry. But it had long ago occurred to Asha that a girl as beautiful, capable, and self-sacrificing as Manju might make a marriage so advantageous it would lift up her whole family. The Mauritius man was rich, supposedly, but Asha was uneasy about sending her only daughter to Africa, where she'd heard that pretty girls got sold into slavery. She decided not to decide, for now. Instead, she encouraged Manju to widen her social circle, which would increase the odds of a superior offer.

Asha believed a person seeking betterment should try as many schemes as possible, since it was hard to predict which one might work. Manju's first idea had been to sell insurance, as one of her college classmates had done. The Life Insurance Corporation of India was offering free training to aspiring agents in an office building down the road from the Hotel Leela.

Asha was intrigued by the television ads for this insurance, which allowed those who could afford it to insulate themselves from some of the volatility of Indian life. The young husband in one of the commercials had cared enough to buy medical insurance for his wife before the traffic accident. Now, miraculously, she was rising from her wheelchair! Life insurance was turning funerals into celebrations! Selling such policies would put Manju in touch with affluent people, while bringing more money to the household.

The children in Manju's hut school came early to support her as she learned the English names of the policies: Future Confidence II, Wealth Confident, Invest Confident, Aspire Life. The children's vocabularies momentarily expanded to include the terms *surrender value*, *rider premium*, and *partial withdrawal*.

In training, Manju learned that she wouldn't sell anything if she referred directly to tragedy or death. You had to emphasize the profit angle — tell the story of a man who bought forty policies and left his family eye-high in rupee notes.

Manju practiced her pitches and rebuttals until she was fluent, and passed the final exam with high marks. Then: nothing. Who did she know who could afford to buy insurance?

"Everybody wants their profit," she told the children one day, shaking her head. "They say, if I do this, how much will I make? In college, the girls talk like that, even when they're talking about each other. 'Why talk to that weird girl, Pallavi? What's the profit? What's the use?' "

The brothelkeeper's eleven-year-old daughter, Zubbu, understood Manju's concern with profit obsession better than the other children. Her parents were trying to sell her, and the girl felt as if she were going mad. Manju could only pray that Zubbu's parents would be as unsuccessful in this entrepreneurial venture as they were in all their other ones.

Teaching girls like Zubbu, Manju felt her own luck. Next spring, if she passed her state board exams, she'd have a B.A. degree. With another year of study, to be financed by selling one of the rented rooms in their hut, she'd be a qualified teacher, with a B.Ed. She had no hope of securing a permanent job at a government school, since such jobs typically required paying enormous bribes to education officials. Small private schools were a likelier bet, although most of them paid so little that her classmates in the B.A./B.Ed program had begun to worry that they'd invested in a chump profession. One girl intended to work at a call center upon graduation; another figured she'd make more money as a chef. Manju alone in the group still wanted to teach. But the Annawadi hut school where she honed her skills was irritating her mother more by the day. Asha didn't see a long-term benefit in networking with low-class children.

The central government funded Manju's "bridge school" and hundreds like it in Mumbai through contracts with nonprofit organizations. Although public funds for education had increased with India's new wealth, the funds mainly served to circulate money through the political elite. Politicians and city officials helped relatives and friends start nonprofits to secure the government money. It was of little concern to them whether the schools were actually running.

Manju's school came under the auspices of a Catholic charity, Reach Education Action Programme, or REAP, that took its obligation to poor students more seriously than some other nonprofits did. The priest who headed the organization resisted paying kickbacks, and his schools were gradually being shut across Mumbai. The Annawadi school was one of the survivors, and a supervisor for the charity came every month or so to sit in on the class and examine the records. He'd caught on that the school Asha was supposed to be running was really being taught by Manju, but he'd let it slide because her students were learning.

One afternoon, the children were mastering the English words *chariot, knee, mirror, fish,* and *hand.* "And what do you do with these hands of yours?" Manju wanted to know.

"Eat!"

"Wash clothes!"

"Fill water!"

"Dance!"

"Raise them to show somebody I'm going to beat him up—"

Heads turned. Asha was in the doorway, enraged.

"How urgent is this teaching?" she shouted at Manju. "What is more important? These children or keeping this house in order for me?"

Dirty children were sprawled on the floor. Notebooks were scattered about. It was a scene unbefitting the home of an almost-slumlord and aspiring elected official. Supplicants would be arriving momentarily to present their problems to Asha. The morning's laundry was damp. "Wonderful," Asha said to Manju, feeling a towel. "You put the clothes on the string inside, when the sun is shining outside. Can't you do one thing properly in my absence?" Manju turned away to keep her students from seeing her face.

After that, Manju began teaching her class every other day, or every third day. The children understood that the choice was not her own. When a new school opened in the pink temple by the sewage lake, many of them gravitated to it, but it closed as soon as the leader of the nonprofit had taken enough photos of children studying to secure the government funds.

In Manju's newly free time, she pursued a second idea for widening her social networks. She joined the Indian Civil Defense Corps, a group of middle-class citizens trained to save others in the event of floods or terror attacks.

Like many people in Mumbai, she was increasingly concerned

about terrorism. In July, there had been bomb blasts in Bangalore, then blasts in Ahmedabad—nineteen explosions in the heart of the city. The bombers weren't Maoists: Maoists were rural India's problem. The urban hazard was religious militants, some of them acting in the name of Allah, as they wrote in their emails to newspapers.

Mumbai, the financial capital, was an obvious target, so sniffer dogs joined the security phalanxes at the five-star hotels. At the airport, sandbag bunkers proliferated. On the Western Express Highway, electronic signboards urged the citizenry to be alert: STRANGER IN YOUR AREA? CALL POLICE. The Civil Defense Corps seemed to Manju a more substantial way to protect her city than calling the police about strangers.

In the cavernous basement of a government building, she and forty other Maharashtrians—middle-aged women and two idealistic college boys—simulated crises and practiced techniques for saving lives. *In a bomb blast, stay calm and make sure you are safe first. Then calm the others and lead them to safety. In a flash flood, pumpkins and empty plastic water bottles may be used as flotation devices. Tie your dupatta to someone too weak to swim, and pull them behind you.*

Of the cadre, Manju was the slenderest, and too weak for the all-important "farmer's lift," so her usual assignment in the training exercises was to be deadweight—the injured object of rescue. Splayed on the linoleum floor, hair fanned, she worked all the distress moves she could think of from Hindi movies, from the chest heave to the terrified eye-flit to the old sigh-and-tremble. Then she'd get thrown over someone's shoulder and carried to safety. Being touched was permissible here, and loveliest when she let her body relax in the arms of Vijay, an earnest, square-jawed college boy who led the battalion. He appreciated the sincere effort Manju put into being a victim.

One night, as Manju left the training in her new jeans and the peach tunic, Vijay called her name. As they crossed the road to the bus stop together, he gripped her hand. Her first time. Manju's hopes pressed against her well-honed tendency toward realism, which insisted that the city's Vijays had better options than a not-yet-first-class girl.

IT WAS HARD TO KEEP secrets in a slum. As Asha understood, secrets successfully kept were a kind of currency. People could say what they liked about where she went at night, and what she did with whom, but until they caught her, she was going to deny it.

Now it was the night of her fortieth birthday—a scant moon in a low sky, no rain. Manju passed out slices of cake, a heap of potato chips on the side, and Asha put her arms around her sons. Even her husband Mahadeo was in a celebratory mood as he plundered one of her gifts, a plastic treasure chest filled with gold-wrapped chocolate coins. "They should have been real coins, since it's my fortieth," Asha said, smiling, as she set into her cake.

Her cellphone rang again. It had been ringing for most of the last fifteen minutes, and she'd been enfolding it ever deeper into the lap of her dark blue sari. A police officer named Wagh was impatient to see her.

"An emergency?" Manju asked after a while. "Calling so many times."

"It's that woman Reena, *shakha* work," Asha lied. Shiv Sena women's-wing business. Then a minute later, she said, uncertainly, "Maybe I will need to go."

"What? Tell her you can't come—it's your birthday party," Manju commanded cheerfully, just before Asha answered the phone.

"Can't," she said into the receiver. Long pause. "No, not possible. Tomorrow? You see—" Long pause. "Listen, I . . ."

Suddenly she was standing at the mirror, powdering her cheeks with talcum, adjusting her sari, combing her thick hair off her face. She could see her husband and Manju staring at her through the mirror.

"My necklace must look real," she chattered, nervous. "A guy at the train station today told me to put it away or it would get stolen. Did you know coriander is only five rupees at the Ghatkopar market? I went to my friend's house for tea there earlier, then missed the bus. Good, fresh coriander, better than we get here—"

"Mother," said Manju quietly. "Don't go."

The cellphone rang again.

Asha said, "Yes, I said I'm coming. I *am* hurrying. But where?"

The talcum powder was all over the cellphone, streaking down her neck. She was sweating. Her husband's eyes had filled with tears.

"Mother," Manju said again, reaching for her hand. "Please. Mother."

But Asha spun out of her daughter's grasp, walked fast across the maidan, past the road boys in the video parlor, past the Hyatt, not pausing until she reached the bus stop outside the imperious Grand Maratha hotel.

This pink hotel was the most expensive of the lot. Golden-pink now, as hundreds of lights illuminated the curves of its Jaipur-stone front. Asha glowed, too, standing on the other side of the fence, a slash of white talc across one cheek.

She suspected, rightly, that at home, Manju's tears were falling on a slice of chocolate cake. For years, Asha had hoped that her daughter wouldn't guess about the men. Now she wished she had raised Manju to be worldly enough to understand. This wasn't about lust or being modern, though she knew that many first-class people slept around. Nor was it just about feeling loved and beautiful. This was about money and power.

Her mind moved more quickly than other people's. The politicians and policemen had eventually recognized this dexterity, come to depend on it. Even so, it had not been enough. At twenty, she was a poor, uneducated refugee from the droughtlands whose husband had no appetite for work. Tonight, at forty, she was a kindergarten teacher and the most influential woman in her slum. A woman who had given her daughter a college education and soon, she hoped, a brilliant marriage. The flourishing of Manju, alone, had justified the trade-offs. Even the nightmares about dying of AIDS.

She should get the blood test done. She knew that. She should be watching Airport Road for the arrival of the officer. But a society wedding was spilling out onto the Grand Maratha's lawn. This day was an auspicious one in the Hindu calendar, astrologist-certified for weddings. She had forgotten. A brass band was playing music she didn't recognize. Paparazzi were jostling for photos, blocking her view of the bride. Bits of red and pink confetti blew over the fence and landed at her feet, before the gusts winged them off. A white police van pulled up. For her. Asha slowly turned from the lights and the band and the celebration, as the back door of the van slid open.

10.

Parrots, Caught and Sold

ONE DAWN IN LATE JULY, Sunil found a fellow scavenger lying in the mud where Annawadi's rut-road met the airport thoroughfare. Sunil knew the old man a little; he worked hard and slept outside the Marol fish market, half a mile away. Now the man's leg was mashed and bloody, and he was calling out to passersby for help. Sunil figured he'd been hit by a car. Some drivers weren't overly concerned about avoiding the trash-pickers who scoured the roadsides.

Sunil was too scared to go to the police station and ask for an ambulance, especially after what was rumored to have happened to Abdul. Instead he ran toward the battleground of the Cargo Road dumpsters, hoping an adult would brave the police station. Thousands of people passed this way every morning.

Two hours later, when Rahul left Annawadi for school, the injured man was crying for water. "This one is even drunker than your father," one of Rahul's friends teased him. "Drunker than *your* father," Rahul retorted unimaginatively as they turned onto Airport

Road. Rahul wasn't afraid of the police; he'd run to them for help when his neighbor dumped boiling lentils on Danush, his sickly baby. The man on the road was just a scavenger, though, and Rahul had to catch a bus to class.

When Zehrunisa Husain passed an hour later, the scavenger was screaming in pain. She thought his leg looked like hell, but she was bringing food and medicine to her husband, who also looked like hell far across the city in the Arthur Road Jail.

Mr. Kamble passed a little later, milky-eyed and aching, on his tour of businesses and charities, still seeking contributions for his heart valve. He had once been a pavement dweller like the injured man. Now Mr. Kamble saw nothing but his own bottomless grief, because he knew miracles were possible in the new India and that he couldn't have one.

When Rahul and his brother returned from school in the early afternoon, the injured scavenger lay still, moaning faintly. At 2:30 P.M., a Shiv Sena man made a call to a friend in the Sahar Police Station about a corpse that was disturbing small children. At 4 P.M., constables enlisted other scavengers to load the body into a police van, so that the constables wouldn't catch the diseases that trash-pickers were known to carry.

Unidentified body, the Sahar Police decided without looking for the scavenger's family. Died of tuberculosis, the Cooper Hospital morgue pathologist concluded without an autopsy. Thokale, the police officer handling the case, wanted to move fast, for he had business with B. M. Patil Medical College in Bijapur. Its anatomy department required twenty-five unclaimed cadavers for dissection, and this one rounded out the order.

A few days later, a young scavenger working in the rains discovered another body at the airport: a disabled man lying on an access road to the international terminal, a handmade crutch beside him.

Unidentified, no autopsy. A third body turned up on the far side of the sewage lake, in a hole where people went to shit. Everyone using the open-air toilet had noticed that the smell was worse than usual. The decomposed body was of an autorickshaw driver named Audhen, though he, too, was marked unknown, his cause of death recorded as "illness." On airport scrubland across from the Hyatt, a fourth corpse turned up, head smashed flat: an Annawadi man who loaded luggage at the airport.

Annawadians suspected that the One Leg had left a curse, and that the whole place was now ruined, rotten, *barbad*. There were rumors that Annawadi and the other airport slums would be demolished after parliamentary elections next year.

Some Annawadians were confident that Corporator Subhash Sawant could delay the arrival of the bulldozers. But at a nearby crisscross, a political poster flapped, suggesting that deals were being made. "You pretend you've hit me. I pretend I'm crying. You people who live on airport lands are familiar with this phony drama. Now the other party says it will be the one to stop the airport from destroying your homes. So why are they meeting in secret with the government and the developers?"

SUNIL WAS SPOOKED by the deaths and the rumors, but of more immediate concern was the fact that his younger sister had grown another inch, increasing the height gap between them. In the monsoon, there wasn't nearly enough airport garbage to get him growing. He was never more dispirited than when he caught a glimpse of another scavenger boy from Annawadi, built like a blade of grass, lugging a sack so full that it bent him.

This was Sonu Gupta, the blinky boy. He lived seven huts down from Sunil, and was two years older. A few years back, when scavenging at the airport had been less competitive, they'd worked the Cargo Road dumpsters together—a partnership that had ended when Sunil accidentally broke Sonu's nose. Lately, though, Sonu seemed to be signaling his forgiveness. Sunil sometimes found him loitering on their slumlane before dawn, a look of let's-work-together spreading over his face.

The face itself was off-putting: wizened, with one of the blinky eyes rolling up. Sonu was half deaf, too, and on hot days his nose spurted blood—some birth disorder that ran in his family. Sunil was old enough now to imagine what other boys would say should he renew such a substandard alliance. Still, he was curious about how the blinky boy secured so much trash. In any season, let alone the monsoon, bad eyesight was a serious disadvantage for a scavenger.

One day, Sunil followed Sonu as he worked. He was surprised to find that a kid with no friends in Annawadi possessed profitable relationships outside it—chiefly, with the security guards at one entrance of the vast Air India compound. In the predawn darkness, Sonu waited outside a set of gates on Cargo Road, a tatty broom in hand. Eventually, an Air India guard let him in, and he began to sweep with comical fury. He cleaned the walkways, the security kiosk, the walkways again, erasing the trace of his small footprints, bending so low that he inhaled the whorl of his sweeping.

It was a display so abject that Sunil felt prepared to disdain it, until the guard emptied two large trash cans at Sonu's feet. Then Sunil saw the cunning. In the middle of unruly, cutthroat Cargo Road, a slight teenaged boy had all to himself, behind security gates, a wealth of plastic cups, Coke cans, ketchup packets, and aluminum foil trays from a canteen where Air India workers ate.

Somehow—his pathetic aspect?—blinky Sonu had achieved with the compound's guards what Sunil had failed to achieve with the rich women who came to the orphanage. Sonu had distinguished himself from the raggedy mass. Soon, only a little embarrassed, Sunil was walking out of Annawadi beside him.

Sunil had to shout at Sonu to be heard, and at first he barely bothered. A monosyllabic routine was sufficient for their days: sweeping at Air India, trying to secure bottles and trash from the managers of beer bars and food joints, then splitting up to cover more ground. Sunil excelled at scaling walls and running from airport guards who caught him too close to the terminal. Sonu had no interest in being beaten by guards. His skills were consistency and systematic planning. He'd paid the Air India guards to give him trash the first time, but then they'd stopped asking for money.

The scavenger Sonu supplanted at Air India had beaten him up, and still cursed him when their paths crossed, but Sonu, having been a mockery-magnet all his life, didn't worry about other people's opinions. Finishing his daily rounds, he'd stand on Airport Road facing traffic, tightening the strings of his fat sack with crisp tugs, his whole body radiating pride.

"You've taught me how to do this properly," Sunil told Sonu one day. Sonu was kind enough to split their earnings down the middle: most days, forty rupees, or a dollar, each.

They started to talk more as they worked. First, little stuff: that toes were almost as useful as fingers for judging the recyclability of goods; that Sonu's family owned a radio that shocked your hand when you turned up the volume. Then bigger stuff, for Sonu liked to give concise lectures as he scavenged. Imbibing water from the sewage lake gives you jaundice, he argued, against Sunil's contention that teasing people with jaundice gives you jaundice. Sonu also advised against any involvement with male tourists who stayed in the luxury hotels, given what had happened to his little brother. He suggested that Sunil might want to brush his teeth more than once in a thousand years, since his breath smelled worse than that of the slum's rotten-food-eating pigs.

One day at the Mithi River, Sonu found a cigarette stub before Sunil could pocket it. Crouching, Sonu began to bash the precious stub with a stone. The tobacco came out, the filter shredded, and he nodded toward to the pulverized remains. "If I see you smoke again, Sunil? I will beat you with a stone like this."

Sonu objected with equal passion to Sunil's fascination with Kalu, the garbage thief who acted out movies for the benefit of boys who could not afford to see them. "You stay up half the night listening to this Kalu, and I have to waste so much time trying to get you up the next morning," Sonu complained. Sonu didn't understand oversleeping. He pointed out, "Every morning, my eyes open on their own." Sunil was unused to being worried over, and liked it.

Sonu's father was a more colorful drunk than Sunil's father. Occasionally, he tore up the rupee notes he'd earned that day doing roadwork, saying, "Fuck this! What does money matter?" Sonu was fortunate in his mother, though. At night, she and her four children pulled the stringy manufacturing remnants from pink plastic clothespins—piecework for a nearby factory. During the day, she sold packets of ketchup and tiny jars of jam, past their expiration date, on a sidewalk near the Hotel Leela. Airline catering companies had donated the jam, along with plastic-wrapped packets of cake crumbs, to Sister Paulette, for her needy young wards. Instead the nun sold the expired goods to poor women and children, who in turn tried to resell them. Sonu resented Sister Paulette even more than Sunil did.

Sonu was enrolled in seventh grade at Marol Municipal. Though he couldn't go to class because of his work, he registered for school annually, studied at night, and returned at year's end to take exams. Sonu thought Sunil should do the same. One morning he cocked his head as if to drain the deafness from his ear, and announced: "Educate our-selves, and we'll be making as much money as there is garbage!"

"You will, boss," Sunil said, laughing. "And I'll be the poor peo-ple, okay?"

"But don't you want to *be* something, Motu?" Sonu asked. Sonu had taken to calling Sunil "Motu"—Fatty—a description that fit Sunil only in relation to Sonu.

Sunil did want to be something, but it didn't seem to him that a municipal school education gave Annawadi boys better opportuni-ties. Those who finished seventh or eighth grade just ended up scav-enging, doing roadwork, or boxing Fair and Lovely lotion in a factory. Only boys who went to private schools had a chance to finish high school and go to college.

When Sunil and Sonu returned to Annawadi from their garbage-gathering, they stopped talking, and their hips no longer bumped together as they walked. They were skinny kids making a little money—prey. Older boys slapped down the wet road, and suddenly Sunil and Sonu were facing a piledrive, getting a noseful of buffalo shit. A son of Robert the Zebra Man offered them protection from the older boys, for thirty or forty rupees a week. When they didn't pay, he pummeled them himself.

Sunil envied those children who seemed to have more than their share of protection. It was understood that a Shiv Sena gang would kick the ass of anyone who messed with Asha's kids, so no one did. The Husain children had another sort of backing, a family the size of a cricket team. The Hindu boys said that Muslims fucked constantly, in order to make enough babies to outnumber the Hindus. Sunil considered big families of any religion a fine thing, since all he really had was the overgrown irritant Sunita.

Kalu the garbage thief looked out for Sunil when he was around, though Kalu was pretty small himself. Late in the afternoon, he sometimes joined Sunil on a warm pile of rubble at the far side of the sewage lake, where the slant of light before dusk made the shadows of both boys gigantic. Here, well out of the blinky boy's sight lines, Sunil could enjoy his daily cigarette in peace. Kalu smoked too, despite the tuberculosis he'd contracted a few years earlier.

The two boys liked studying Annawadi from a hidden vantage, across the water. From the rocks, they could see how crazy-lopsided all the huts were against the straight lines of the Hyatt and Meridien hotels that rose up behind them. It was as if the huts had fallen out of the sky and gotten smushed upon landing.

The other marvels on the far side of the lake were a little farm that felt like a secret in the city, and a jamun-fruit tree where parrots nested. Some of the other road boys had been capturing the parrots one by one to sell at the Marol Market, but Sunil brought Kalu around to the belief that the birds should be left as they were. Sunil listened for their squawks when he got up each morning, to make sure they hadn't been abducted in the night. Sunil thought of Kalu as the parrot of road boys, although the older boy had recently seemed subdued. Even the movies he enacted were growing darker.

Kalu's expertise was in the recycling bins inside airline catering compounds. Private waste-collectors emptied these dumpsters on a regular basis, but Kalu had mastered the trash trucks' schedules. The night before pickup, Kalu would climb over the barbed-wire fences and raid the overflowing bins. He'd managed to secure discarded aluminum serving trays from inside Chef Air, Taj Catering, Oberoi Flight Services, and Skygourmet. The Oberoi dumpsters, he said, had been the most ferociously defended.

Kalu's routine had become known by the local police, however. He kept getting caught, until some constables proposed a different arrangement. Kalu could keep his metal scrap if he'd pass on information he picked up on the road about local drug dealers.

A white-suited cocaine dealer named Ganesh Anna did a galloping business at the airport, and twice a week sent some of his distributors—Annawadi men in their early twenties—to pick up the bulk cocaine in another suburb. Though Ganesh Anna paid the police to stay off his back, the constables weren't satisfied with their cut. In return for good information about the time and place of drug buys, they would leave Kalu's trash pilferings alone. Kalu kept a scrap of paper with the officers' cellphone numbers in the side pocket of his cargo pants—red-and-brown camouflage, Mirchi castoffs.

Kalu was equally afraid of the police and of Ganesh Anna. He felt like bait fish. He kept bringing up the film *Prem Pratigyaa,* in which a slum hoodlum feels so trapped by his life that he decides to kill himself with liquor—at which point the glorious Madhuri Dixit saunters to the rescue. Kalu routinely struck out with the girls who waited at the water taps, and both he and Sunil thought it unlikely that any new girl would appear, Madhuri-style, to extricate him from this entanglement. Getting out of Mumbai was the safer bet, and his estranged father had offered him a plausible escape.

His father and elder brother, itinerant pipe fitters, had a hut in a nearby slum that hung perilously onto a hillside; Kalu sometimes cried about how unwanted he'd felt in that home before he came to live on the road outside Annawadi. "I grew up in a second when my mother died," he told Sunil. "My father and brother didn't understand me." Being misunderstood was better than being trapped between a drug dealer and the police, however. His father and brother were decamping for a construction project in the hill country near Karjat, two hours away from Annawadi. Kalu had learned to pipe-fit as a child, and there would be work on the site for him, too.

Sunil wished Kalu didn't have to go. Annawadi would lose a lot of its color without him. It would lose the dramatic, hip-propelled re-

enactments of *Om Shanti Om* and the subtler entertainment of Kalu's hair, which changed in accordance with his favorite movies.
Recently he'd grown it long and lank like the crazy college boy played
by Salman Khan in that old film *Tere Naam*.

Moreover, thieves like Kalu had status that garbage-pickers
lacked, and with Kalu's departure, Sunil would be more firmly fixed
in his own identity as a scavenger, like Sonu the blinky boy—the kind
of person other people allowed to suffer unaided and die alone on the
road.

A few days before leaving, Kalu told Sunil, "My real name is
Deepak Rai. Don't tell anyone. Also, my main god is Ganpati." He
thought Ganpati, the elephant god, the remover of obstacles, should
be Sunil's main god, too. To convince him, Kalu took him on a barefoot nine-mile penitents' pilgrimage to the Siddhivinayak temple in
central Mumbai.

Which saints and gods to follow was something about which
many road boys had strong feelings. Some said Sai Baba was quicker
than fat Ganpati. Others contended that Shiva could open his third
eye and explode both of them. Sunil's mother had died before she
could teach him about the gods, and he was too unsure of their respective merits to decide upon a favorite. Still, from what he had observed in Annawadi, the fact that a boy knew about the gods didn't
mean the gods would look after the boy.

ONE AFTERNOON, Abdul's mother arrived at the Dongri detention
facility rain-soaked, the skin under her eyes dark as mango stones.
Abdul was sulking when he came out of the barrack—kept his head
down, kicked a hard clump of mud. She had come to take him home.
A judge had decided he wasn't the type to run away before his trial in

juvenile court, releasing him with strict instructions: Until the trial, report to Dongri every Monday, Wednesday, and Friday to prove you haven't absconded.

Abdul followed his mother down a long stinking hallway packed with children, across the courtyard, and out onto the street. The rain had turned to drips, and there was a weak sun, low and paling. "So when's my trial?" he asked her. "When is my father's trial?"

"No one knows, but don't worry," Zehrunisa said. "Just leave everything to God and keep praying. Now we have a lawyer who will say the right words, and then it will end, because the judge will pick up the truth."

"Pick up the truth," he repeated skeptically. As if truth were a coin on a footpath. He changed the subject.

"How is my father?"

"They don't give medicine in Arthur Road Jail, and there's no room to sleep. Oh, it is terrible to see him there—his face has become so small. But Kehkashan says it is not so bad in her jail. She prays a lot, for all of us. She says it's what Allah wants, troubles coming at us from all four sides at once."

"Why didn't you get Father out first?" he asked. "It's not right that I get out before him."

Sighing, Zehrunisa told him of all the relatives and friends who had declined to help with the bail, and of her humiliation before the family of his supposed fiancée.

"For these others, what has happened to us is just entertainment— something to talk about when they're bored," Abdul said grimly. "Now we know for certain that no one cares about us."

A rich silence followed. Then he asked his mother about his garbage business.

Under Mirchi's supervision, it had collapsed. The scavengers all sold to the Tamil who ran the game parlor.

Abdul emitted a sound like an amplified hiccup. He might have guessed it. His parents had raised Mirchi for something better than garbage work. Even Abdul had wanted something better for Mirchi.

"Okay," he said after a while, pressing a finger deep into his twitching lower lip. It was only mostly hopeless. He would start over, work harder than before, and try not to resent losing three days a week going back and forth to Dongri. Additional income would be forfeited to his decision to walk down the virtuous path recommended by The Master at Dongri, and to stay out of police interrogation cells for the rest of his life. He would no longer buy stolen goods.

His mother seemed fine with his decision. He hoped she'd actually been listening. She seemed half absent in her exhaustion, and definitely hadn't been listening later, when he asked if his suffering might be rewarded with an iPod.

THE SCAVENGERS FOUND Abdul to be more talkative on his return from Dongri. At the scales, he kept asking whether they had procured their goods honestly. Between rounds of this newly interrogatory purchasing, he made weird little announcements: "Can I tell you something?" "This is the thing I have to say." Upon which, he talked endlessly about a teacher at Dongri who had seen the *taufeez*, the refinement, in his nature.

Abdul claimed that he spoke to The Master all the time—that the guy had been so taken with Abdul that he'd given him his cellphone number. Everyone knew the garbage sorter was lying. Road boys didn't mind deception; extravagant fabrications passed the time. They were just amused that he would lie about a friendship with a teacher. The only other boy who told that kind of loser-lie was Sunil, who liked to pretend to new boys that he was a fifth-grade student, top of his class.

Abdul had a fresh audience for his stories about The Master when his semi-friend Kalu returned from the Karjat construction site in mid-September. Kalu had gained weight, on account of the shortage of Eraz-ex outside the city.

Zehrunisa, surprised to see Kalu back so soon, called him into the house for a plate of leftovers, of which there were more than usual, since the Husains were fasting for the month of Ramadan. Zehrunisa was fond of Kalu, thought he was in need of mothering. Kalu did not dispute this. He'd been calling Zehrunisa *Amma*, or Mother, for a year—an endearment that made Abdul a little tense.

"Your father is still there in the mountains?" she asked.

"Yes, but Amma, I had to leave it. I didn't want to be out in the country now." Mumbai was in the midst of the giddy festival in honor of his beloved Ganpati. Two days from now, to the sound of drumbeats and cheering, millions of citizens from across Mumbai would bring lovingly crafted idols of the elephant god to the sea to immerse them. It was a celebratory practice of which environmentalists took a dim view, but which marked the high point of Kalu's year.

"You should have stayed," Zehrunisa admonished him. "I can barely recognize you, you're so healthy. Why forget your father like that? You'll just slip back into your old bad ways, being here."

"I'm not getting back into stealing," he promised her. "I'm good and improved now, can't you see?"

"Yes, good and improved now," Zehrunisa agreed. "But can thieves really change? If they can, I haven't seen it."

The next day, Kalu scavenged for trash at the airport with Sunil. In the evening, after selling the trash to Abdul, they lingered with him outside the game shed. The three boys were ranging across the usual subjects—food, movies, girls, the price of waste—when a disabled man named Mahmoud, stoned and glassy-eyed, slugged Abdul in the chest for reasons known only to himself. Another raging One

Leg. Of course Abdul wasn't going to fight him. He headed home to sleep. Sunil did, too.

Kalu had no home to retreat to. He decided to go to the airport, taking off across the thoroughfare toward the bright blue signs that lead the way to the international terminal. ARRIVALS down. DEPARTURES up. HAPPY JOURNEY.

The following morning, Kalu lay outside Air India's red-and-white gates: a shirtless corpse with a grown-out Salman Khan haircut, crumpled behind a flowering hedge.

11.

Proper Sleep

A HULKING, MUSTACHIOED CONSTABLE named Nagare rode his motorcycle into Annawadi, the disabled junkie who'd punched Abdul the previous night balanced on the seat behind him. The motorcycle braked hard in front of Zehrunisa, who was haggling with a scavenger. She began to shake when she saw the constable's face. This Nagare did not wear the face a policeman usually wore when coming to ask for money. His was a tense, bad face she didn't know how to read. So he would be bringing some fresh trouble to compound the trouble her family was already in.

No, she was being paranoid like Abdul. The constable simply wanted to know the whereabouts of Kalu's relatives, and Mahmoud, the disabled junkie, had told him she was likely to know. Zehrunisa felt lightheaded with relief, until Nagare told her why he was asking.

"Boy's dead," he said with a frown, and she barely had time to grieve when he sped away, because the next thing she heard was the sound of Abdul breaking down.

For weeks her eldest son had tried to forget what had happened to him in the police cell. Now, in an instant, something sealed inside him had split open. He couldn't remember the mechanics of breathing, and began to speak in a clipped, frantic tone. Kalu, his only sort-of friend: dead. So now he would be arrested for the murder. The police would trap him, just as Fatima had done. "I know it," he kept saying. The addict, Mahmoud, would already have told the police that Abdul had been standing on the road with Kalu the night before. This would be the evidence on which Abdul would be convicted. There would be more police beatings and, after that, decades in Arthur Road Jail. He crouched and gulped, then rose and ran inside his hut, where even Kehkashan, now out on bail, could not console him. He felt he needed to go into hiding again, but not, this time, in his trash pile—

"Kalu got murdered! Eyes poked out! Sickle up his ass!"

Other boys, less traumatized by life, had run to see the body, and their reports now flew through the slumlanes. Sunil refused to believe them, needed to see for himself. He took off, dodging the cars on Airport Road.

The other boys had said that Kalu's body was in the garden, but which garden? Two years into the aesthetic makeover of the airport, led by the conglomerate GVK, the place was choking with flowers. There were also gardens by the Hotel Leela, weren't there? In his distress, Sunil's mental map of his airport terrain got turned around.

When he finally arrived at the correct garden, Air India and GVK executives had gathered, and the police were keeping everyone else far away. Another boy told Sunil that crows had taken Kalu's eyeballs and dropped them in the coconut trees.

Sunil watched from a distance as Kalu's half-naked corpse was loaded into a police van. He watched the van drive away. All that remained to stare at was yellow police tape—dumb plastic ribbon twisting through a stand of orange heliconia, their flowers like the open beaks of baby birds.

Sunil turned and walked home, past the immense pilings of the elevated expressway being constructed in the middle of Airport Road, past a line of signs GVK had planted that said WE CARE WE CARE WE CARE, past the long wall advertising floor tiles that stay beautiful forever. He felt small and sad and useless. Who had done such a thing to his friend? But the fog of shock and grief didn't fully obscure his understanding of the social hierarchy in which he lived. To Annawadi boys, Kalu had been a star. To the authorities of the overcity, he was a nuisance case to be dispensed with.

OFFICIALLY, THE SAHAR police precinct was among the safest places in Greater Mumbai. In two years, only two murders had been recorded in the whole precinct, which included the airport, hotels, office buildings, and dozens of construction-site camps and slums. Both murders had been promptly solved. "All murders we detect, 100 percent success," was how Senior Inspector Patil, who ran the Sahar station, liked to put it. But perhaps there was a trick to this success rate: not detecting the murders of inconsequential people.

Succumbed to an "irrecoverable illness" was the swift conclusion of Maruti Jadhav, the inspector in charge of Kalu's case. At the morgue of Cooper Hospital, the nature of the "irrecoverable illness" was decided. Fifteen-year-old Deepak Rai, known as Kalu, had died of his tuberculosis—the same cause of death tagged to the bleeding scavenger who had slowly expired on the road.

Active, fence-climbing boys don't suddenly drop dead of tuberculosis; one thing Annawadians know as well as pathologists is that TB deaths are torturously slow. But the evidence of Kalu's body was swiftly turned to ash in a pyre at the Parsiwada Crematorium on Airport Road, the false cause of death duly noted in an official register that had been burned through the middle by a resting cigarette. Then photos of the boy's corpse, taken in accordance with police regulations, vanished from the files at the Sahar station.

As Abdul and his family had already learned, the police station was not a place where victimhood was redressed and public safety held dear. It was a hectic bazaar, like many other public institutions in Mumbai, and investigating Kalu's death was not a profit-generating enterprise. The death did, however, provide the police with an opportunity to clear the airport grounds of other Annawadi road boys.

AFTER KALU'S DEATH, five of the road boys were picked up and taken to the Sahar Police Station's "unofficial" cell. They were beaten in the name of an investigation and released with the understanding that, if they didn't stay away from the increasingly elegant airport, they might find themselves charged with Kalu's murder. The boys didn't know that the police had already filed away the case as a natural death.

One of the released boys, named Karan, fled Annawadi, fled the city, and never returned. Another, Sanjay Shetty, frantically collected garbage and took it to the Husains in order to finance his own getaway.

Zehrunisa gasped when she saw him. "What happened to your face?" she asked. "Why are you crying?"

Sixteen-year-old Sanjay stood out from the other road boys for his uncommon height, his beauty, and his pronounced South Indian drawl. "Every word you say has a loving sound," Zehrunisa had once teased him. "You will melt a person, the way you talk." Now Sanjay could barely make words.

"Calm yourself," Zehrunisa told him. "Say what happened."

Between sobs he told her he had seen Kalu attacked by a gang of men in the darkness by the Air India gate. Then he told her of his own beating, in the police station. Sanjay didn't know what to fear more: that Kalu's attackers would discover he'd been a witness and come after him, or that the cops would pick him up for another round of violent interrogation.

He couldn't sleep on the Annawadi rut-road any longer and was heading to his mother's house, because he couldn't think of anywhere else to go. After his family's hut at the airport had burned down, she'd moved five miles south to Dharavi, the largest slum in the city.

Zehrunisa agreed that Dharavi was a better place than Annawadi for a boy to get lost in. She put the money in Sanjay's hand and watched him run.

When Sanjay reached Dharavi, his fourteen-year-old sister, Anandi, was making tomato chutney for dinner. She nearly dropped the bowl when she saw the fear in his face. The two were close, and recently, in rare possession of disposable income, he'd had her first initial tattooed next to his own on his forearm. Anandi often chided him that any brother who loved his sister as much as he professed to would come home more often. But their sixty-square-foot hut was too small for three people, and Sanjay liked to be near the airport—said it made him feel he had a chance to get away.

Sanjay took his sister's hand, and as they sat knee-to-knee on the floor, told her of seeing a group of men swarm Kalu all at once. "They killed my friend," he kept repeating. "Just threw him off." Like he was garbage.

Recovering himself, Sanjay began to lecture Anandi: that she shouldn't cause heartache for their mother, who was still at work, tending to an elderly woman in a middle-class neighborhood; that she should take her studies more seriously.

His sister looked at him, confused. "What are you saying, Sanjay? Study? Like you, I have to work and earn. And you're the one who gives Mother tension, not me."

"You also should sleep properly," he said, not hearing her. "I don't think you sleep so good."

Anandi didn't know what to make of her brother's paternal tone. Was it Eraz-ex? She stood up, impatient. She was sorry that this Kalu had been murdered. She'd met him once; he'd praised her cooking, made her laugh. But she couldn't just sit here holding Sanjay's hand when she had the vegetables and rice to do. As she turned back to the stove, Sanjay stretched on the floor and closed his eyes, perhaps to model his idea of proper sleep.

When his mother walked in an hour later, Sanjay was up and restless, listening to a duet from an album called *Phir Bewafaai: Deceived in Love*. "Sanjay's broken-heart music," his mother liked to call it, rolling her eyes.

"Just a single misunderstanding," the guilty husband was singing, as his betrayed wife sang back her plan of revenge. Sanjay's mother's voice rose above them both: "Going to be sick! Oh, I ate something rotten at lunch!"

Bolting for the toilet, she called, "Wait, Sanjay. Don't run off."

"I won't," he promised. When his mother returned, his sister was hysterical and he was convulsing on the floor. Pulling Sanjay up, thinking that he was having a seizure, his mother caught a chemical reek on his breath. His sister retrieved a white plastic bottle from the corner of the room. She'd seen him toying with it earlier, assumed it contained soap for blowing bubbles—Sanjay was crazy for soap bubbles. But the empty plastic bottle was rat poison.

Sanjay rolled over to face the wall, refusing the salt water his mother prepared to force him to vomit. He lived for two hours after reaching the public hospital. After midnight, returning home to Dharavi ancient with grief, his mother tossed into the gutter the prescriptions the doctor had written for Sanjay. There had been no time to go out to the road and fill them.

The police inquiry into her son's death was closed as swiftly as the inquiry into Kalu's death had been. In the public record, Sanjay Shetty would be neither a vulnerable witness to a murder nor the victim of police threats and beatings. He would be a heroin addict who had decided to kill himself because he couldn't afford his next fix.

IN DELHI, POLITICIANS and intellectuals privately bemoaned the "irrationality" of the uneducated Indian masses, but when the government itself provided false answers to its citizens' urgent concerns, rumor and conspiracy took wing. Sometimes, the conspiracies became a consolation for loss.

Trying to make sense of the deaths of Kalu and Sanjay, Sunil and Abdul grew closer. Not quite friends—rather, an unnameable, not-entirely-willing category of relationship in which two boys felt themselves bound to two boys who were dead. Sunil and Abdul sat together more often than before, but when they spoke, it was with the curious formality of people who shared the understanding that much of what was said did not matter, and that much of what mattered could not be said.

Sunil felt certain that Air India security guards had murdered

Kalu upon catching him in their recycling piles. Abdul suspected Kalu had been killed by drug dealers on whom he'd informed. "It was a dog's death, either way," Abdul said, often, which made Sunil think of the strangled dog in the Will Smith movie that he and Kalu had seen at Pinky Talkie Town.

Mirchi felt both boys should drop the subject. "Yeah, he stole garbage, but it was *their* garbage. So of course he was going to die like that."

Road boys blamed other road boys. "Mahmoud—my full doubt is on him." "Karan probably did it then ran away." A corrosive, free-floating distrust worked its way down the slumlanes. Fatima's ghost may or may not have been involved.

Kalu's father turned against the woman whose Airport Road stall Kalu had frequented for chicken-chili rice. She heard things, and Kalu's father had counted on her to tell him what had really happened. "Kalu what? Kalu who?" she had said, staring into her cookpot. In the end, for the refusal of the police and the morgue to tell the truth about the death of his son, he would blame the chicken-chili rice woman most of all.

Sanjay's mother didn't know whom to blame. For weeks after her son's suicide, she walked unsteadily through Annawadi, asking everyone she passed if they could tell her why her son had taken his life. "How do I sleep without knowing?" she asked her daughter. "The whole world is in my head, and it doesn't make sense."

Sunil and the road boys were torn when they saw Sanjay's mother coming. They'd known her before she'd moved to Dharavi. That she now looked three hundred years old suggested just how much she'd loved her son. But how to explain Sanjay's death without talking about Kalu's, without talking about the Sahar police? Even the Tamil who ran the game shed, and whose police contacts were intimate, was afraid to say Kalu's name. So Sanjay's mother learned only what another mother, who slept on pavement, dared to whisper: "Your boy died with fear in his heart."

The soil outside the red-and-white Air India gates was good and loamy. Gradually, with the ministrations of the airport gardening crew, a boy-sized break in the flowers filled in. One afternoon, Sunil crouched there, studying the skin of the earth. He could find no trace of damage.

PART FOUR

up and out

Don't confuse yourself by thinking about such terrible lives.

—ZEHRUNISA HUSAIN   ·

12.

Nine Nights of Dance

BY LATE SEPTEMBER 2008, Asha was in control of Annawadi. There had been no clinching event, no slum-boss coronation. Rather, it had been a campaign of small advances toward the moment when the line of supplicants extended outside her hut, policemen promptly returned her calls, and Corporator Subhash Sawant, on hand to address the residents, offered her the plastic chair beside his own. Her patron had regained his confidence, now that the faked-caste-certificate case against him seemed tied up in court. Seated beside him on the stage by the sewage lake, Asha looked nearly his equal, sporting a gold chain much like his own. Hers had been financed by her self-help group and the high-interest loans it made to poorer women.

Relaxing into her authority, Asha stopped making elaborate excuses to her family about the men she met late at night. When her husband threatened suicide, she consoled him but made no promise to change. She let herself gain ten pounds, which softened the lines beneath her eyes—a last trace of her years in the fields.

Her main regret was the lack of a confidante with whom to relish this fledgling triumph. Her secrets had isolated her from other women; she'd had to close certain doors to herself. "What friend do I really have," she would say to Manju. But now even her daughter seemed remote. On the rare occasion that Manju met her eye, she would bring up Asha's least favorite subject, the One Leg.

WHILE THE DEATHS OF KALU and Sanjay shook the boys who lived on the road, Fatima's death was the one that strobed in and out of the minds of Annawadi women. Two months after the public spectacle of her burning, it had insinuated itself into countless private narratives. Fatima's regret at what she'd done had been forgotten, her act reconstrued as a flamboyant protest.

What, exactly, she had been protesting was subject to interpretation. To the poorest, her self-immolation was a response to enervating poverty. To the disabled, it reflected the lack of respect accorded the physically impaired. To the unhappily married, who were legion, it was a brave indictment of oppressive unions. Almost no one spoke of envy, a stone slab, a poorly made wall, or rubble that had fallen into rice.

One night the brothelkeeper's wife doused herself with kerosene in the maidan, called out Fatima's name, and threatened to light a match. Another night, a woman beaten by her husband *did* light the match. She survived in such a state that Manju and her friend Meena, in their secret nightly meetings at the public toilet, began discussing more foolproof means of suicide.

Only fifteen-year-old Meena knew that Manju had considered taking her life the night that Asha had run out on her fortieth birthday party, and on other nights after that. As Manju became consumed with shame and worry over her mother's affairs, Meena could only offer perspective. Her own parents and brothers beat her regularly, with force, and the big expeditions punctuating her housekeeping-days were visits to the public tap and the toilet. In Meena's opinion, any mother who financed her daughter's college education, rarely slapped her, and hadn't arranged her marriage at age fifteen could be forgiven for other failings.

Meena encouraged Manju to express the worst of her thoughts. It was said to be the modern, healthy way of coping. "You always say that the flowers I put in my hair never turn sticky and brown," she told Manju one night at the toilet. "My flowers live because I don't keep anything dark in my heart. I let the bad things come out into the air."

Manju winced. She didn't want her mother's behavior to be more in-the-air than it already was. "My heart must be black, then," she replied, deflecting. "The flowers in my hair die in two hours."

Manju thought it wiser to practice the denial about which she'd been learning in psychology class—just stop thinking about her mother altogether. "If I don't block it out, I won't be able to study," she said. The exams that would determine whether she would become Annawadi's first female college graduate were only a few months away.

> Based on his theory of the unconscious, Freud tells us how a fantasy is an unsatisfied wish which is fulfilled to the imagination. He divides fantasies into two main groups:
> a) ambitious wishes
> b) erotic
> Young men have mostly ambitious wishes. Young women have mostly erotic ones. The ordinary person feels ashamed of his fantasies and hides them.

By-hearting the psychology notes her teacher provided, Manju realized she needed to block out a second painful subject: Vijay, the middle-class hero of the Civil Defense Corps, who had once gripped her hand. "In my next birth, you can be my wife," he had recently told her. "Not this time."

Late September was the season of romantic contemplation for many young women in Annawadi. The annual flirtfest, the Navratri festival, was about to begin.

The holidays the boys anticipated most were Holi and Haandi. On Holi, they attacked each other with balloons full of colored water; on Haandi, they made human ladders and belly-flopped into the mud. Slum girls weren't allowed to roll in mud. Navratri—nine nights of dance—was the festival in which they could be equals, even betters, of the boys. Over these nights at the end of the monsoon season, the goddess Durga was said to battle the evil of the universe and triumph. Feminine divinity was celebrated, and even Meena received parental permission to dance and shine.

On the first night of the previous Navratri, Meena and Manju had spent hours getting ready. A dark blue sari for Manju, who could pull it off now that she had breasts and hips, like her mother. Stylish red salwar kameez for Meena, who stayed reedy no matter how many Good Day biscuits she put away.

Meena found it hard work not to be dazzled by Manju: her figure, her fairness, her ability to stand back straight, butt in, perfectly still. Meena's own deportment was fidget-and-twist. But when she threw back her head and laughed, teeth gleaming, hers was the edgier beauty. She looked like one of those girls who made exciting things happen. Exciting things didn't happen, though—and certainly not on the Navratri of 2007. The two girls had swanned onto the maidan for the first night of dancing only to be drenched by the season's final downpour. The stage by the sewage lake was the only mudless place. The feral pigs that camped beside it reeked of a too-long monsoon.

The Navratri of 2008 could only be better, since Asha would be choreographing it. She knew what these nine nights meant to girls. Among her plans were a band, a deejay with powerful speakers, a large pandal to house an idol of the goddess Durga, and fairy lights strung up over the maidan, under which the dancing would wheel. The leaders of Shiv Sena and the rival Congress Party had contributed money for this extravaganza. Elections were approaching and, with millions of slum voters to be won over, the city's political class was in a generous mood.

Annawadians were in need of exuberant distraction, as a recession that had begun in the West arrived in India. Suddenly, once-profitable links to the global markets were pushing the slumdwellers backward. The price of recyclable goods declined. Temp work in construction dried up as projects that had stopped in the monsoon stalled again for lack of foreign financing. Meanwhile, the price of food was soaring, largely on account of poor rains and harvests in Vidarbha and other agricultural strongholds.

The political response to this hardship—deejays and colored lights—was a time-honored tradition in Mumbai. On festival days before elections, the city slums became as bright as the wealthy neighborhoods with their *pucca* buildings, and ten times louder. Meena was all for bands, amps, and twinkling lights. This would be her last Navratri before starting a life she dreaded, as a teenaged bride in a Tamil Nadu village.

MEENA HAD ONCE TAKEN pride in having been the first girl born in Annawadi. But as she prepared to leave Mumbai, it troubled her that domestic labor in the slum was all she had learned of her city. Nothing a girl cleaned in Annawadi stayed clean. Why did people see it as a failure of the girl? Why did her mother scream at her when, like everyone else, she lost two hours of her morning standing in line for water at a dribbling tap?

Everything on television announced a new and better India for women. Her favorite Tamil soap opera was about an educated single girl who worked in an office. In her favorite commercials, a South Indian movie siren named Asin was recommending, along with Mirinda orange soda, more fun, a little wildness.

This new India of feisty, convention-defying women wasn't a place Meena knew how to get to. Maybe Manju would get there, with her college degree. Meena couldn't say, not knowing any woman who had finished college. But watching the soap operas and Mirinda commercials, she sometimes felt her own life to be a husk of an existence. Things were inflicted upon her—regular beatings, the new engagement to marry. But what did she ever get to decide?

A boy, not her fiancé, had recently fallen in love with her. In the soap operas, such a thing would be explosive. In her constricted life, it was a small but welcome distraction. The boy was a friend of her older brother: a factory worker from a nearby slum who was about to take a housecleaning job in the Persian Gulf—the only way he thought he could make enough money to someday support a wife and family. One night, while visiting her brother, he slipped Meena his phone number. Another night, at a public phone, she dialed it. During the sixth or eighth illicit phone call, he said she was the future wife for whom he was striving.

The flirtation had gone too far. Meena gave him what she thought was a respectable response: "It's okay if you love me. I'm glad that you do. But I am going to be married to someone else, so you must think of me only as a friend."

Manju was relieved to hear it, since Meena was a see-through kind of girl, poorly suited to sneaking around. Her brothers had twice caught her on the phone and slapped her for it.

"Anyway," Manju pointed out, "you said last month that you liked the village boy."

Meena did like the village boy, who called on Sundays. He washed his own dinner plate—an astonishment to Meena and Manju, since he could have ordered his sister to do it for him. The boy was not the problem; the problem was an arranged marriage at age fifteen.

Meena's father spoke rapturously of the feeling she was supposed to have, being engaged: "The first time your hearts meet, nothing else is left."

Manju's father took a more cynical view: "No marriage is happy after it happens. It's only before, thinking of it, that it's happy."

But Meena didn't feel euphoric anticipation. She couldn't see how love would alter the daily practicalities. What if over the verge of marriage stretched an adult life even more confined than her childhood had been?

To both Meena and Manju, marrying into a village family was like time-traveling backward. In Asha's village, people of the Kunbi caste still considered Dalits like Meena contaminated: unhygienic people relegated to the outskirts of town and tolerated in Kunbi homes only when picking up garbage or dredging drains. If a Dalit touched a cup in such a house, it had to be destroyed. Those villagers would be appalled if they saw how Manju leaned against her friend, or learned that the two girls shared a sky-blue sari.

Manju had worn the sari on the Maharashtrian New Year, the previous spring. Meena had worn it, draped with narrower pleats, for the Tamil New Year. "I feel too fluffy and puffy, wearing it your way," she told Manju. Meena would rightfully get to wear it for her final Navratri in Mumbai.

"I'm afraid my mother will decide to marry me to that soldier from the village," Manju said one night in the toilet, where they always made a point of turning their backs to the slum. Ever since Asha had taken Manju home to Vidarbha, Rahul had been teasing her about her rural future: "You'll have to cover your head and clean and cook for your mother-in-law, and your husband will be away in the army and you'll be so lonely."

"So what will you do if your mother sets up such a marriage?" Meena asked.

"I'll run to my aunt, I think. She would protect me. How could I spend my life like that?"

"Maybe it's better just to do what Fatima did," Meena said. "Escape the situation if you know you're going to be miserable. But I would kill myself by eating poison, not by burning. If you burned yourself, the last memory people would have of you is with your skin all spoiled and scary."

"Why are you still thinking like that?" Manju admonished. "You were sick for a week after you saw Fatima's body lying there. You'll get sick again if you don't push such thoughts out of your mind the way I do."

As they whispered, they couldn't help looking around every once in a while, to make sure there was no sign of the One Leg. Although her curses floated through Annawadi, wreaking havoc in any number of huts, her actual ghost was known to be lodged in these very toilets. Slumdwellers remembered her walking there, *tink-tink-tink*, dolled up in lipstick. Many of them had decided it was safer to shit outside.

"Don't worry," Rahul told the girls. "The One Leg didn't take her crutches with her when she died, so her ghost won't be able to run and catch you." Manju more or less believed this, and also knew that first-class people did not subscribe to ghost talk.

Meena was unapologetically superstitious, though. Recently, her mother reported seeing a snake slither across a menstrual cloth that Meena had too casually discarded. Her mother had been hysterical—said it foretold that Meena's womb would shrivel up.

Manju suspected that Meena's mother hadn't really seen a snake, and was simply getting more creative in her attempts to keep Meena docile before marriage. But Meena was shaken. "I'm going to dry up and die," she cried one night. Married women without children were suspect in Mumbai. And to be barren in a village?

Meena started to feel skittish at the toilet; the serpent curse and Fatima's ghost struck her as a risky convergence. Still, she lingered, couldn't not linger. The minutes in the night stench with Manju were the closest she had ever come to freedom.

THE DAY BEFORE ASHA'S Navratri began, the maidan underwent a fury of beautification. Abdul and his garbage piles were banished, and women swept and swept. A teenaged boy shimmied up the flagpole to anchor the strings of lights, while other boys climbed onto hut roofs to affix the ends of the strings to corrugated eaves. Tonight, Manju and Asha would fetch the idol of Durga from a nearby neighborhood, the arrival of which would complete the holiday preparations. Now, returning from college in the early afternoon, Manju rushed across the maidan wondering how she could teach school, memorize a plot summary for English literature, and do the housework on a day when the goddess-getting would consume at least an hour.

"Will come before dinner!" she called out to Meena, who was waving from the doorway of her hut. Manju didn't intend to be caught with unfinished laundry on a week when dancing privileges could be taken away.

Four hours later, clothes on the line and the final round of Head-Shoulders-Knees-and-Toes completed, Manju walked over to Meena's. Her friend was sitting in her doorway, looking out at the tidy maidan. This was odd. Meena's parents didn't let her sit on the stoop—said it gave a girl a loose reputation.

Manju settled in beside her. Late afternoon was the time many girls and women of Annawadi took a break from housework, before beginning their dinner preparations. When they were younger, Meena and Manju had spent their free minutes playing hopscotch in front of the hut, but marriageable teenaged girls couldn't jump around. Meena looked wan, and wasn't as fidgety as usual, but she was fasting as she did every Navratri, to please the goddess Durga.

From time to time, Meena bent over and spit in the dust. "Are you getting sick?" Manju asked after a while.

Meena shook her head and spit again.

"So what are you doing?" Manju said in a low voice, suddenly suspicious. "Chewing tobacco?" With her mother right there inside the hut?

"Just spitting," Meena said with a shrug.

Feeling a little aggrieved at Meena's failure to entertain her, Manju rose to return to her work. "Wait," said Meena, holding out her hand. In her palm was an empty tube of rat poison.

Meena met her eyes, and Manju went flying into the hut, where Meena's mother was grinding rice to make idlis. Manju's words came forth in a torrent—*rat poison, Meena, foolish, going to die.*

Meena's mother kept grinding the rice. "Calm down. She's playing a trick," she told Manju. "She said a few weeks back that she'd eaten poison, and nothing happened."

Meena's mother was fed up with her daughter. The prospect of dancing had apparently caused the girl to lose her senses. Meena had been discovered talking on the phone to the city boy at 2 A.M., and taken a beating for it. At lunchtime, she refused to make her younger brother an omelet because she was fasting and didn't want to be tempted by food. Took a beating for that, too. Her brother was about to give her the third beating of the day, for sitting outside the house, when she concocted this story about having eaten poison.

Manju was momentarily reassured by Meena's mother. But if Meena was manufacturing a drama, wouldn't she let Manju in on it? Manju went back outside, leaned into her friend's face, and sniffed.

Manju thought of cartoon dragons, exhaling fire and smoke. Later, she kept thinking she *saw* smoke coming out of Meena's mouth and nose—as if the girl had set herself on fire from the inside. No, that was impossible. Rat poison only. Her mind was looping. If she screamed for help, the whole slum would know that Meena had attempted suicide, which would ruin her reputation. Quiet seemed essential. She ran to a pay phone to call Asha.

"Mummy," she whispered, "Meena ate rat poison, her mother doesn't believe, and I don't know what to do!"

"Oh, shit!" said Asha. "You've got to force her to swallow tobacco right away. That will make her puke everything out."

But what would people say if Manju was seen buying tobacco? Manju chased down some Tamil women on Meena's slumlane, hoping they would have a better idea. "She poisoned herself!" she hissed. "Help me! I don't know what to do!"

They shook their heads. "So many fights in that family lately," someone said.

"No!" Manju cried, forgetting to be quiet. "Don't be calm! You have to *do* something!"

Meena had come over, was standing beside her.

"Did you really swallow it?" one of the women asked.

"I did," Meena said, her voice mild.

"Did you take *all* of it?" Manju demanded. A woman on this slumlane had recently consumed half a tube of the same brand of poison, Ratol, and survived.

"All of it," Meena said, then leaned forward to gag, spirals of hair spilling over her face. When the gagging stopped, she started to talk very fast. That the Ratol cost forty rupees at the Marol Market. That she had stolen change from her brothers and father to buy it. Something about always getting beaten. Something about her brother and an omelet, but not just about that. She wasn't acting out of anger, as Fatima had done. She'd thought it through—had consumed two tubes of rat poison on two other days, but had started to vomit, which led her this time to mix the poison with milk. She hoped the milk would keep the poison in her stomach long enough to kill her.

This was one decision about her life she got to make. It wasn't a choice easily shared with a best friend.

Meena sat again with a heaviness that had nothing to do with her weight. A woman materialized with a bowl of water and salt. "This will make her vomit," she said, tipping back Meena's head. She swallowed. Everyone waited. Dry heaves. Nothing.

Water and laundry soap, another woman suggested, running home to chop up a foul-smelling bar of Madhumati. Meena held her nose as the second brew went down her throat. Finally, she vomited a jet of bright green froth.

"I feel better," Meena announced, eventually. "It's all out." Her face slick with sweat, she stood unsteadily, and her mother led her inside to sleep off the effects of the poison. As the door shut behind them, the women of the slumlane exhaled. Feminine discretion had averted a scene, perhaps saved a wedding. Meena's future in-laws might not come to hear that they'd chosen an impetuous bride.

The shopkeeper two huts down kept selling milk and sugar, unaware. Construction workers returning from work tramped through soapy green vomit. Manju registered through a screen of exhaustion that it was evening and that she needed not to be standing, disheveled, outside her friend's closed door. She needed to wash her face and get the goddess Durga.

As she and Asha left to pick up the idol, Meena's elder brother arrived home, learned that his sister had consumed rat poison, and beat her for it. Meena wept and went to sleep. Just before midnight, she started to cry again. Eventually her father realized that this was not sad crying.

On the first night of Navratri, as the young people of Annawadi, minus Manju, danced in the illuminated clearing, Meena answered the question of a police officer who had come to her bedside at Cooper Hospital. Had anyone incited her to attempt suicide? "I blame no one," said Meena. "I decided for myself."

On the third night of Navratri, Meena stopped talking, at which point Cooper Hospital doctors extracted five thousand rupees from her parents in the name of "imported injections."

On the sixth day of Navratri, Meena was dead.

"She was fed up with what the world had to offer," the Tamil women concluded. Meena's family, upon consideration, decided that Manju's modern influence was to blame.

The lights of Navratri came down. Rahul tried to make Manju laugh again, and thought she'd smiled a little the day he pointed out that Meena's younger brother had lost something, too. "That boy will never want to eat an omelet again."

In a certain morning light, Manju could see the name MEENA traced faintly in a broken piece of cement just outside the toilet. "Only in that light," she said, "and even then, it's barely there." Another, lesser Meena lived in Annawadi, and a man who loved that Meena had once carved her name on the inside of his forearm. Manju thought he'd probably written MEENA in the wet cement, too. It stood to reason. But she preferred to believe that Meena's own finger had made the letters, and that the first girl born in Annawadi had left some mark of herself on the place.

13.

Something Shining

IN NOVEMBER, THE WASTE MARKET in free fall, the Tamil who
owned the game shed tried to help the scavengers grasp why their
trash was worth so little. "The banks in America went in a loss, then
the big people went in a loss, then the scrap market in the slum areas
came down, too": This was how he explained the global economic
crisis. A kilo of empty water bottles once worth twenty-five rupees was
now worth ten, and a kilo of newspaper once worth five rupees was
now worth two: This was how the global crisis was understood.

The newspapers Sunil collected said that a lot of Americans were
now living in their cars or in tents under bridges. The richest man in
India, Mukesh Ambani, had also lost money—billions—although
not enough to impede construction on his famed twenty-seven-story
house in south Mumbai. The lower stories would be reserved for cars
and the six hundred servants required by his family of five. Far more
interesting to young slumdwellers was the fact that Ambani's helicop-
ters would land on the roof.

"Things will get better soon," Abdul told Sunil and the other scavengers, because that was what his father told him. Although the global markets were volatile, the behavior of tourists could be predicted. They inundated Mumbai in the winter. Indians who lived abroad began arriving in November, for the Diwali holiday. Europeans and Americans came in December. The Chinese and Japanese came soon after, and the hotels and airport boomed until January's end. With the influx of travelers, Annawadians decided, the losses of monsoon and recession would be recovered.

One night in late November, Sunil was in the game shed after an unprofitable day of scavenging, watching two boys at one of the red consoles play Metal Slug 3. On the video screen, guerrillas were fighting policemen and mutant lobsters in the streets of a bombed-out city. Outside the game parlor, other Annawadians started getting loud. Sunil eventually realized that the commotion was not the usual Eraz-ex bullshit. People were pressed against the window of the hut where the game-shed owner lived, watching a news report on the man's TV. Muslim terrorists from Pakistan had floated in rubber boats onto a Mumbai beach, and were running loose in the city.

The jihadis had taken over two luxury hotels, the Taj and the Oberoi, slaughtering workers and tourists. People were also dead at a place called Leopold Cafe, and reports of more than a hundred other casualties were coming in from the city's largest train station. Before long, a photo of one of the terrorists filled the television screen. Black T-shirt. Knapsack. Running shoes. He looked like a college kid, except for the automatic weapon.

The attacks were taking place seventeen miles from Annawadi, in the wealthy southern part of the city—to Sunil, a reassuring remove. He was interested when the television people said the terrorists might have bombs. The bombs in his second-favorite video game, Bomberman, were black and round with long sizzle-fuses. Circus music played when they exploded.

But a taxi had blown up near Airport Road, and older boys were saying that the airport itself would be a logical target. Manju speculated that if the terrorists had invaded five-star hotels in south Mumbai, they might also come to the five-star hotels by the airport. Might even come through Annawadi to get to these hotels. Mercifully, her unit of the Indian Civil Defense Corps was not being called upon to aid in this particular crisis. She went into her house and shut the door.

Abdul's parents were afraid to do the same. What if Annawadi Hindus decided the slum's Muslims were part of some plot? Door open, Karam Husain turned on the TV. As Abdul covered his head with a sheet, one of his little brothers drew close to the screen. The architecture in the colonial part of the city was beautiful to the younger boy— the red turrets rising up behind the reporters at the Taj, the ornate façade of the train station. Here in Annawadi, every home looked a little like the family who had made it. But even when besieged, this south Mumbai seemed to him majestically coherent—"like a single mind made the whole place."

Early the next morning, Sunil and Sonu the blinky boy set off for work, only to discover that scavenging was out of the question. The airport perimeter was sealed, and military commandos with long black guns clustered on Airport Road. The boys ran back to Annawadi and the television of the man who owned the game shed. The Taj Hotel had been burning, terrorists and tourists were still inside, and the newscaster said people all over the world were following the drama. Outside the hotel, well-dressed people wiped away tears as they told reporters what the Taj meant to them.

Sunil understood that the rich people were mourning the devastation of a place where they had relaxed and felt safe. In his equivalent place, the 96-square-foot game shed, no one cried about the siege of south Mumbai, or about the hundreds of people dead and injured. Instead, slumdwellers worried for themselves. By the time the attack ended, sixty hours after it had begun, many Annawadians had accurately predicted the chain of economic consequences.

A city in which terrorists killed foreign tourists in hotels was not a place other foreign tourists would want to spend their winter holidays. There would not be a peak season in Annawadi this winter. The airport would be quiet, the hotels empty. When midnight came on January 1, there would be few partiers at the Intercontinental shouting "Happy New Year."

Instead, 2009 arrived in the slum under a blanket of poverty, the global recession overlaid by a crisis of fear. More Annawadians had to relearn how to digest rats. Sonu deputized Sunil to catch frogs at Naupada slum, since Naupada frogs tasted better than sewage-lake ones. The deranged scavenger who talked to the luxury hotels stopped accusing the Hyatt of plotting to kill him. Instead, he pleaded to its nonreflective blue-glass front, "I do so much work, Hyatt, and earn so little. Will you not take care of me?"

ONE JANUARY AFTERNOON, Sunil took a bath in an abandoned pit at the concrete-mixing plant. Pushing away the algae, he examined his reflection with care. He was a thief now, and Sonu said it showed in his face.

Sunil knew what his friend meant. He'd seen a change come over the faces of other boys who turned to stealing—a change security guards recognized in an instant. He decided he still looked the same: same big childish mouth, wide nose, sunken torso. Same thick hair, sticking up and out now, but about which he had no complaint when he thought about his sister Sunita. Rats had bitten them both while they slept, and the bites had turned into head boils. But she had recently become a baldie, because her boils had erupted with worms.

Sonu wanted Sunil to renounce his new line of work, and to that end had recently slapped his face four times, hard. Sunil neither slapped back nor changed his mind. Sonu was probably the most virtuous boy at Annawadi, but he also had a mother and younger siblings working to supplement the household income. Sunil, unable to feed himself by scavenging, had to consider his airport terrain afresh, and locals who fenced stolen goods were glad to help him. For Sunil's first solo mission, a teenaged thief-wrangler, himself with a worm-bald sister, provided a bicycle for a high-speed getaway. By morning, the airport fire brigade was stripped of copper faucet valves. The game-shed man handed over his cutting tools, and metal supports disappeared beneath dozens of concrete sewer covers. As construction workers prepared a cavernous airport car park for its opening, Sunil set to dismantling bits of it, screw by screw.

He was well suited to his work as a new-economy microsaboteur. His climbing ability had been honed on Airport Road coconut trees, his small size helped deflect suspicion, and he didn't balk at calculated risks, like the ones he took when jumping down to the garbage-filled ledge above the river. The only problem was that his hands and legs shook every time he picked up a piece of metal—a nervous tic other thieves found hilarious.

One of them, Taufeeq, had been asking him all month, "Should we go into the Taj tonight?" The Annawadi boys' Taj was not the hotel that the terrorists attacked. Their Taj was Taj Catering Services, a squat building on airport grounds owned by the hotel company. Behind high stone walls topped with rows of barbed wire, meals to be served on flights got made. Recently, Sunil had noticed orange netting and iron scaffolding rising above the walls: an indicator that something was being built inside, and that there might be metal on the ground for the taking.

In his day, Kalu had scaled the barbed wire to raid the dumpsters. Sunil cased the Taj for an easier way in, discovering a small hole concealed by brush at the base of one wall. The fact that the hole sat at the end of an unlit gravel lane made a stealing expedition practically compulsory. Sunil kept putting off the mission, though.

His fellow thief, Taufeeq, complained that other boys would discover the hole if they hesitated any longer. But this Taj Catering made Sunil think of Kalu and of death, as did the military men in blue berets lately crouching behind bunkers, as did the Sahar Police, who seemed to have grown meaner in the months since the terror attacks. Recently, a guard at the Indian Oil compound had caught Sunil sneaking around in search of metal and delivered him to an inebriated constable named Sawant. At the station, the constable had stomped on his back and beaten him so viciously that another officer apologized to Sunil and brought a blanket to cover him.

Given the risks, Sunil wanted to spend more nights watching the Taj guards through the hole, assessing the odds of getting caught. In the meantime, he got money for food by working the four-story car park nearing completion by the international terminal.

By now he knew the best way in: past rows of bright red-and-yellow barricades; past bulldozers and a generator, shrouded at night; past a checkpoint where guards with flashlights were opening car trunks; past an awesome mountain of gravel; past a bitter almond tree whose leaves had reddened, which meant the nuts had gone from sour to sweet; past two of the security bunkers.

One midnight in January when he visited the dark garage, he couldn't make out which animals were scurrying underfoot. Rats or bandicoots, possibly, but he'd never encountered them in the car park before. Guards he had often encountered, but tonight he couldn't tell where they were. He moved carefully to a stairwell near an exterior wall made of horizontal steel slats. The slatted wall let in a bit of the blue-white light bathing the international terminal, where travelers were still hugging their families goodbye. Being near the light increased the risk of being seen by a guard, but it allowed for proper surveillance.

He was searching for what Annawadians called German silver—aluminum or electroplate or nickel. Lately, the term was spoken with reverence. The price for German silver had recently dropped from a hundred rupees per kilo to sixty, but the price for everything else had fallen further.

Sunil worked his way up the stairwell, taking care, on each landing, to peer through a small hole in the floor. He supposed that a water pipe would eventually run through the holes, but for now, they allowed him to ascertain whether guards were slinking up the stairs behind him. Nepali watchmen scared him most, because they were sort of Chinese, like Bruce Lee.

On the third tier, in a corner, were two long strips of aluminum. He darted out to grab them, surprised that some other thief hadn't found them. He thought they might have been parts of a window frame, although the car park didn't have windows. The practical function of the items he stole at the airport didn't matter to his work, but he still wondered.

He carried the metal strips up to the roof, where the only German silver he'd ever found was inside a red cabinet marked FIRE HOSE BOX—a flimsy holder for a fire extinguisher, worth little. The roof was also where he was most likely to encounter watchmen, who went there to smoke. Still, he tried to get up to this roof on every visit. At four stories, it was the highest roof he'd ever been on, but what made it exhilarating was the vista of open space, a rarity in the city.

The roof had two kinds of spaces, really. One kind was when he stood exactly in the middle and knew that even if his arms were thirty times longer he'd touch nothing if he spun around. That kind of space would be gone when the lot was open and filled with cars, a month from now. The space that would last was the kind he leaned into, over the guardrails.

He liked seeing red-tailed Air India planes taking off. He liked the bulbous municipal water tower. He liked the building site of the massive new terminal. He didn't care for the smokestack of Parsiwada crematorium, where Kalu's body had burned. Better to spot the glowing Hyatt sign and try to pinpoint which of the dark patches beneath it was Annawadi. Best, though, was watching the rich people moving in and out of the terminal.

Other boys who visited this roof liked watching the moving people because they looked so small. For Sunil, seeing the people from above made him feel close to them. He felt free to watch them in a way he couldn't when he was on the ground. There, if he stared, they would see him staring.

Every month that passed, he felt less sure of where he belonged among the human traffic in the city below. Once, he had believed he was smart and might become something—not a big something, like the people who frequented the airport, but a middle something. Being on the roof, even if he had come up to steal things, was a way of not being what he had become in Annawadi.

Enough time-pass: He had to get home with his German silver. He carried the aluminum strips down the stairs and, before leaving the building, unzipped his pants and slid the metal through the legs of his underwear. German silver against the skin didn't feel good, but when he tried to carry it outside his underwear, it slipped around.

He limped, stiff-legged, past the security checkpoints and the Sahar Police Station. Soon he was at Annawadi, curling up to sleep in the back of a lorry. The next afternoon, he used the game-parlor man's tools to steal tire locks that the airport parking police clipped onto autorickshaws.

When he returned to the game shed after dark, everyone was talking about a woman who had just tried to hang herself, and failed. Her indebted husband had sold their hut, and she didn't want to live on the pavement.

Too many Annawadi females wanted to die, it seemed to Sunil. He felt especially sad about Meena, who had been nice to him. And all for an egg, people said.

Abdul contended that what Meena had done was daring. People had called Kalu daring, too. Now the Tamil who owned the game shed said that he, Sunil, was Annawadi's daring boy: "The number-one thief!" Sunil saw through the guy's words to his motive. The Tamil was trying to bolster his confidence so that he'd do the theft at the Taj and sell him the goods. Sunil didn't have that confidence tonight.

On the road outside the shed, his father was careening past, and Abdul was talking animatedly to another boy, who wasn't listening. As Abdul talked, he was twisting his neck back and forth, same as a water buffalo standing behind him. Sunil laughed as he walked over. It was the kind of goofy behavior Kalu would have mimicked. Abdul and the buffalo were probably flinging back and forth the same killer mosquitoes.

"Do you ever think when you look at someone, when you listen to someone, does that person really have a life?" Abdul was asking the boy who was not listening. He seemed to be in one of the possessions that came over him from time to time, ever since he got locked up at Dongri.

"Like that woman who just went to hang herself, or her husband, who probably beat her before she did this? I wonder what kind of life is that," Abdul went on. "I go through tensions just to see it. But it is a life. Even the person who lives like a dog still has a kind of life.

Once my mother was beating me, and that thought came to me. I said, 'If what is happening now, you beating me, is to keep happening for the rest of my life, it would be a bad life, but it would be a life, too.' And my mother was so shocked when I said that. She said, 'Don't confuse yourself by thinking about such terrible lives.' "

Sunil thought that he, too, had a life. A bad life, certainly—the kind that could be ended as Kalu's had been and then forgotten, because it made no difference to the people who lived in the overcity. But something he'd come to realize on the roof, leaning out, thinking about what would happen if he leaned too far, was that a boy's life could still matter to himself.

IN FEBRUARY, the impatient Taufeeq beat Sunil up and assumed control of the operation to rob Taj Catering Services. Sunil was relieved to be demoted to one of four soldiers. The boys went through the hole in the stone wall once a week for three weeks, acquiring twenty-two small pieces of iron. One night, when security guards came running, the boys pelted them with stones. Sunil now had enough to eat, plus ten extra rupees to buy a skull-shaped silver-plate earring that he'd seen outside the Andheri train station. He'd always wanted to own something shining.

There was more German silver in the car park, and in the industrial warehouses over the river. A ladder hoisted from a security kiosk was worth a thousand rupees, divided five ways. Weeks passed in which Sunil was mostly not hungry, and in which he was granted a wish for something greater than a silvery earring.

At first he didn't believe it—thought it was a trick of shadow and light-slant on the wall of his hut. But standing back to back with Sunita, it was confirmed. He was taller. As a thief, Sunil Sharma had finally started to grow.

14.

The Trial

WHILE ABDUL'S FATHER PRIVATELY believed that the only Indians who went on trial were those too poor to pay off the police, he had raised his children to respect the Indian courts. Of all the public institutions in the country, these courts seemed to Karam the most willing to defend the rights of Muslims and other minorities. In February, his own trial approaching, he began to follow trials across India in the Urdu papers the way some other Annawadians followed soap operas. Though he disputed many a specific court resolution, and understood that some judges were corrupt, his relative faith in the judiciary obtained.

"In the police station, they tell us only to be silent," Karam said to Abdul, who remembered enough not to need telling. "In the courts, though, what we say may get heard." Karam was still more hopeful when he learned that his case had been assigned to the city's Fast-Track Sessions Court.

In normal courts, five or eight or eleven years sometimes passed between the declaration of charges and the beginning of a trial. To people without permanent work—the vast majority in India—every court appearance involved a forfeit of daily wages. Long trials were economically ruinous. But by fiat of the central government, the massive case backlogs were now being addressed by fourteen hundred high-speed courts across the country. In Mumbai, verdicts were flying out of fast-track courts so quickly that the number of pending trials, citywide, had declined by a third in three years. Many notorious cases, including organized-crime ones, went directly to fast track, since the public was presumably eager to see them resolved. But in addition to the publicized cases, which brought television trucks to the fast-track courthouse, were thousands of small, unnewsworthy trials, like the Husains'.

A judge named P. M. Chauhan had been assigned to decide whether Karam and Kehkashan had driven their neighbor to self-immolation. Abdul would have a separate trial in juvenile court at a later date and would not see the inside of Judge Chauhan's courtroom. As such, the trial felt to him as if it were happening oceans away, no matter what his sister said about a sixty-minute bus-and-train ride to a south Mumbai neighborhood called Sewri. The matter was one of many in his life that he considered out of his hands. He simply counted on Kehkashan, a more reliable narrator than his father, to keep him apprised of how worried he should be.

The courthouse in Sewri had previously been a pharmaceutical company. "This hardly seems like a court," Kehkashan said to her father, concerned, on the day the trial began. No teak banisters; nothing stately. The hallways were clotted with encampments—families of other accused people eating, praying, sleeping, leaning against a greasy tile wall upon which signs threatened fines of twelve hundred rupees for spitting. The whole place seemed to lack a resident crew of waste-pickers. In the courtroom, empty plastic bottles and cans wreathed the base of the high platform from which Judge Chauhan presided.

"This lady judge is strict," a police officer had said. "She does not let the accused go free." Kehkashan saw at once that this Judge Chauhan was impatient. Pursing her dark red lips, the judge shouted at her father, who had shown up this first day without a lawyer. "It's a *bhaari* case, a grave one! Don't delay me, start it fast, get it going!"

The impatience was structural. Like most fast-track judges, Chauhan conducted more than thirty-five trials simultaneously. A given case wasn't heard beginning to end, the way Kehkashan had seen on TV serials. Rather, it was chopped into dozens of brief hearings that took place at weekly or fortnightly intervals. On an average day, the judge heard bits of nine trials, so the accused bench where Kehkashan and her father sat, under police supervision, was a crowded affair. There were men on trial for murder, for armed robbery, and for electricity-thieving, many of them shackled. Karam was the oldest man on the bench, Kehkashan the solitary female. Their seats were against the back wall of the courtroom, behind a great assembly of white plastic chairs for witnesses and observers and two tiers of metal desks where a proliferation of clerks, prosecutors, and defenders paged through files. To Kehkashan, the witness stand and the judge with the lipstick seemed very far away.

At the next lightning-fast hearing, the Husains' lawyer materialized, and a medical officer from Cooper Morgue testified, falsely, that Fatima had been burned over 95 percent of her body. Hearing over. "Now what? What's next?" asked the judge, pulling out a new file and moving to another case.

Another week, a Sahar police officer testified about the conclusion of the station's investigation: that the Husains had beaten Fatima and driven her to suicide. "Now what? What's next?" asked the judge.

What came next was the part of the trial the Husains dreaded. Beginning this March day, and continuing in brief sessions for untold weeks, would be the testimony of neighbors whom the police had chosen to interview from Annawadi, and whom the prosecution had chosen to make its case.

Peculiarly, most of these "witnesses" had not been on hand for the fight that had preceded the burning. Among them were Fatima's husband and her two closest friends.

On the accused bench, Kehkashan was glad for her burqa, which obscured the fact that she was dripping sweat. She'd contracted jaundice in jail, and a lingering fever had just shot up, which she attributed to her anxiety. She considered her family's behavior on the crucial day to have been ragged and shameful. She wished she hadn't said, during the fight with Fatima, that she would twist off her neighbor's other leg; she wished her father hadn't threatened to beat Fatima up. But ugly words were unlikely to send them to prison. They would go to prison if enough of the supposed witnesses backed Fatima's revised hospital statement to the police about being throttled and beaten.

Poornima Paikrao, special executive officer of the government of Maharashtra, had helped craft that hospital statement, after which she'd told Zehrunisa that the accounts of other witnesses would be equally damaging, unless the Husains paid her off. She'd made her second attempt at extortion this morning, right outside the courthouse.

The Annawadi witnesses might remember new, devastating details of the night in question, the special executive officer had told Karam. She herself might have to testify about Fatima's dying declaration in such a manner that a guilty verdict was all but guaranteed. The special executive officer didn't want to do it. She wanted to help them. "But what else can I do?" she asked, palms up, as always. "Think again about what might happen. You and your children will go to jail. So what do you suggest?"

"I won't pay," Karam had sputtered. "Already my son and daughter have seen the inside of the jail—the terrible things you threaten have already happened. But we're paying the lawyer, not you, to fix it. The lawyer will make the judge see the truth. And if this judge doesn't see it," he had concluded with bravado, "I will take it all the way to the Supreme Court!"

Awaiting the first of their neighbors in a trashed-out courtroom, both father and daughter hoped this belief in the Indian judiciary had a basis in reality.

First to the wooden witness stand was one of Fatima's two close confidantes, a destitute girl named Priya. Priya was probably the saddest girl in Annawadi, and Kehkashan had known her for years. This morning, the two young women had shared an autorickshaw from the slum to the train station, sitting thigh to dampening thigh, each in her own unhappy bubble. Avoiding Kehkashan's eyes, Priya had hugged herself, repeating, "I will not go, I am not going." Priya had avoided most people's eyes since the burning. "Fatima was the only person who knew my heart's pain," she once said. A tougher girl might have been able to forget her friend's cries for help, her thrashings. But at the stand, as in Annawadi, Priya wore her damage like a slash across the face.

It wasn't the kind of damage that turned a girl into a fabulist, though. Trembling, Priya told the prosecutor she hadn't been on the maidan when the fight occurred, and had seen Fatima only after she'd been burned. Fatima provoked a lot of fights in the slum, Priya allowed to the defender before being dismissed from the stand.

Succeeding her in front of the judge was a handsome, articulate man named Dinesh, who loaded luggage at the airport. Kehkashan had never spoken to him, but she'd heard rumors that his testimony would be damaging. She felt sicker than ever when she saw him take the stand with a clenched jaw, a livid face. Because he was speaking in Marathi, some minutes passed before Kehkashan figured out that his anger was not directed at her family but at the Sahar Police.

Shortly after the burning, an officer had recorded a witness statement under Dinesh's name describing the fight. The statement was false, Dinesh told the judge. He'd been at home in another slumlane, hadn't seen the fight, and didn't see why he'd been called as a key prosecution witness. He cared little about the Husains or whether they ended up in prison. What he cared about was having to forgo a day's income because of an inaccurate police statement.

The surprised prosecutor quickly wrapped up his questioning, the hearing came to an end, and Kehkashan and her father returned to Annawadi feeling almost giddy.

Despite the insinuations of the special executive officer, the first witnesses hadn't lied in order to ruin them. Looking back, Kehkashan would remember this afternoon's shock of optimism, before the seams of the celebrated fast-track court began to show.

BY APRIL, THE CASE AGAINST the Husains was poking along in bitty hearings, and Judge P. M. Chauhan was annoyed. Her stenographer, adept in only the Marathi language, was hopeless at translating the slum Hindi of the Annawadi witnesses into the English required for the official transcript. Impatient at the translation delays, the judge began telling the stenographer what to write. And so a slumdweller's nuanced replies to the prosecutor's questions became monosyllabic ones—the better to keep the case moving along. At the end of a particularly tedious hearing, the judge rose for lunch and sighed to the prosecutor and defender, "Ah, fighting over petty, stupid, personal things—these *women*. All that and it reached such a level they made it a case." It was becoming apparent that the outcome of the trial mattered only to the people of Annawadi.

For Kehkashan and her father, ten years of incarceration were at stake. But as the weeks progressed, they found it impossible to understand what was being said for or against them in the front of the courtroom. The windows had been opened on account of the April heat, so instead of hearing the testimony upon which their liberty depended, they heard the cacophony of an industrial road. Car horns. Train horns. Throttling engines. The beep-beep of trucks reversing. This outside noise seemed to be sucked in by the ceiling fan, churned and flung outward by its metal blades. Hearing over. Next hearing. Now something had gone wrong with the fan, and its whirring had become a loud clatter.

What was the policeman telling the judge? What was the judge telling the prosecutor? The prosecutor had an orange comb-over, stiff with hair spray, and when he nodded vigorously, one clump of hair came loose and traveled upward. More vigorous nodding and it was straight in the air, like a finger pointing to the heavens. Hearing over. Come back in a week. Kehkashan stopped leaning forward, started sagging in her seat. She was so poised the day Fatima's husband took the stand.

A FEW MONTHS BACK, Fatima's husband, Abdul Shaikh, had brought his daughters to the Husain home for Eid, the holiest day of the Muslim year. Young Abdul had dejugulated a goat on the maidan, and old Abdul had worked with him shoulder to shoulder, stripping back the muscle to mine the meat for the feast. Same as they'd always done at Eid. A good goat this year, a good time. But the trial was a matter of honor for Fatima's husband, just as it was for the Husains.

The old garbage sorter had been able to hear more than the Husains could, from his seat in the middle of the courtroom. As the trial progressed, he realized that Fatima's deathbed account of a beating and a throttling was being undermined. Witnesses kept saying the fight had been one of hot words. Abdul Shaikh was disturbed by this contradiction of the first and last official statement of his wife.

He and Fatima had not been happy, after the first warm year. They'd fought regularly about her lovers, the force with which she beat the children, the force with which he beat her when drunk. He didn't have it in him to prettify their history. But day in and day out since Fatima's death, he had had to live beside the Husains, hearing Zehrunisa singing to her daughters, hearing Mirchi making everyone laugh. Fatima's suicide had thieved him of the chance, however remote, of finding peace with his wife and giving his beloved daughters a happy home.

He wanted to blame someone other than his wife for this loss of future possibility. He wanted the judge to convict the Husains. The problem was that he wasn't sure what the Husains had or hadn't done to Fatima, and had said so in his original statement to the police. He'd been at work, arriving home only to see his wife grotesquely injured. His daughters, underfoot during the fight, had told him that no one had hit anyone. But where did that leave those girls? He didn't want them to grow up knowing that their mother had burned herself, lied, and died.

His daughters were back at Annawadi now. He'd removed them from Sister Paulette's care upon finding bruises on their arms and legs. They'd been elated to leave. "Always we had to say 'Thank you, Jesus' to a picture of a white man," his younger daughter said. "It was so boring!" Since coming home, they hadn't once asked about their mother, but Noori, who'd seen the burning through the window, had changed. She'd stand in the road as if she wanted the oncoming cars to hit her, and had developed a nervous habit of chewing her head scarf.

Today, though, she'd been excited to take the train across the city to the courthouse, and especially enthusiastic about the television cameras set up outside. "Some big trial must be happening today," Abdul Shaikh had told his daughters, who'd run in front of one camera to smile and wave. Other Annawadians said the younger daughter, Heena, smiled just like her mother. Abdul Shaikh thought this was correct, though he didn't have a great mental reserve of Fatima smiles to reflect on.

"Will they show us on TV now?" Noori had asked as the three of them went through a low metal security gate. Turning to answer, Abdul Shaikh banged his head hard on the gate. He still felt dazed an hour later, standing in the wooden witness box.

In his right hand he clutched a creased plastic bag containing his wife's death certificate, two photos of her dressed nicely—the pink outfit and the blue—and the government document about her disability that had secured her metal crutches, free of charge. These remainders of her presence stank of mildew and contained words he couldn't read, but he wanted them in his hands as he gave the testimony he hoped would put the Husains in prison.

The judge looked at him kindly while swearing him in, but when the prosecutor cleared his throat, Abdul Shaikh's knees buckled. He had to grab the stand to stay upright. He had never been in such a place, talking to such intimidating people. At the most basic questions of the prosecutor—a man he understood to be on his side—he grew flustered.

"Who do you live with?" the prosecutor asked.

His wife, he said, as if she were not dead. To the next question, he insisted he was thirty-five years old. He got his daughters' names right, but his home address eluded him. He wasn't sure where he was supposed to look when he answered. Should he look at the judge, who was considering him placidly from her perch high above the stand, or at the prosecutor, who stood opposite him, on his level? When he looked at the defense lawyer, he became still more confused, for the defender was grinning at the judge for no discernible reason.

He decided to look only at the judge. To her, he got out his account of finding Fatima at home and taking her to the hospital.

"Was your wife in a condition to speak to you that night?"

This was the first crucial question that Abdul Shaikh had to answer. He had to rally, and did. "Yes, she could speak," he said forcefully. He appeared relieved that the words came out right.

"What did your wife tell you on the way to Cooper Hospital?"

"She told me they called her a prostitute and would take her other leg," he began. This was what he'd told the police in his original statement, nine months earlier, but it did not sound awful enough in this courtroom—just ordinary Annawadi words. After a long pause, he continued. "She told me they beat her." Another long pause, thinking. Then he said, "She told me that they held her by the neck and beat her with a big stone."

There. The words of a dying woman that he hoped might turn around the case.

The prosecutor seemed delighted, and the Sahar policemen in attendance were happy, too. As the Husains' mop-haired, pin-striped defender began the cross-examination, Abdul Shaikh's composure continued to grow. No, his wife had not been depressed after their daughter Medina drowned in a pail. No, his wife hadn't poured kero-

sene on herself twice before. By the time he staggered off the stand
and collapsed into a white plastic chair, he believed he had avenged
his children's loss.

"Now what, what next?" said Judge Chauhan, by way of calling
the final Annawadi witness to the stand.

Cynthia Ali, Fatima's best friend, had resented the Husains ever
since her husband's garbage business went under. Late on the night
of the burning, as Abdul hid in his storeroom, she'd stood in the
maidan trying to convince her neighbors to march to the police station and demand the arrest of the whole Husain family.

Although Cynthia hadn't seen the fight between Fatima and the
Husains, the following day she had given the police a witness statement to the contrary. Then, through the brothelkeeper's wife, she
had informed the Husains that her testimony would send them to
jail, unless they paid her twenty thousand rupees before she took the
stand. The Husains, having refused to pay, had been bracing for her
vengeance for months.

"I feel as if I am going crazy," Zehrunisa had said to Abdul the
previous day as they waited for scavengers at the scales. She had a
wild look in her eyes that he hadn't seen since she'd stood at the window of the Sahar Police Station's unofficial cell. "After lying in court,
what honor will she have?" Zehrunisa asked. "If you lose your honor,
how can you show your face in Annawadi?"

Abdul found his mother's question absurd.

Cynthia had washed her hair for her court date and put on her
best sari, purple with a blue-and-gold border. There was nothing to
be done about the teeth. In recent days, she'd envisioned her testimony as a decisive occasion, laying her anticipated performance
against climactic trial scenes in Hindi movies.

It had been painful to watch the Husains' income grow as her
family's foundered. She thought that Zehrunisa had been lucky, hav-

ing a sorting machine like Abdul come out of her body, but Zehrunisa acted as if she'd been smart. Moreover, Zehrunisa gossiped about how Cynthia, a Christian, had once worked in an exotic-dance bar—a chapter of Cynthia's life long closed. Lately, she called herself a social worker and was trying to get into the anti-poverty business, just like Asha. There was a lot of government and international money going around.

When Judge Chauhan called her forward, she stood pole-straight, confidently announcing her name and the new profession of social work. Only when the prosecutor began asking questions did her head start to cock.

This prosecutor was nothing like the prosecutors in the movies. He wasn't looking at her intently, despite her spectacular sari. He seemed as bored by the trial as the judge.

Cynthia's brows knitted together. She felt the prosecutor was rushing her. Didn't the judge want to hear the details of the fight she was pretending to have seen? Her story about how she'd helped break down the door to save her smoldering friend? She'd barely warmed up when the prosecutor's questions stopped coming, and the Husains' private defender rose for the cross-examination.

This guy *did* seem like a lawyer in the films. Uncharacteristically alert in the face of a dubious witness—the last witness of a tedious trial—he sprang.

Yes, she admitted to his questioning, her family business had failed as the Husains' had prospered.

Yes, she said, she lived in a hut some distance from the Husains, in another slumlane.

Yes, her home was far from where the fighting had taken place. Yes, she had been home chopping vegetables for dinner.

So how could you have seen what happened? the defender wanted to know.

"But I saw it," she insisted, frowning. "She was my neighbor!"

"I don't think so," the defender said. "You said earlier that you saw the fight, but that wasn't true. You lied."

The judge repeated for her inept stenographer a nonsensical combination of this question and answer: "I lied and I saw the fight." Cynthia's eyes went wide.

Cynthia's son had studied English in a Catholic school, and she'd picked up a little as she helped him study. What she understood was that the judge had told the stenographer to write that she had admitted she was a liar. She wanted a correction. She wanted time to think, regroup. "Wait," she cried so loudly that Kehkashan and her father heard her over the din of the street. But this was fast-track court— a nothing case in fast-track court. No one was going to wait.

Her witness services were no longer required. Judge Chauhan was calling another case. A policeman was gesturing toward the door. But how could she leave the stand, having been misunderstood? How could she get this false iteration of her own false words out of the stenographer's computer? She shook with anger. But at whom? The judge? The lawyers? The justice system? She decided to blame the Husains, hunched on the accused bench in the back.

"I will show you!" she yelled as she left the courtroom, raising her fist in high *filmi* style. But her performance was over, and no one was filming. The misconstrued witnesses and the mystified accused all got on the same train to return to their regular, contentious lives in Annawadi, where they would stew about what they thought had happened but couldn't know for sure. Closing arguments were to come in two weeks.

15.

Ice

ONE AFTERNOON, ABDUL, MIRCHI, and their parents stood, hands behind backs, contemplating a motley cache of garbage in the storeroom. They'd tried to forestall a trip to the recycling plants because prices were so low, but now they had no choice. They had sold the storeroom to pay for the lawyer. Although Abdul had been working maniacally on the days he didn't have to report to Dongri, he was making little money. The Sahar Police had effectively put the Husains out of business.

As the trial proceeded, the whole family had tried to follow the virtuous path of Abdul's teacher at Dongri: not buying anything that might have been stolen. Although this decision reduced the family income by 15 percent, it didn't decrease the attention of the police. Officers came to demand money every day now—"licking at us like dogs, sucking what is left of our blood," Zehrunisa cried one afternoon. Unable to accuse the family of possessing hot goods, the officers threatened to arrest Abdul for sorting his garbage on the maidan.

A usurpation of public space! A crime against Annawadians' quality of life!

The officers hinted that a new charge might be used to show the judge that the family had a pattern of criminality. So Zehrunisa paid bribe after bribe, as her husband searched for a storeroom in another police district where officers might not know about the court case.

Karam tried to be optimistic about what they would make by selling off the last of their recyclables. "There must be five kilos of German silver here," he said. "Maybe two kilos of copper."

"Bullshit," snapped Zehrunisa. "It is much less than that. Like father like son—Mirchi is like you. Doesn't want to work, only wants to eat. Both of you want everything for free."

Mirchi winced. Growing up, he'd been the first to call himself lazy. He'd liked to show his friends a bleached-out photo of Abdul and himself as toddlers. "See how Abdul is moving while I am sitting? It was like that even then!" But the family catastrophe had changed him. He'd become a fast, competent garbage sorter and taken every other job he could find.

He'd worked construction with his best friend, Rahul, finishing two swimming pools in a new boutique hotel on Airport Road. Then he scored the temp work of his dreams: setting up for parties at the Intercontinental hotel. A subcontractor had liked the looks of him and handed him a clip-on bow tie and a uniform coat. The coat's cloth was as black and glossy as a crow's wing; his mother had grown silent when she touched it. At the end of the workweek, though, the subcontractor reclaimed the beautiful coat and paid him only a fifth of what he'd been promised. When Mirchi traveled across the city to the man's office to collect the remainder, security guards turned him away.

His next temp job was at Skygourmet, which made meals served on airplanes. Arriving at work, Mirchi stood under a blower that blasted the city dirt from his body, then loaded food onto pallets inside a cavernous freezer. It was miserable labor, carrying heavy containers when he was too cold to manage his limbs. Ice formed inside his runny nose, and when his flesh touched metal, it stuck. Still, he made two hundred rupees a day, until management cut back the temp staff.

Many businesses dependent on the airport were downsizing as the effects of the terror attacks and the recession persisted. Asha's political party, Shiv Sena, had been protesting these cuts, sometimes violently. After layoffs at the Intercontinental, a Shiv Sena gang smashed up its elegant lobby, demanding more work for the Maharashtrians—a rampage of which Rahul was one beneficiary. He secured a six-month stint cleaning air-conditioning ducts. Mirchi was happy for Rahul, and only a little resentful that his own parents' best connections were with scavengers.

"There's this guy who counts cars in a parking lot, and he said he saw the talent in me," Mirchi reported one evening at home, breathless in his hope that this new contact might lead to steady work. But there were millions of other bright, likable, unskilled young men in this city.

AS THE HUSAINS WAITED for closing arguments in their case, the rest of Mumbai began following another fast-track trial. The lone surviving gunman of the terror attack, a twenty-one-year-old Pakistani named Ajmal Kasab, had his hearings in a dedicated, high-security courtroom at Arthur Road Jail.

Abdul's father said that what Kasab had done was wrong—that the Koran didn't entitle Muslims to kill innocent civilians, some of whom had also been Muslim. Still, Kasab seemed lucky to Abdul. "They will probably beat him lots in the jail," Abdul said one day, "but at least Kasab knows in his heart that he did what they said he did." That had to be less stressful than being beaten when you were innocent.

The popular rage about Kasab didn't seem to transfer to other Muslims in Mumbai, Abdul was relieved to find on the three days a week he traveled by train to Dongri. In the clammy, crowded train cars, he was no one's proxy. The Hindus were just going where they had to go, as he was. Like him, they were coughing, eating lunch, looking out windows at billboards on which Bollywood heroes hawked cement and Coca-Cola. They were bent protectively over prized documents in prized plastic bags like his own, which said, TAKE A BREAK, HAVE A KIT KAT. It was all as it had been, which was hopeful.

Mumbai's wealthy were also hopeful in the months after the terrorist attacks. Many had begun to engage in politics for the first time, intent on bringing about government reform. Rich Indians typically tried to work around a dysfunctional government. Private security was hired, city water was filtered, private school tuitions were paid. Such choices had evolved over the years into a principle: The best government is the one that gets out of the way.

The attacks on the Taj and the Oberoi, in which executives and socialites died, had served as a blunt correction. The wealthy now saw that their security could not be requisitioned privately. They were dependent on the same public safety system that ill served the poor.

Ten young men had terrorized one of the world's biggest cities for three days—a fact that had something to do with the ingenuity of a multi-pronged plot, but perhaps also to do with government agencies that had been operating as private market-stalls, not as public guardians. The crisis-response units of the Mumbai Police lacked arms. Officers in the train station didn't know how to use their weapons, and ran and hid as two terrorists killed more than fifty travelers. Other officers called to rescue inhabitants of a besieged maternity hospital stayed put at police headquarters, four blocks away. Ambulances failed to respond to the wounded. Military commandos took eight hours to reach the heart of the financial capital—a journey that involved an inconveniently parked jet, a stop to refuel, and a long bus ride from the Mumbai airport. By the time the commandos arrived in south Mumbai, the killings were all but over.

Parliamentary elections would be held at the end of April, and middle- and upper-class people, especially young people, were registering to vote in record numbers. Affluent, educated candidates were coming forward with platforms of radical change: accountability, transparency, e-governance. While independent India had been founded by high-born, well-educated men, by the twenty-first century few such types stood for elections, or voted in them, since the wealthy had extra-democratic means of securing their social and economic interests. Across India, poor people were the ones who took the vote seriously. It was the only real power they had.

ANOTHER GARBAGE TRADER had set up shop at Annawadi, filling the niche created by the demise of the Husains' business. Abdul now spent his days in a tiny rented storage shed at the edge of the Saki Naka slums. His efforts at trading came to little. The Saki Naka scavengers had preexisting allegiances. But sitting idly in the doorway of the new shed, looking out over an alien maidan, Abdul found that he felt light. Annawadi tragedies did not rank here. No one knew of Fatima, or of his family's trial, or of Kalu's death, or that Sanjay and Meena had eaten rat poison. Afternoons, a man turned a small Ferris wheel with a hand crank, and children took rides for a rupee. The police came to take bribes from other businesses but left him alone, probably because any fool could tell he wasn't making money. He had almost as much time to think as he'd had at Dongri, and maybe because of the boiling April sun, he thought about water and ice.

Water and ice were made of the same thing. He thought most people were made of the same thing, too. He himself was probably little different, constitutionally, from the cynical, corrupt people around him—the police officers and the special executive officer and the morgue doctor who fixed Kalu's death. If he had to sort all humanity by its material essence, he thought he would probably end up with a single gigantic pile. But here was the interesting thing. Ice was distinct from—and in his view, better than—what it was made of.

He wanted to be better than what he was made of. In Mumbai's dirty water, he wanted to be ice. He wanted to have ideals. For self-interested reasons, one of the ideals he most wanted to have was a belief in the possibility of justice.

It wasn't easy to believe, just now. The lawyer for Kehkashan and Karam had been confident about exoneration after Cynthia's ragged performance as a prosecution witness. But just before closing arguments, Judge Chauhan had been transferred to a court on the other side of the state. A new judge would have to be appointed and, using the flawed court transcript, try to pick up where the first judge had left off.

The Husains were crushed, a fact not lost on the special executive officer with the gold-rimmed spectacles. She came for a third time to try to extort payment from them, this time accompanied by Fatima's husband.

The new judge was severe and likely to find the Husains guilty, the special executive officer said. Fortunately, Fatima's husband was willing to take back the case. He would cancel his testimony and the testimony of his late wife, upon which the trial would shut down. The price for ending the trial would be two lakhs—more than four thousand dollars.

The special executive officer seemed to be banking on the ignorance of slumdwellers: that the Husains wouldn't understand that the case against them was a criminal one, brought by the state of Maharashtra, and that Fatima's husband didn't have the power to call it off, no matter how much the Husains paid.

Before telling the woman off, Abdul's father checked his facts with his lawyer. He wanted to make sure that what he'd gleaned about legal process from reading Urdu newspapers was correct. It was. Finally, a small triumph of information over corruption.

EVERY COUNTRY HAS its myths, and one that successful Indians liked to indulge was a romance of instability and adaptation—the idea that their country's rapid rise derived in part from the chaotic unpredictability of daily life. In America and Europe, it was said, people know what is going to happen when they turn on the water tap or flick the light switch. In India, a land of few safe assumptions, chronic uncertainty was said to have helped produce a nation of quick-witted, creative problem-solvers.

Among the poor, there was no doubt that instability fostered ingenuity, but over time the lack of a link between effort and result could become debilitating. "We try so many things," as one Annawadi girl put it, "but the world doesn't move in our favor."

Three days a week, going through the child-size security gate at Dongri, Abdul scanned the courtyard for The Master. He wanted to tell him about the government official who had tried to trick his parents, and about how well the trial had been going until the female

judge was sent away, and how his Annawadi business had been un-
done by the police. Abdul had told so many lies about The Master,
back at Annawadi, that he had started to believe the man actually
cared how he was faring.

Abdul didn't find The Master, though. After signing his name in
a register, he returned to the street wondering how he could delay
going back to a shed in Saki Naka where he was failing to make his
family's living. One day, trying to recover his energy, he walked an
hour from the juvenile jail to Haji Ali, the city's storied Muslim gathering place.

"I won't go long," he had promised his mother. "Just long enough
to fill my heart."

The mosque and tomb of Haji Ali sat on an islet in the Arabian
Sea, connected to the mainland by a rocky promontory. Salty gusts
turned the burqas in front of Abdul into hundreds of black balloons,
floating slowly down the promontory toward the glittering dome of
the mosque. On either side of him, merchants with fold-up tables
were selling paste jewelry and plastic water guns. Above him, the sky
was batting gullwings. It was beautiful—like he was walking into an
Urdu calendar. Then he registered what no calendar ever showed.

The narrow road to Haji Ali was lined with One-Legs. No Legs,
too. Stretching before him for hundreds of yards were disabled beg-
gars, prostrate, keening and tearing their clothes. It was like a mad
multiplication of Fatimas.

He departed Haji Ali in haste. The confusion he felt wasn't going
to be addressed by feasting his eyes on something lofty. It could be
eased only by a court deciding that he hadn't attacked a disabled
woman, throttled her, and driven her to a violent suicide.

Abdul could control many of his desires, but not this one. He
wanted to be recognized as better than the dirty water in which he
lived. He wanted a verdict of ice.

16.

Black and White

ASHA HAD CONCEIVED of a hundred escape routes from Annawadi, but in the first months of 2009 those paths kept dead-ending, and she began to feel scooped out and sad. Possibly an electrical shock was to blame for disrupting her normal, optimistic mental circuits. Possibly Mr. Kamble had left a curse when he finally died for want of a heart valve. For shortly after his cremation, his pretty widow, in debt to a loan shark, stole one of Asha's most useful male companions.

It was hardly the first time Asha had been dismissed by a man without warning. In earlier times, though, she'd managed to seal the disappointment in some tidy interior compartment and bustle forth in pursuit of something new. The questions had even entertained her: What to try, whom to try, next? But now, such questions merely illuminated the fact that her previous answers had been wrong. Gold pots flaked away, revealing mud pots.

Asha's slavish attention to Corporator Subhash Sawant was the biggest mud pot. Shortly after her spectacular Navratri, a judge had expelled her political patron from office for pretending to be low-caste. But her list of disappointments was long. The grocery store for which she'd received a government loan, and which she'd hoped her husband could run from the hut. The tedious, still unremunerative slumlording. The idea of Manju as insurance agent to the Mumbai elite. The idea of Manju as a profit-center bride. The windfall that was supposed to have come from securing flats for Sahar police officers to conduct their side businesses. Other schemes that had sucked up months before sputtering out.

The parliamentary elections were closing in, and she was supposed to be leafleting the slums. Shiv Sena people called five times a day to remind her. The newly installed Corporator, from the Congress Party, also called. To win the slumdwellers' affection, he had installed elegant paving stones on the maidan, plus a black-marble monument to the Congress Party. Now he needed an Asha. Her power at Annawadi had transcended party affiliation.

But Asha was as reluctant to pledge allegiance to another politician as she was to leaflet. She wanted to stay inside and cry. Coming home from kindergarten, she wrapped herself in a blanket and murmured a Marathi poem she had copied from a bulletin board in Mankhurd.

> *What you don't want is always going to be with you*
> *What you want is never going to be with you*
> *Where you don't want to go, you have to go*
> *And the moment you think you're going to live more,*
> *   you're going to die.*

Manju was distressed to see her mother curled up, making a cave of herself, though she knew better than to ask why. Instead she said, "Not like you, Mummy, sitting still."

Said the next day, handing over a steaming teacup, "I'm tired, too, from my exams."

Said the next day, "I'll copy this poem over, and do it nicely." Asha had smeared the ink with her tears.

That evening, when Asha pulled her head out of the blanket, she found her ode to low expectations neatly printed, laminated, and hanging from a tack on the wall.

Although Manju attributed her mother's grief entirely to a secret heartache, Asha's heart at forty was stubborn and knowing. Her brain was the troublesome thing. When not reflecting on the cause of past failures, she brooded on the smallest of slights: a police officer who no longer returned her phone calls; Reena, a Shiv Sena colleague who had a special puja and failed to invite her. The normal Asha would have been happy not to visit Reena, who was grumpy and had the face of a cow. But in her current mood, small affronts were bundled with larger disappointments and became a body of evidence. Something bright in her had been eclipsed.

Asha had always prized her competitiveness, a quality that she'd failed to pass on to her children. Perhaps because they lacked it, she had valued it more in herself. But over time, the compulsion to win could become self-deceiving. Instead of admitting that she was making little progress, she had invented new definitions of success. She had felt herself moving ahead, just a little, every time other people failed. She had outflanked the Husains, for one, and Mr. Kamble, in a way. But the facts of her days had barely changed. She was still living with a drunken husband in a cramped hut by a sewage lake. Her vanity—a quality she *had* passed on to all three children—was being undermined. She had failed to crack the code of the wider city, while at home, many of her neighbors had started to loathe her.

Annawadians agreed upon the moment when their respectful

wariness of Asha had turned to vibrant dislike. It was during her attempt to capitalize on what they feared: that in 2010 or 2011, the airport slums would start being razed.

Since it was election season, and airport slumdwellers were known to vote, some politicians were still talking about fighting the demolition. But plans were well underway. A small part of the cleared acreage would be used to serve the expanding airport, and the rest would be leased on the open market. In place of thirty-odd slums, there would be more hotels, shopping malls, office complexes, perhaps a theme park.

The airport clearance would roughly follow the state's slum-redevelopment scheme. Under it, private developers were granted rights to build on slum land only if they agreed to construct apartments for those slumdwellers who could prove they'd lived in their huts since 1995 or 2000, depending on the slum. Corruption in the scheme was endemic; organized-crime syndicates had become major players. But the program had overt limitations as well. Although in the previous two years 122,000 huts had been demolished, two-thirds of the affected families hadn't lived in their huts long enough to qualify for rehousing. So they had crowded into other slums, or built new slums on the outskirts of the city.

The general failure of Mumbai slum clearance efforts made removing the *airport* slums even more important. The job was manageable in scale and outsized in resonance. It would signify to the world that Indian leaders were making headway on their goal of a "slum-free Mumbai."

It irked Asha that officials saw the slums simply as monuments to backwardness. "And if they need space at the airport so badly," she said one day, "why don't they bulldoze the hotels?" But luxury hotels were not perceived as the problem; swimming pools and lawns would be preserved. So what was she supposed to do, as a leader of one of the eyesores said to be holding back the fortunes of a nation? Unite her neighbors in some fruitless opposition? It had seemed to her more realistic to pursue her private ambitions and make some money.

She had identified an opening in land speculation, of which there was much at Annawadi lately. The apartments promised to displaced airport slumdwellers would be tiny—269 square feet—but would have running water, which made them a valuable asset in a city starved of affordable formal housing. Hence overcity people had been buying up shacks in the slums and concocting legal papers to show that *they* were longtime Annawadi residents.

Most of the speculators intended to use the rehabilitation flats as rental or investment properties. "The flat I'll get will be worth ten times what I paid for this place," said the businessman who bought Abdul's storage hut. A small-time politician named Papa Panchal had secured a large block of huts by the sewage lake on behalf of a major developer, hiring thugs on commission to persuade the occupants to sell.

Asha had anticipated her own commission when she arranged for a middle-aged hotel supplier to buy the hut of an illiterate young mother of three named Geeta. The fake papers, showing that the businessman was a veteran slumdweller, had come out nicely. Then Geeta began to have second thoughts at high volume.

Such shouting, up and down the slumlanes! Asha had tricked her! Her children would be out on the pavement! Geeta refused to leave her hut, and tried to register a complaint with the police. Asha handled the police end of things, of course. The problem arose when the businessman sent a gang of drunken men to expedite Geeta's exit—on a Sunday afternoon, when all of Annawadi was on hand to watch.

Asha dispatched her son Rahul to supervise as the men dragged the tiny, flailing Geeta out into the slumlanes by her hair, dumped her belongings into the sewage lake, called her a whore, and poured kerosene over her last bag of rice. Sobbing, Geeta's young children had crouched to pick up the spoiled rice grains, one by one.

Bad visuals. Damaging to the stature of a slumlord, especially one who had been seen sitting at home, face hard as a knuckle, while the violence in the slumlanes had transpired. Ever since that Sunday, the whispers of her neighbors had trailed Asha like jet streams.

"She's become like an animal in her greed," said a Nepali woman, putting her hand to her mouth.

"Always she was sly, but now we know there is no one she won't hurt for money," said a Tamil woman.

"She probably made ten thousand rupees in the end," said Zehrunisa. This hurt the most, when it got back to Asha. Ten thousand would have been tremendous—would have made up for the lost reputation. Instead, the businessman had stiffed her on the commission.

It was an experience so disheartening that when another corrupt and powerful person approached her, promising that, this time, her efforts would be rewarded with a share of the proceeds, she was skeptical.

And the moment you think you're going to live more, you're going to die. She firmly held this position of pessimism until the day she saw she *would* be living more, which was the day the government check cleared the bank.

THE IDEA THAT SECURED her family's future was not her own. It belonged to an administrator named Bhimrao Gaikwad at the Maharashtra Department of Education. His charge was to implement in Mumbai an ambitious central government program, supported by foreign aid, called Sarva Shiksha Abhiyan. Its aim was to make ele-

mentary education universal, bringing tens of millions of child laborers, girls, and disabled children to school for the first time.

In newspaper interviews, Gaikwad spoke of his search for un-
schooled children and his hope of giving them the sort of education
that would lift them out of poverty. His less public ambition was to
divert federal money to himself. Working with community development officials across the city, he found frontmen to receive government funds in the name of educating children. Then he and his
colluders would divvy up the spoils.

Later, Asha wished that she had come to the attention of Gaikwad
because of her intelligence, or even her looks. But his interest was
based on something more mundane: the fact that she had a nonprofit
organization. In 2003, another man with another scheme had set up
the nonprofit for her, promising a city sanitation contract that had
failed to materialize.

"Properly registered?" Gaikwad wanted to know.

"Yes, properly." And on that basis she was chosen to help him
defraud the central government's most important effort to improve
the lives of children.

Government officials prepared documents attesting that for several years her nonprofit had been running twenty-four kindergar-
tens for poor children. The government would pay her 4.7 lakhs, or
more than ten thousand dollars, for this fictitious work. More money
would come later in the year for her supposed management of nine
bridge schools for former child laborers. From this windfall, Asha
would write checks to a long list of names that Gaikwad provided—
theoretically teachers and assistants at the schools. What business
was it of hers to ask who they were? Her business was to hand-deliver
twenty thousand rupees in cash to Bhimrao Gaikwad, plus five thousand rupees to the community development official who had helped
to fix the contract.

In the first year, Asha wouldn't make big money after all the pay-offs. But Gaikwad had assured her that there would be more money in the years ahead.

A minor hitch occurred when the first installment of govern-ment money—429,000 rupees—showed up in the bank account of the moribund nonprofit. The checks to be dispersed required a co-signer, but the neighbor whom Asha had named long ago as the nonprofit's secretary was in a state. "Will we be rich?" the woman asked, and then, tearfully, "What if we get caught?" She resisted signing the checks, so Asha fired her and appointed a more compli-ant secretary. The checks went out, and the government officials got their cash.

Triumphant, Asha felt confirmed in a suspicion she'd developed in her years of multi-directional, marginally profitable enterprise. Be-coming a success in the great, rigged market of the overcity required less effort and intelligence than getting by, day to day, in the slums. The crucial things were luck and the ability to sustain two convic-tions: that what you were doing wasn't all that wrong, in the scheme of things, and that you weren't all that likely to get caught.

"Of course it's corrupt," Asha told the deferential new secretary of the nonprofit. "But is it *my* corruption? How can anyone say I am doing the wrong when the big people did all the papers—when the big people say that it's right?"

The new secretary nodded at Asha's analysis, but ever since she had co-signed the checks, her mouth had been slightly tight. How could she argue? Asha was her mother.

"Now you don't have to do a real job once your studies are fin-ished," Asha told Manju of the empire of schools they were pretend-ing to be running. "You'll take it over from me. I'll have to put your name down as the person in charge anyway, since all these schools are supposed to be run by someone with an education."

Although Manju was troubled by this legacy, she wasn't about to refuse the secondhand computer that soon came through the door. Meena had been the hot resister of daughterly responsibilities, not she. Asha also provided a dial-up Internet connection, which Rahul used to join Facebook, though his interest in social networking receded when his red Honda motorcycle arrived.

Manju loved her computer, as did the children she had taught in her slum school. They popped in regularly to contemplate its splendor. The children still called her "Teacher" and looked at her expectantly, unwilling to believe that their education was over. But the schools Asha and Manju were pretending to run made the income derived from a real school unnecessary.

Manju had recently memorized a plot summary of *Dr. Faustus*, which told of an ultimate reckoning—the moment when a "person who wanted to be the supreme person" discovered that the payment for a good life, badly acquired, had come due. Though this Christian hell was something she couldn't quite picture, she felt that punishment might be in the offing.

One quiet evening, shortly before the day on which she graduated from college, she looked up from her keyboard, alarmed. There were two, no, five eunuchs at the door! The eunuchs were nothing like the lithe and beautiful one who had once mesmerized her in the temple by the sewage lake. These she-males had hairy hands, mustache traces, and a practice of coming to the doors of families who'd had good luck and throwing down a curse to reverse it.

She was terrified, and the eunuchs felt bad, making her tremble like that. They had come on different business. Asha being the most powerful person they knew, they hoped she would help them register to vote in the election, a week away. Like most Annawadians, they wanted to be part of the exhilarating moment when politics was forced from its cryptic quarters and brought into the open air.

———

THE PARLIAMENTARY ELECTIONS would be the largest exercise of democracy in the history of the world: nearly half a billion people standing in line to vote for their representatives in Delhi, who would in turn select the prime minister. The parliamentarian who would represent Annawadians was hardly in doubt. It would be the incumbent from the Congress Party, Priya Dutt, a kind, unassuming woman who personified two historical weaknesses of the Indian electorate: for *filmi* people and for legacies. Her parents had been Bollywood superstars, and her father had held the parliamentary seat before her.

The previous week, a Congress Party truck had pulled up outside Annawadi, and workers unloaded eight stacks of concrete sewer covers. A crowd amassed on the road, excited at the pre-election gift. Thanks to Priya Dutt's party, the slumlanes would have no more open sewers.

A few days later, the Congress Party workers returned in the truck. Instead of installing the sewer covers, they reclaimed them. The covers were needed in one of the district's larger slums, where the prop might influence a greater number of voters. Older Annawadians laughed as they watched the truck depart. The blatancy was refreshing.

The eunuchs, who were migrants from Tamil Nadu, saw little difference among the political parties, but they were eager to vote nonetheless. Their problem was that district elections officials sometimes failed to process registration forms submitted by migrants and other reviled minorities. While Asha and her husband had voter cards and I.D. numbers that allowed them each two votes, in two different precincts, many non-Maharashtrians in Annawadi had yet to secure their one vote. Zehrunisa and Karam Husain were local record holders in disenfranchisement, having spent seven years trying unsuccessfully to register to vote.

To the excluded Annawadians, political participation wasn't cherished because it was a potent instrument of social equality. The crucial thing was the act of casting a ballot. Slumdwellers, who were criminalized by where they lived, and the work they did, living there, were in this one instance equal to every other citizen of India. They were a legitimate part of the state, if they could get on the rolls.

The tallest eunuch bowed toward Asha, then crouched at her feet. "Teacher," the eunuch said, "one year ago we went to register at the office but still we have not received our voting cards. We have done the needfuls but then, nothing. The election is so near. Will you take our forms and give them to the right people and make them give us a vote?"

Asha picked up a hand mirror.

The eunuch coughed. "Can you help? Teacher?"

Manju furrowed her brow. Her mother was acting as if the eunuchs were not even there. Asha picked up a tub of moisturizing cream and rubbed her face, slowly. She poured talc on her palms and massaged it onto her cheeks. She was getting ready to go someplace else.

"What! Putting on makeup!" hissed one of the eunuchs to another, too loudly. But in the someplace for which Asha seemed already to have departed, she didn't hear.

Asha had quit being slum boss. She was done with politics. Done with disenfranchised eunuchs and all the other inhabitants of Annawadi, "finished with all these small deals that keep me running here and there." Whether the Husains went to prison or an entire slumlane expired of TB or Fatima's ghost got bored with her hauntings and took it upon herself to clean the toilets, which badly required it: not of interest. Asha might have to live in this slum, for the time being. But she was a member of the overcity now: the director of a charitable trust, a philanthropic organization with a city vendor number, and maybe, someday soon, foreign donors. She was a re-spectable woman in the land of make-believe, who also happened to be late for a date.

"At the petrol pump," the man had said on the phone. "In the pink housedress, the one I like."

So behind the lace curtain, smiling, Asha wound around her body a silk sari in a tasteful black-and-white print. What *she* liked. The person she had become.

"You look good," said Manju, upon consideration. "Better than that pink."

"Oh ho, nice," concurred one of the eunuchs sullenly, as the new Asha stepped into the dark.

17.

A School, a Hospital,
a Cricket Field

IN MID-MAY, THE ELECTION RESULTS came in. The reform-minded elites had not turned out to vote, after all. Most of the incumbent parliamentarians were reelected, they returned the prime minister to office, and the radical improvements in governance promised before the voting were quietly shelved. A few weeks later, the bulldozers of the airport authority began to move across the periphery of Annawadi.

The Beautiful Forever wall came down, and in two days, the sewage lake that had brought dengue fever and malaria to the slum was filled in, its expanse leveled in preparation for some new development. The slumdwellers consoled one another, "It's not us yet, just at the edges." The demolition of airport slums would occur in phases over several years, so there was still plenty of time for the residents to unite to ensure that the businessmen and politicians who'd been buy-

ing up huts wouldn't be the only beneficiaries of the promised rehabilitation.

In the meantime, the earth-flattening at Annawadi's borders gave
the children something to do. They stood where the sewage lake used
to be, rapt, as the bright yellow bulldozers churned the ground. The
machines were unearthing the recyclable remainders of an earlier
city: a suede oxford, once white; rusty screws and other bits of plastic
and metal. Salable commodities, all.

One Saturday afternoon, the little Husains wandered out with
Fatima's daughters to join other child prospectors at the edge of the
site. As the children kept their eyes on the shovels, they debated what
was going to be built on the newly reclaimed land.

"A school," someone said.

"No, a hospital is what I heard it is going to be."

"One of those hospitals for babies being born."

"No, fool. What they're doing is for the airport. A taxi stand. And
planes will come here also."

"That ground is too small for planes. They are making a place for
us to play cricket only."

Fatima's younger daughter tensed. Something was gleaming at
the edge of a new gash in the earth. She sprinted out toward a bulldozer, darting under a lowering shovel.

"Don't," yelled a woman passing by. The little girl did: crouched
and tugged, jumped back just in time to avoid getting clocked, and,
after the bulldozer passed, squatted again to dig. It was a whole,
real something—a heavy steel cooking pot! She seized it and tore
back to Annawadi, beaming, her bare feet kicking up dirt clouds as
she ran.

The old pot was worth at least fifteen rupees, and at the sight of it
two women in the maidan began to laugh. From progress and mod-

ernization, at least one Annawadian would make a profit. Fatima's daughter lifted her treasure high for all of her envious peers to see.

A FEW WEEKS LATER, the children found a still more exciting diversion: journalists bearing cameras with long black snouts. Suddenly, Annawadi was in the news.

The proximate cause was a cheerful, if illegal, June tradition — a Sunday afternoon horse-and-carriage race on the gleaming Western Express Highway. Small bets were placed, and people lined the highway to watch.

The deposed slumlord, Robert the Zebra Man, was running two of his horses harnessed to an undermaintained carriage, freshly painted red and blue. Late in the race, as the pretty cart reached the crest of an overpass, one of its wheels rolled away. The carriage veered, harnesses broke, and the unnerved horses plunged off the bridge. A newspaper photographer was on hand to capture their grisly landing on the road below. And so began a campaign to find and penalize their negligent owner — Robert having fled the scene, leaving only a false address behind.

Public outrage built, and newspaper headlines multiplied. "On the Dead Horse Trail: An Exclusive Investigation." "Minutes After Horses' Death, Cops Knew About It; No Case Even Now!" "Exclusive! Where the Two Horses Lived Before Their Painful Death."

One day, Sunil, Mirchi, and other children watched as activists from a group called the Plant & Animals Welfare Society, or PAWS, brought in the media and representatives of the city's Animal Welfare League for a "raid" on Robert's horse shed. Several horses were determined to be malnourished. Cuts and sores were found on painted zebras. The Animal Welfare League spirited the neediest of the beasts to a therapeutic horse farm. "Horses Rescued!" was the headline of the following day.

The persistent activists then turned their attention to Robert's prosecution. The officers at the Sahar police station, having enjoyed a long, mutually profitable relationship with the former slumlord, declined to register a charge of cruelty to animals ("Culprit Goes Scot-Free!"). So the animal-rights group took its photographic evidence to the commissioner of the Mumbai Police. Finally, the former slumlord and his wife were charged under the Prevention of Cruelty to Animals Act for failing to provide adequate food, water, and shelter to their four-legged charges.

The forces of justice had finally come to Annawadi. That the beneficiaries were horses was a source of bemusement to Sunil and the road boys.

They weren't thinking about the uninvestigated deaths of Kalu and Sanjay. Annawadi boys broadly accepted the basic truths: that in a modernizing, increasingly prosperous city, their lives were embarrassments best confined to small spaces, and their deaths would matter not at all. The boys were simply puzzled by the fuss, since they considered Robert's horses the luckiest and most lovingly tended creatures in the slum.

THE ACTIVISTS HAD been few in number but, working together, they'd made their anger about the horses register. At Annawadi, everyone had a wrong he wanted righted: the water shortage, brutal for three months now; the quashing of voter applications at the election office; the worthlessness of the government schools; the fly-by-night subcontractors who ran off with their laborers' pay. Abdul was one of many residents who were angry at the police. Elaborate fantasies about blowing up the Sahar Police Station had become the secret comfort of his nighttimes. But the slumdwellers rarely got mad *together*—not even about the airport authority.

Instead, powerless individuals blamed other powerless individuals for what they lacked. Sometimes they tried to destroy one another. Sometimes, like Fatima, they destroyed themselves in the process. When they were fortunate, like Asha, they improved their lots by beggaring the life chances of other poor people.

What was unfolding in Mumbai was unfolding elsewhere, too. In the age of global market capitalism, hopes and grievances were narrowly conceived, which blunted a sense of common predicament. Poor people didn't unite; they competed ferociously amongst themselves for gains as slender as they were provisional. And this undercity strife created only the faintest ripple in the fabric of the society at large. The gates of the rich, occasionally rattled, remained unbreached. The politicians held forth on the middle class. The poor took down one another, and the world's great, unequal cities soldiered on in relative peace.

AS THE RAINS BEGAN in June, the new judge presiding over the trial of Kehkashan and her father started calling witnesses. This judge, C. K. Dhiran, had bony hands and sleepy eyes behind his spectacles, and he ran through cases even faster than the first judge had. Approaching his courtroom, on the top floor of the building, Kehkashan turned her head to a small window, where over an expanse of wet tile roofs she could make out the Arabian Sea.

What was the point of trying to mind-read another judge? She was still weak from jaundice and tension, and as the weeks passed it seemed futile to try to understand what was being said or to predict whether or not she and her father would go to prison. Her mother was worried enough for all of them, with her terrible dreams and her new habit of running across the maidan in her sleep. Kehkashan simply sat on the bench with the other accused people and murmured prayers until she was free to join the rest of the family in devising new ways to make money. As Mirchi put it, they were now "down to earn-and-eat."

They had given up on the idea of restarting their garbage business in Saki Naka. The rent on the shed there had been greater than Abdul's monthly income. So Abdul now spent his days driving the rattletrap three-wheeled truck from slum to slum, looking for jobs transporting other people's waste to recyclers. Mirchi took the temp jobs he could find, in addition to discreetly trading garbage at Annawadi when the police were not around. Their younger brother Atahar dropped out of school, paid for fake papers that said he was of working age, and broke rocks on the road. Atahar said he didn't mind quitting school to help his family, but Kehkashan minded, very much.

On the last day of July, the prosecutor and the defender made their closing arguments. The judge looked at Kehkashan for what seemed to her to be the first time, and cracked a joke about her burqa: "Are we certain this is the accused? It could be someone else. Who can recognize her, dressed like this!" When the judge finished laughing and the lawyers finished saying whatever it was they were saying to the judge, in English, the judge told Kehkashan and her father to come back in ninety minutes. There would be a verdict.

As they left the courtroom, the judge was saying, "Now I am only waiting for the pay hike to take effect and then I should retire. Maharashtra is such a narrow-minded state—only here they ask for the receipts and bills from judges. In Andhra Pradesh and Gujarat, the judge receives the petrol money along with the salary without having to produce bills. . . ."

Outside the courthouse, a city garbage truck rolled over a dog. It yelped and died, and Kehkashan and her father decided the courthouse canteen was a better place to wait. Kehkashan sat on the floor and stared at her shoes, which were new and plastic and hurt her. When she walked back into the courtroom she was limping and barefoot.

"What do you do?"

At the witness stand, Kehkashan answered the first and last question that the judge had directed to her.

"Housewife," she said. She wasn't about to tell him about leaving her husband and the photos of the other woman in his cellphone.

"And what is your business?" the judge asked Karam, who had clasped his hands to stop them from trembling.

"Sir, I am of plastics," Karam replied. He thought it sounded better than "of empty water bottles and polyurethane bags."

"Well, because of you," the judge said, "one woman's life has gone."

"No, sa'ab!" Karam cried out. "She did what she did by herself."

The judge said nothing for a while, then looked to the prosecutor with the stiff orange comb-over.

"So what to do with these ones, then? Should I sentence them to two years or three years?"

Kehkashan froze. Then the judge smiled and held up his hands.

"Go, leave them," he said to the lawyers. "*Jao, chhod do.*" He declared the Husains not guilty. It was over.

The judge's conclusion was succinct. "There is nothing on record to show that the accused in any manner instigated the deceased to commit suicide. Thus, prosecution has miserably failed to establish guilt against accused beyond reasonable doubt."

Move along now. The judge had other cases to hear, and wanted to clear the witness stand, to which Kehkashan and her father appeared to be glued. "You can go," the defense attorney said a second time, more emphatically, and Kehkashan and her father flew.

———

NOW ONLY ABDUL'S TRIAL in juvenile court—the judgment on *his* honor—remained. In September 2009, the clerk at the juvenile court said, "Next month it is likely to start." In October, the word was, "Three months' time, maybe." A Sahar police officer whom Abdul kept running into at Dongri was at least consistent. "Admit you did those things to the One Leg! There is a solution to everything! Your case will go on forever if you don't admit it, and if you do admit it, they will let you go today."

As 2009 drew to a close, Zehrunisa was taking special measures to hasten Abdul's trial and vindication. She visited a Sufi mystic on Reay Road who specialized in improving futures, relieving tensions, removing curses, and appeasing ghosts—the latter an important part of the draw for Zehrunisa, who thought Fatima's ghost might be behind Abdul's legal limbo. The mystic tied a red thread on Zehrunisa's wrist and sent her to tie another red thread around a tree in a courtyard where her fellow pilgrims were spinning and chanting to drumbeats. The spirits would be friendlier now, the mystic had promised, taking the money. Still, Zehrunisa thought it couldn't hurt to go to the mosque and do a mannat in Abdul's name, for seven Fridays.

As 2010 progressed and Zehrunisa's efforts bore no fruit, the special executive officer of the government of Maharashtra resurfaced to suggest that money would start a trial faster than prayer. Zehrunisa rewarded the suggestion with some of the finest curses she had ever invented.

By the end of 2010, she and Abdul had concluded that a suspended state between guilt and innocence was his permanent condition.

Abdul still looked for The Master when he went to Dongri. He wanted to tell the teacher that he had tried to be honorable in his final years as a boy, but wouldn't be able to sustain it now that he was pretty sure he was a man. A man, if sensible, didn't make bright distinctions between good and bad, truth and falsehood, justice and that other thing.

"For some time I tried to keep the ice inside me from melting," was how he put it. "But now I'm just becoming dirty water, like everyone else. I tell Allah I love Him immensely, immensely. But I tell Him I cannot be better, because of how the world is."

With three Husain boys earning, the family was slowly gaining again, and when Annawadi was demolished, they believed they just might get one of the rehabilitation flats: 269 square feet for a family of eleven, far from the airport and its garbage, but considerably better than pavement. Abdul grew dark only when he thought back to the start of 2008, his business thriving, the first installment made on a small plot of land outside the city. The Vasai plot had now been sold to another family, and the Husains' deposit had not been returned.

Abdul's father had developed an irritating habit of talking about the future as if it were a bus: "It's moving past and you think you're going to miss it but then you say, wait, maybe I won't miss it—I just have to run faster than I've ever run before. Only now we're all tired and damaged, so how fast can we really run? You have to try to catch it, even when you know you're not going to catch it, when maybe it's better just to let it go—"

Abdul wanted no part of this malaise. Fortunately, he had hauling work to do. Early mornings, he would start humbling up to supervisors at sheds in large industrial slums: "Anything to take to the recyclers?" He was learning all the back roads and spiny byways of the city, since three-wheeled vehicles like his own were barred from some of Mumbai's smooth new thoroughfares.

There were days when he spent more on gasoline, looking for work, than he earned from commissions, but there were good days, too, humping down the road, his tiny truck overloaded with trash. There was no place he wouldn't go for money, the farther from An-nawadi the better. He went over the state border to Vapi, in Gujarat. He went to Kalyan, to Thane. But mostly he stayed in Mumbai.

Driving his circuit late at night, he sometimes imagined not re-turning to his family in a slum he now thought of as "just another kind of prison"—imagined pressing forward and disappearing into some distant, perhaps better, unknown. Eventually, though, his city would jerk him back to his senses. The buses and SUVs barreling toward him, swerving. The children stepping obliviously from the roadsides into traffic, as Fatima's daughter was always doing, as if they didn't know the value of their lives.

"One mistake at the wheel, and it will finish me," Abdul would complain to his mother upon the inevitable return to Annawadi. "It's so much tension out there—the mind cannot wander. Every second you have to be alert."

In truth, he felt powerful moving through midnight traffic, his tired eyes narrowed to pinpoints. If there was no mastering this vast, winking city, he could still master a few feet of gummy road.

EARLY ONE MORNING, Abdul was perched on a black garbage bag by the video shed, contemplating another fruitless trip to Dongri and the "Anything to move?" routine of the evening to follow, when Sunil nestled into the garbage bag beside him. They hadn't seen each other in a while, with Abdul away, driving. Sunil leaned in close, as an almost-friend will sometimes do.

"Lend me two rupees for something to eat?"

Abdul reared back. "Ugh! Talking to me so close and you haven't washed your mouth! It's horrible. And your face. Go wash your face! I get scared just looking at you."

"Okay, okay, I will," Sunil said, laughing. "Just got up."

"Early for a thief."

"Not doing that anymore."

Garbage prices had been inching back up, police beatings had been intensifying, and security guards at the airport had stripped him naked and shaved his head. Sunil had decided to return to scavenging. In fact, this decision to scavenge was why he was sitting with Abdul on a garbage bag on the road. The Tamil who owned the game shed was angry at the loss of Sunil's stolen goods and wouldn't let him sit there anymore.

The blinky boy, Sonu, had almost forgiven Sunil for becoming a thief, but not for his habit of waking after dawn. Sunil wanted to join up with Sonu again, and was working on the early rising. He was also developing a formula for not hating himself while doing work that made him loathsome to his society. Eraz-ex worked, Sunil had discovered, but not for very long.

"Always I was thinking how to try to make my life nicer, more okay, and nothing got better," Sunil said. "So now I'm going to try to do it the other way. No thinking how to make anything better, just stopping my mind, then who knows? Maybe then something good could happen."

Abdul swatted him. "I lose my head, listening to you," he said. He felt old, sitting next to someone who still had ideas. When the slum got demolished, they'd probably never see each other again. Sunil wanted to start his life over somewhere outside the city, where there were trees and flowers, but Abdul thought it likelier that Sunil would end up sleeping on city pavement. These last days of Annawadi might be the best days Sunil would get.

A large, glossy leaf gusted across the road and landed at Abdul's feet. The filth in the air had barely browned it. He reached for it, took a rusty razor blade from his pocket, sliced the leaf into tiny pieces, then blew into his palm. Green confetti settled on Sunil's eyebrows, in his lashes, and on top of his rough-shorn head.

"So what now?" asked Sunil after a minute.

"What now? So wash your mouth and go to work! Already you're late. What's going to be left on the ground at this hour?"

"Okay, bye," said Sunil, jumping up, brushing off the leaf bits, and starting to run. Abdul watched him go. Weird and decent kid—he wished the boy luck, and half an hour later Sunil would find it, on a narrow ledge high above the Mithi River.

Soon, the taxi drivers who littered this ledge with garbage would be pushed elsewhere, as the new airport fulfilled its talismanic role: becoming an elegant gateway to one of the twenty-first century's most important world cities. But for now, eleven cans, seven empty water bottles and a wad of aluminum foil rested on a long spit of concrete, awaiting the first child with the courage to claim them.

Author's Note

TEN YEARS AGO, I fell in love with an Indian man and gained a country. He urged me not to take it at face value.

When I met my husband, I'd been reporting for years from within poor communities in the United States, considering what it takes to get out of poverty in one of the richest countries in the world. When I came to India, an increasingly affluent and powerful nation that still housed one-third of the poverty, and one-quarter of the hunger, on the planet, parallel questions persisted.

I quickly grew impatient with poignant snapshots of Indian squalor: the ribby children with flies in their eyes and other emblems of abjectness that one can't help but see within five minutes of walking into a slum. For me—and, I would argue, for the parents of most impoverished children, in any country—the more important line of inquiry is something that takes longer to discern. What is the infrastructure of opportunity in this society? Whose capabilities are given wing by the market and a government's economic and social policy?

Whose capabilities are squandered? By what means might that ribby child grow up to be less poor?

And another set of questions nagged, about profound and juxtaposed inequality—the signature fact of so many modern cities. (The scholars who map levels of disparity between wealthy and impoverished citizens consider New York and Washington, D.C., almost as unequal as Nairobi and Santiago.) Some people consider such juxtapositions of wealth and poverty a moral problem. What fascinates me is why they're not more of a practical one. After all, there are more poor people than rich people in the world's Mumbais. Why don't places like Airport Road, with their cheek-by-jowl slums and luxury hotels, look like the insurrectionist video game Metal Slug 3? Why don't more of our unequal societies implode?

I wanted to read the book that would begin to answer some of my questions, because I felt I couldn't write it, not being Indian, not knowing the languages, lacking a lifetime of immersion in the context. I also doubted my ability to handle monsoon and slum conditions after years of lousy health. I made the decision to try in the course of an absurdly long night at home alone in Washington, D.C. Tripping over an unabridged dictionary, I found myself on the floor with a punctured lung and three broken ribs in a spreading pool of Diet Dr Pepper, unable to slither to a phone. In the hours that passed, I arrived at a certain clarity. Having proved myself ill-suited to safe cohabitation with an unabridged dictionary, I had little to lose by pursuing my interests in another quarter—a place beyond my so-called expertise, where the risk of failure would be great but the interactions somewhat more meaningful.

I had felt a shortage in nonfiction about India: of deeply reported accounts showing how ordinary low-income people—particularly women and children—were negotiating the age of global markets. I'd read accounts of people who were remaking themselves and triumphing in software India, accounts that sometimes elided early privileges of caste, family wealth, and private education. I'd read stories of saintly slumdwellers trapped in a monochromatically miserable place—that is, until saviors (often white Westerners) galloped in to save them. I'd read tales of gangsters and drug lords who spouted language Salman Rushdie would envy.

The slumdwellers I'd already come to know in India were neither mythic nor pathetic. They were certainly not passive. Across the country, in communities decidedly short on saviors, they were improvising, often ingeniously, in pursuit of the new economic possibilities of the twenty-first century. Official statistics offered some indication of how such families were faring. But in India, like many places in the world, including my own country, statistics about the poor sometimes have a tenuous relation to lived experience.

To me, becoming attached to a country involves pressing uncomfortable questions about justice and opportunity for its least powerful citizens. The better one knows those people, the greater the compulsion to press. Although I had no pretense that I could judge a whole by a sliver, I thought it would be useful to follow the inhabitants of a single, unexceptional slum over the course of several years to see who got ahead and who didn't, and why, as India prospered. There being no way around the not-being-Indian business, I tried to compensate for my limitations the same way I do in unfamiliar American territory: by time spent, attention paid, documentation secured, accounts cross-checked.

The events recounted in the preceding pages are real, as are all the names. From the day in November 2007 that I walked into Annawadi and met Asha and Manju until March 2011, when I completed my reporting, I documented the experiences of residents with written notes, video recordings, audiotapes, and photographs. Several children of the slum, having mastered my Flip Video camera, also documented events recounted in this book. Devo Kadam, one of Manju's former pupils, was an especially passionate documentarian.

I also used more than three thousand public records, many of them obtained after years of petitioning government agencies under India's landmark Right to Information Act. The official documents — from agencies that included the Mumbai Police, the state public health department, the state and central education bureaucracies, electoral offices, city ward offices, public hospitals, morgues, and the courts — were crucial in two ways. They validated, in detail, many aspects of the story told in these pages. They also revealed the means by which government corruption and indifference erase from the public record the experiences of poor citizens.

When I describe the thoughts of individuals in the preceding pages, those thoughts have been related to me and my translators, or to others in our presence. When I sought to grasp, retrospectively, a person's thinking at a given moment, or when I had to do repeated interviews in order to understand the complexity of someone's views — very often the case — I used paraphrase. Abdul and Sunil, for instance, had previously spoken little about their lives and feelings, even to their own families. I came to my understanding of their thoughts by pressing them in repeated (they would say endless) conversations and fact-checking interviews, often while they worked.

Although I was mindful of the risk of overinterpretation, it felt more distortive to devote my attention to the handful of Annawadians who possessed a verbal dexterity that might have provided more colorful quotes. Among overworked people, many of whom spent the bulk of their days working silently with waste, everyday language tended to be transactional. It did not immediately convey the deep, idiosyncratic intelligences that emerged forcefully over the course of nearly four years.

———

WHEN I SETTLE INTO A PLACE, listening and watching, I don't try to fool myself that the stories of individuals are themselves arguments. I just believe that better arguments, maybe even better policies, get formulated when we know more about ordinary lives.

While I spent time in other slums for comparative purposes, I chose to focus on Annawadi for two reasons: because of the sense of possibility there, as wealth encroached on every side, and because its scale was small enough to allow door-to-door household surveys—the vagrant-sociology approach. The surveys helped me start to differentiate between isolated problems and widely shared ones, like the disenfranchisement of Annawadi's migrants and hijras.

My reporting wasn't pretty, especially at first. To Annawadians, I was a reliably ridiculous spectacle, given to toppling into the sewage lake while videotaping and running afoul of the police. However, residents had concerns more pressing than my presence. After a month or two of curiosity, they went more or less about their business as I chronicled their lives.

The gifted and generous Mrinmayee Ranade made this transition possible. She was my translator in the first six months of this project, and her deep intelligence, scrupulous ear, and warm presence allowed me to come to know the people of Annawadi, and for them to know me. Kavita Mishra, a college student, also translated ably in 2008. And beginning in April of that year, Unnati Tripathi, a brilliant young woman who had studied sociology at Mumbai University, joined the project as a translator. She was skeptical of a Westerner writing about slumdwellers, but her attachments to Annawadians proved greater than her reservations. She quickly became a fierce co-investigator and critical interlocutor; her insights litter this book. Together, over the course of three years, we wrestled with the question of whether days in rat-filled

Annawadi garbage sheds and late-night expeditions with thieves at a glamorous new airport had anything to contribute to an understanding of the pursuit of opportunity in an unequal, globalized world. Maybe, we firmly concluded.

I witnessed most of the events described in this book. I reported other events shortly after they occurred, using interviews and documents. For instance, the account of the hours leading up to Fatima Shaikh's self-immolation, and its immediate aftermath, derives from repeated interviews of 168 people, as well as records from the police department, the public hospital, the morgue, and the courts.

As I reported this and many other aspects of the narrative in which facts were hotly contested, I found Annawadi children to be the most dependable witnesses. They were largely indifferent to the political, economic, and religious contentions of their elders, and unconcerned about how their accounts might sound. For instance, Fatima's daughters, present during the arguments that ended with their mother's burning, were consistent in their exoneration of Abdul Husain, as were other Annawadi children on whose sharp eyes and wits I had learned, over time, to rely.

Being present for events or reporting them soon afterward was crucial, since as years passed, some slumdwellers recalibrated their narratives out of fear of angering the authorities. (Their fear was not irrational: Sahar police officers sometimes threatened slumdwellers who spoke to me.) Other Annawadians rearranged narratives for psychological solace: giving themselves, in retrospect, more control over an experience than they had had at the time. It was considered inauspicious and counterproductive to dwell on unhappy memories, and Abdul spoke for many of his neighbors when he protested one day, "Are you dim-witted, Katherine? I told you already three times and you put it in your computer. I have forgotten it now. I want it to *stay* forgotten. So will you please not ask me again?"

Still, from November 2007 to March 2011, he and the other Annawadians worked extremely hard to help me portray their lives and
dilemmas. They did so even though they understood that I would
show their flaws as well as their virtues, and with the knowledge that
they wouldn't like or agree with everything in the book that resulted.

I feel confident in saying they didn't participate in this project out
of personal affection. When I wasn't dredging up bad memories, they
liked me fine. I liked them more than fine. But they put up with me
largely because they shared some of my concerns about the distribution of opportunity in a fast-changing country that they loved. Manju
Waghekar, for instance, spoke frankly about corruption in the hope,
however faint, that doing so would help create a fairer system for
other children. Such choices, given the socioeconomic vulnerability
of those who made them, were simply courageous.

Just as the story of Annawadi is not representative of a country as
huge and diverse as India, it is not a neat encapsulation of the state of
poverty and opportunity in the twenty-first-century world. In every
community, the details differ, and matter. Still, in Annawadi, I was
struck by commonalities with other poor communities in which I've
spent time.

In the age of globalization—an ad hoc, temp-job, fiercely competitive age—hope is not a fiction. Extreme poverty is being allevi-
ated gradually, unevenly, nonetheless significantly. But as capital
rushes around the planet and the idea of permanent work becomes
anachronistic, the unpredictability of daily life has a way of grinding
down individual promise. Ideally, the government eases some of the
instability. Too often, weak government intensifies it and proves better at nourishing corruption than human capability.

The effect of corruption I find most underacknowledged is a con-
traction not of economic possibility but of our moral universe. In my
reporting, I am continually struck by the ethical imaginations of

young people, even those in circumstances so desperate that selfishness would be an asset. Children have little power to act on those imaginations, and by the time they grow up, they may have become the adults who keep walking as a bleeding waste-picker slowly dies on the roadside, who turn away when a burned woman writhes, whose first reaction when a vibrant teenager drinks rat poison is a shrug. How does that happen? How—to use Abdul's formulation—do children intent on being ice become water? A cliché about India holds that the loss of life matters less here than in other countries, because of the Hindu faith in reincarnation, and because of the vast scale of the population. In my reporting, I found that young people felt the loss of life acutely. What appeared to be indifference to other people's suffering had little to do with reincarnation, and less to do with being born brutish. I believe it had a good deal to do with conditions that had sabotaged their innate capacity for moral action.

In places where government priorities and market imperatives create a world so capricious that to help a neighbor is to risk your ability to feed your family, and sometimes even your own liberty, the idea of the mutually supportive poor community is demolished. The poor blame one another for the choices of governments and markets, and we who are not poor are ready to blame the poor just as harshly.

It is easy, from a safe distance, to overlook the fact that in undercities governed by corruption, where exhausted people vie on scant terrain for very little, it is blisteringly hard to be good. The astonishment is that some people *are* good, and that many people try to be—all those invisible individuals who every day find themselves faced with dilemmas not unlike the one Abdul confronted, stone slab in hand, one July afternoon when his life exploded. If the house is crooked and crumbling, and the land on which it sits uneven, is it possible to make anything lie straight?

Acknowledgments

My deepest debt is to the residents of Annawadi. I am also grateful for the support and insight of the following people and institutions:

Bharati Chaturvedi, Vijaya Chauhan, Benjamin Dreyer, Naresh Fernandes, Severina Fernandes, Mahendra Gamare, Shailesh Gandhi, Matthew Geczy, David Jackson, James John, Kumar Ketkar, Cressida Leyshon, The John D. and Catherine T. MacArthur Foundation, Nandini Mehta, Sharmistha Mohanty, Sumit Mullick, Shobha Murthy, Kiran Nagarkar, Alka Bhagvaan Nikale, Brijesh Patel, Gautam Patel, Jeet Narayan Patel, Rajendra Prasad Patel, Anna Pitoniak, Vikram Raghavan, Lindsey Schwoeri, Mike and Mark Seifert, Altamas Shaikh, Gary Smith and the American Academy in Berlin, Hilda Suarez, Arvind Subramanian, M. Jordan Tierney, and Madhulika and Yogendra Yadav.

Binky Urban and Kate Medina for believing, against considerable evidence, that I could do this.

David Remnick for his commitment to work that is slow to do and not necessarily appealing to advertisers.

David Finkel and Anne Hull for their sustaining counsel at every stage of this project.

Unnati Tripathi for her genius and bravery.

Mrinmayee Ranade for her teaching, her optimism, and her perceptiveness about the domestic lives of ordinary women.

Luca Giuliani, Joachim Nettelbeck, and the staff of the Wissenschaftskolleg zu Berlin for providing the haven where I recovered from the reporting and wrote the first draft of this book.

Lorraine Adams, Jodie Allen, Evan Camfield, Elizabeth Dance, Ramachandra Guha, Anne Kornhauser, Molly McGrath, Amy Waldman, and especially Dorothy Wickenden for—among other things—smart and crucial reads that made this book better than it would have been.

My family, who years ago invested in the question of how to do justice to the lives and imaginations of Abdul Husain and his neighbors, and who guided me, editorially and emotionally, through this project: my late father, Clinton Boo; John and Nick Boo; Tom Boo and Heleen Welvaart; Catherine Tashjean; Asha Sarabhai; Kyla Wyatt Leonor; Mary Richardson; Matt Buhr-Vogl, who helped me see the connections; Jack Boo, canniest twelve-year-old editor ever; two Mary Boos—my fierce, brilliant sister and my mother, who remains my most trusted reader and inspiration; and Sunil Khilnani, my love, my better world.

ABOUT THE AUTHOR

KATHERINE BOO, a staff writer for *The New Yorker*, has spent the last twenty years reporting from within poor communities, considering how societies distribute opportunity and how individuals get out of poverty. Her reporting has been honored by a MacArthur Foundation "genius" grant, a National Magazine Award for Feature Writing, and the Pulitzer Prize for Public Service.

Boo learned to report at the *Washington City Paper*. She was also an editor of *The Washington Monthly* and, for nearly a decade, a reporter and editor at *The Washington Post*. This is her first book.

ABOUT THE TYPE

This book was set in Electra, a typeface designed for Linotype
by W. A. Dwiggins, the renowned type designer (1880–1956).
Electra is a fluid typeface, avoiding contrasts of thick and thin
strokes that are prevalent in most modern typefaces.